Lecture Notes in Computer Science 6162

Commenced Publication in 1973
Founding and Former Series Editors:
Gerhard Goos, Juris Hartmanis, and Jan van Leeuwen

Zoé Lacroix (Ed.)

Resource Discovery

Second International Workshop, RED 2009
Lyon, France, August 28, 2009
Revised Papers

 Springer

Volume Editor

Zoé Lacroix
Translational Genomics Research Institute
445 North 5th Street, Phoenix, AZ 85004, USA
and
Arizona State University
Tempe, AZ 85281-5706, USA
E-mail: zoe.lacroix@asu.edu

Library of Congress Control Number: 2010930172

CR Subject Classification (1998): H.4, C.2, H.3, D.2, H.5, I.2

LNCS Sublibrary: SL 3 – Information Systems and Application, incl. Internet/Web
and HCI

ISSN   0302-9743
ISBN-10   3-642-14414-4 Springer Berlin Heidelberg New York
ISBN-13   978-3-642-14414-1 Springer Berlin Heidelberg New York

springer.com

© Springer-Verlag Berlin Heidelberg 2010
Printed in Germany

Typesetting: Camera-ready by author, data conversion by Scientific Publishing Services, Chennai, India
Printed on acid-free paper   06/3180

Preface

Resource discovery is the process of identifying and locating existing resources that have a particular property. A resource corresponds to an information source such as a data repository or database management system (e.g., a query form or a textual search engine), a link between resources (an index or hyperlink), or a service such as an application or a tool. Resources are characterized by core information including a name, a description of its input and its output (parameters or format), its address, and various additional properties expressed as metadata. Resources are organized with respect to metadata that characterize their content (for data sources), their semantics (in terms of ontological classes and relationships), their characteristics (syntactical properties), their performance (with metrics and benchmarks), their quality (curation, reliability, trust), etc. Resource discovery systems allow the expression of queries to identify and locate resources that implement specific tasks. Machine-based resource discovery relies on crawling, clustering, and classifying resources discovered on the Web automatically.

The First Workshop on Resource Discovery (RED) took place on November 25, 2008 in Linz, Austria. It was organized jointly with the 10th International Conference on Information Integration and Web-Based Applications and Services and its proceedings were published by ACM. The second edition of the workshop was co-located with the 35th International Conference on Very Large Data Bases (VLDB) in the beautiful city of Lyon, France. Nine papers were selected for presentation at this second edition. Areas of research addressed by these papers include the problem of resource characterization and classification, resource composition, and ontology-driven discovery. The papers included in this volume went through a two-step peer-review process: they were first reviewed by the Program Committee for acceptation to the workshop, then they were extended after the workshop and went through a second review phase. My sincere thanks to the Program Committee members (listed here) for their valuable input and for accepting to contribute to the multiple phases of the review process and to VLBN organizers for their support and the local organization. I am also grateful to the National Science Foundation that supported the workshop with a grant for student travel.

April 2010   Zoé Lacroix

Organization

RED 2009 was organized in cooperation with SIGMOD.

Program Committee

Witold Abramowicz	The Poznan University of Economics, Poland
Sudhir Agarwal	University of Karlsruhe, Germany
Bernd Amann	LIP6, Université Pierre et Marie Curie, France
Omar Boussaid	Université Lyon 2, France
Stéphane Bressan	University of Singapore, Singapore
Antonio Brogi	University of Pisa, Italy
Barbara Catania	Università di Genova, Italy
Óscar Corcho	Universidad Politécnica de Madrid (UPM), Spain
Valeria De Antonellis	Università degli Studi di Brescia, Italy
Federico Michele Facca	University of Innsbruck, Austria
Norbert Fuhr	University of Duisburg, Germany
Abdelkader Hameurlain	Université Paul Sabatier, France
Iraklis Paraskakis	University of Sheffield and CITY College, UK
Philippe Picouet	ENST Bretagne, France
Birgitta Konig-Ries	Friedrich-Schiller-Universität Jena, Germany
Chantal Reynaud	LRI, Université Paris-Sud, France
Ioan Salomie	Technical University of Cluj-Napoca, Romania
Miguel-Angel Sicilia Urbán	University of Alcalá, Spain
Zahir Tari	School of Computer Science, RMIT University, Australia
Maria-Esther Vidal	Universidad Simón Bolívar, Venezuela
Francisco Javier Zarazaga Soria	Universidad de Zaragoza, Spain
Lizhu Zhou	Tsinghua University, China

External Reviewers

Michele Melchiori
Francisco J. Lopez-Pellicer

Sponsoring Institutions

The National Science Foundation (IIS 0944126)	http://www.nsf.gov
The Translational Genomics Research Institute (TGen)	http://www.tgen.org

Table of Contents

Immune-Inspired Method for Selecting the Optimal Solution in Web Service Composition

Cristina Bianca Pop, Viorica Rozina Chifu, Ioan Salomie,
and Mihaela Dinsoreanu,

Department of Computer Science
Technical University of Cluj-Napoca
26-28 Baritiu Street, Cluj-Napoca, Romania
{Cristina.Pop,Viorica.Chifu,Ioan.Salomie,
Mihaela.Dinsoreanu}@cs.utcluj.ro

Abstract. This paper presents an immune-inspired algorithm applied in the context of Web service composition to select the optimal composition solution. Our approach models Web service composition as a multi-layered process which creates a planning-graph structure along with a matrix of semantic links. We have enhanced the classical planning graph with the new concepts of service cluster and semantic similarity link. The semantic similarity links are defined between services on different graph layers and are stored in a matrix of semantic links. To calculate the degree of the semantic match between services, we have adapted the information retrieval measures of *recall*, *precision* and *F_Measure*. The immune-inspired algorithm uses the enhanced planning graph and the matrix of semantic links to select the optimal composition solution employing the *QoS* attributes and the semantic quality as the selection criteria.

Keywords: clonal selection, semantic Web service, Web service discovery, Web service composition, ontology.

1 Introduction

The growing popularity and usage of Web Services, triggers the problem of finding and composing relevant services for a given request. Nevertheless, to discover and compose Web services, one must know some of its details, i.e. what it does, what it requires, what it assumes, what it achieves and to some extent, even how it achieves its purpose. The above information required for discovering and composing Web services is partially represented and supported by the signature of the operations and the message formats, which together form the Web service syntactical interface, captured in the WSDL document. The lack of any machine interpretable semantics in the WSDL document makes the work of automated agents impossible, rendering human intervention in the process compulsory. Semantic Web services relax this restriction by annotating services with semantic descriptions provided by ontologies. These semantic descriptions can be exploited to automate the service discovery, composition and execution.

Z. Lacroix (Ed.): RED 2009, LNCS 6162, pp. 1–17, 2010.

This paper presents a new approach for the automatic Web service composition using the service semantic descriptions referring concepts in a common ontology. The proposed approach combines the AI planning graph with an immune-inspired algorithm in order to find the Web service composition solutions which satisfy the user request. The user request is described in terms of functional and non-functional requirements. As main contributions of this paper we mention: (*i*) the enhancing of the AI planning graph with the concepts of service cluster and semantic similarity link; (*ii*) a Web service composition algorithm based on the enhanced planning graph (*iii*) an immune-inspired solution for finding the optimal composition based on the enhanced planning graph and a matrix of semantic links which stores similarity links and the associated degree of match.

The paper is structured as follows. Section 2 highlights the related work about Web service composition. Section 3 presents a motivating scenario that will be used throughout the paper to illustrate our approach for Web service composition. Section 4 describes our Web service composition method. Section 5 presents the composition algorithm, while section 6 describes the immune-inspired solution for finding the optimal composition. Section 7 presents experimental results. Section 8 concludes the paper and outlines future work.

2 Related Work

Researchers are being conducted in order to find, evaluate and develop new means and methods for automatic Web service composition. In this section we review some of this work which is closely related to our approach.

The use of planning graphs in semantic Web service composition is proposed in [1]. The main drawbacks of this approach are the following: (*i*) it provides a trivial composition solution, (*ii*) it does not consider multiple services providing similar functionality which could lead to a large number of composition solutions and (*iii*) it does not take into consideration *QoS* attributes.

Immune-inspired approaches have gained ground in the context of selecting the optimal solutions obtained through Web service composition. In [2] and [3], two immune-inspired selection algorithms are proposed in the context of Web service composition. Both approaches use an abstract composition plan which is mapped to concrete services, obtaining in this way a graph structure having services in the nodes and *QoS* values on the arcs. The immune-inspired algorithms are applied in both cases to select the optimal composition solution based on *QoS* attributes. The main differences between the two algorithms are the following: (*i*) the encoding of a solution – even if both approaches encode a composition solution as a binary string, the encoding in [2] is longer and more complex than the one in [3] as each stage of the workflow has a sequence of bits associated, where a 1 indicates the service selected; (*ii*) the mutation processes – both approaches perform mutation processes to generate new solutions, but in [3] the mutation is not performed randomly, it rather targets the cells which provide low fitness values to the antibody.

Our Web service composition method is also based on planning graphs but in contrast to the approach presented in [1] we provide the whole set of composition solutions as response to the user request. In addition, we extend the planning graph structure with clusters of services and store the semantic relations between services in the planning graph in a matrix of semantic links. We also consider (i) multiple Web services providing the same functionality and (ii) QoS attributes and semantic quality in ranking the composition solutions. In contrast to the approaches described in [2] and [3] which apply an immune-inspired algorithm on a graph of services built by mapping concrete services to an abstract composition plan, we combine an immune-inspired algorithm with the AI planning graph technique in order to find the optimal composition solution. We evaluate a composition solution in terms of its QoS attributes and semantic quality as opposed to [2] and [3] which take into consideration only QoS attributes.

3   A Motivating Scenario

In this section we present a reference scenario that will be used throughout the paper to illustrate our approach for the automatic Web service composition. This scenario closely follows the classical one for making travel arrangements [8]. Let assume that we want to make the travel arrangements for a trip to Lyon. First, we should search for a flight from Cluj-Napoca to Lyon on August 27. Second, we should search for hotel accommodation and for a car rental company in Lyon. Based on the search results we would book the most convenient flight and hotel and we would rent a car. Consider that all these subtasks (search / book flight, search / book accommodation and search / rent car) are published by businesses as Web services and our goal is to compose them for scheduling the trip to Lyon.

In order to be automatically composed, Web services must have associated machine-processable semantics. We achieve this by semantically annotating the Web service descriptions with concepts from a domain ontology. In this context, we developed a Web service domain ontology which defines the data and functional semantics of the services. The functional semantics defines the concepts that are used to annotate the service operations, while the data semantics defines the concepts that are used to annotate the inputs and outputs of the service operations. Using the concepts and properties captured in the ontology, a Web service can be specified by its functionality and the set of its inputs and outputs. For example, a Web service that searches for a hotel could have its functionality annotated with the concept *SearchHotel*, its input parameters annotated with the concepts *DestinationCity* and *HotelType* and its output parameter annotated with the concept *HotelName*. Besides its semantic description, each service is associated with a set of values corresponding to the following *QoS* attributes: availability, reliability, cost, and response time. The user request is expressed using (*i*) ontological concepts representing the semantic description of the provided inputs and requested outputs for the composed Web service and (*ii*) a set of weights. The weights indicate the user preferences regarding the importance of *QoS* attributes and semantic quality established between the services involved in composition. From the user perspective, we consider two categories of weights: one category refers to the relevance of *QoS* attributes compared to the semantic quality, while the other category establishes the relevance of each individual *QoS* attribute.

4 Web Service Composition Method

The goal of Web service composition is to obtain an inter-connected set of Web services satisfying the user's request. To achieve this goal, we combine the AI planning graph technique [6] with a new formal model called the *matrix of semantic links*. The semantic links are established between the services on different layers in the planning graph. A semantic link stands for the output-input matching between two services and is related to a common ontology used for the semantic description of Web services. We consider three types of semantic matching between an output concept of a service and an input concept of another service: EXACT, PLUG IN, and SUBSUME [4]. To calculate the degree of the semantic match between services, we have adapted the information retrieval measures of *recall, precision* and *F_Measure*.

4.1 The Enhanced Planning Graph Model

A *planning graph* [6] is a directed graph of layers in which edges connect only the entities of the neighbor layers. A planning graph layer contains a tuple (A_i, L_i) of sets of actions and literals. On layer 0, the set of actions A_0 is empty and the set of literals L_0 represents the initial state of the planning problem. On layer 1, the set of actions A_1 includes the actions whose preconditions are the nodes in L_0, while the set of literals L_1 is composed of the literals in L_0 and the positive effects of A_1 actions. This way, the planning graph is extended from the current layer to the next layer, until all the goals are contained in the set of literals L_n of the last layer n, or until a fixed point is reached. Reaching the fixed point means that the sets of actions and literals are the same for the last two consecutive generated layers.

By mapping the *AI planning graph model* to the semantic Web Service composition problem we have obtained an *enhanced planning graph model (EPG)* having the following characteristics:

- An *action* in the *EPG* represents a *service operation* (described by an ontology concept) in the service composition problem.
- The *preconditions* of an action in the *EPG* represent the *input parameters* of a service operation. The input parameters of a service operation are ontology concepts represented in the model as literals.
- The *positive effects* of an action in the *EPG* represent the *output parameters* of a service operation. Similar to input parameters, the output parameters are ontology concepts represented in the model as literals.
- A layer i of the *EPG* contains a tuple (A_i, L_i), where:
  - o A_i is a set of clusters of service operations for which the input parameters are the literals in L_{i-1}. A cluster of service operations groups services providing similar functionality. The inputs and functionality of the services of a cluster may be annotated with *is-a* related ontological concepts.
  - o L_i consists of the literals in L_{i-1} and the sets of A_i service outputs. Parameters of L_i (inputs and outputs) are grouped in clusters of literals where each cluster contains *is-a* related ontological concepts.

o Layer 0 is a particular case, in which A_0 does not contain any cluster of service operations and L_0 is represented by the *user provided input parameters* expressed as ontology concepts.

• The set of *goal literals* L_g in the *EPG* is represented by the *user requested output parameters* expressed as ontology concepts.

The construction of the *EPG* is an iterative process, in which a new layer is added to the graph in each iteration. For each layer $i > 0$, a tuple (A_i, L_i) is added to the *EPG*. Therefore, a semantic level composition is achieved as a result of the *EPG* construction. The mapping of the semantic annotated services, to real services is achieved as a separate stage. The services which contribute to the extension of the *EPG* are provided by a discovery process. The discovery process finds the appropriate Web services in a repository, based on the semantic matching between the services' inputs and the set of literals of the previous layer. Figure 1 shows an example of an *EPG*. In Figure 1a we present an ontology fragment containing concepts used as literals in the *EPG* in Figure 1b. In Figure 1b, a service is represented with a rectangle and a literal with an oval. The services as well as the literals are grouped in clusters. The clusters are represented as rectangles with rounded corners. An example of cluster of literals would be {*E, EE, EEE*} which is linked to the second cluster of services from the first layer, because the services in this cluster, s_2, s_3 and s_4, have *E, EE* and, *EEE* as outputs. A composition solution for the *EPG* of Figure 1 consists of a set of subsets of services: {[s_1 s_2], [s_6, s_7]}. In each solution subset, only one service of its cluster can be considered.

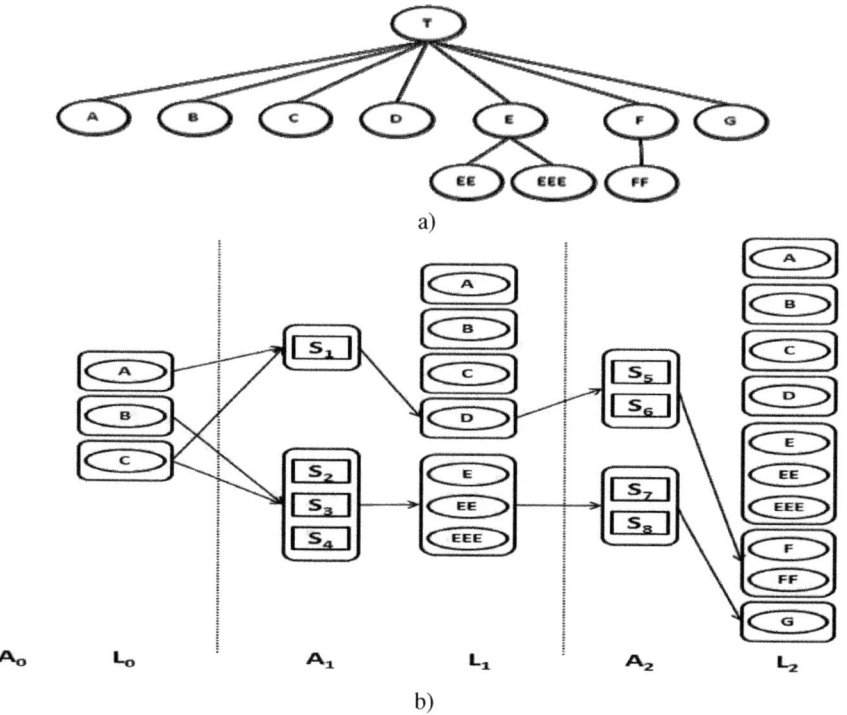

Fig. 1. a) Ontology fragment; b) An example of step-by-step construction of the *EPG*

4.2   The Matrix of Semantic Links

The *Matrix of Semantic Links* (*MSL*) stores the semantic links established between the services on different layers in the *EPG*. One Web service could be linked to several other Web services. We say that there is a semantic link between two services s_1 and s_2 if there is a degree of match (*DoM*) [4] between the set of output parameters of service s_1 and the set of input parameters of service s_2. The *MSL* is built iteratively during the composition process by using the information gathered during the service discovery process and the new information obtained during the *EPG* construction. In *MSL*, both the columns and the rows are labeled with services from the *EPG*. A column and a row having the same index will be labeled with the same service. *MSL* is formally defined as $MSL = [msl_{ij}]_{\ i=1,\dots n,\ j=1,\dots m}$, where an element msl_{ij} of *MSL* is represented as:

$$msl_{ij} = \begin{cases} \phi, & if\ simS(s_i.out_k, s_j.in_k) = 0 \\ sl_{ij}, & otherwise \end{cases} \quad (1)$$

In (1), sl_{ij} represents the semantic similarity link between the service on row i and the service on column j. A semantic similarity link stores a tuple $sl_{ij} = (V, simS)$, where:

- V is a set of pairs of output parameters $s_i.out_k$ of service s_i and input parameters $s_j.in_k$ of service s_j for which $DoM > 0$

$$V = \{(s_i.out_k, s_j.in_k) \mid s_i.out_k \in s_i.out, s_j.in_k \in s_j.in\} \quad (2)$$

- $simS$ is the semantic similarity score computed between the subset of output parameters of service s_i and the subset of input parameters of service s_j. We compute $simS$ between the subset out_k of output parameters of service s_i and the subset in_k of input parameters of service s_j with the following formula:

$$simS(s_i.out_k, s_j.in_k) = \frac{\sum_{t=1}^{m} F\_Measure(s_i.out_{k_t}, s_j.in_{k_t})}{m} \quad (3)$$

In (3), *F_Measure* is an adapted version of the similarity measure from information retrieval and is computed as:

$$F\_Measure(s_i.out_{k_t}, s_j.in_{k_t}) = \\ \frac{(1+a)*prc_g(s_i.out_{k_t}, s_j.in_{k_t})*rec_g(s_i.out_{k_t}, s_j.in_{k_t})}{a*prc_g(s_i.out_{k_t}, s_j.in_{k_t}) + rec_g(s_i.out_{k_t}, s_j.in_{k_t})} \quad (4)$$

where prc_g and rec_g is the *precision* and the *recall* between an output parameter of service s_i and an input parameter of service s_j. For calculating the prc_g and rec_g the following formulas have been used:

$$prc_g(s_i.out_{k_t}, s_j.in_{k_t}) = \sqrt{prc_I(s_i.out_{k_t}, s_j.in_{k_t})*prc_{II}(s_i.out_{k_t}, s_j.in_{k_t})} \quad (5)$$

$$rec_g(s_i.out_{k_t}, s_j.in_{k_t}) = \sqrt{rec_I(s_i.out_{k_t}, s_j.in_{k_t}) * rec_{II}(s_i.out_{k_t}, s_j.in_{k_t})} \qquad (6)$$

In formulas (5) and (6), prc_I and rec_I represent the *precision* and *recall* between an output of a service and an input of another service, while prc_{II} and rec_{II} represent the global precision and recall between all the properties of a service output and of another service input. The *precision* and *recall* have been evaluated according to the formulas presented in [5].

5   The Composition Algorithm

The objective of our approach is to generate the *best* Web service composition according to user specified goals and preferences (see formula (7)). For each service composition request we first determine a set of candidate composition solutions that satisfy the specified goal and then, the best composition is selected by ranking the solutions according to user preferences. This section presents our algorithm for finding the composition solutions, while section 6 describes the immune-inspired algorithm for selecting the best composition solution. Based on the semantic concepts associated to the user provided input and desired output parameters which are part of the service composition request, *SCR*, (issued by a software agent or by a human user) the composition algorithm (**ALGORITHM _1**) builds the *EPG*.

ALGORITHM _1. WEB-SERVICE-COMPOSITION

Input: *SCR* – the Service Composition Request; *R* – repository of available services;
Output: *EPG* – the Enhanced Planning Graph;
Comments: *S* - set of discovered service clusters, sc_{ij} is a cluster in *S*; GET-LAST-LITERAL-SET – returns the last set of literals added to the *EPG*; INITIALIZE-MSL – sets the *MSL* elements to Ø.
begin
　　$A_0 = Ø$; $L_0 = \{SCR.in\}$; $EPG = \{(A_0, L_0)\}$; $i = 1$; INITIALIZE-MSL(*MSL*)
　　repeat
　　　　$S = $ WEB-SERVICE-DISCOVERY(L_{i-1}, *R*); $L_i = L_{i-1}$
　　　　foreach sc_{ij} **in** *S* **do**
　　　　　　begin
　　　　　　if (! EXISTS(sc_{ij})) **then**
　　　　　　　　begin
　　　　　　　　foreach *s* **in** sc_{ij} **do**
　　　　　　　　　　begin
　　　　　　　　　　MSL = BUILD-MSL(*MSL*, *s*)
　　　　　　　　　　BUILD-LITERALS-SET (L_i, *s.out*)
　　　　　　　　　　end
　　　　　　　　$A_i = A_i \cup sc_{ij}$
　　　　　　　　end
　　　　　　end
　　　　$EPG = EPG \cup \{(A_i, L_i)\}$; $i = i + 1$
　　until (($SCR.out \subseteq$ GET-LAST-LITERAL-SET(*EPG*)) $\lor$ FIXED-POINT(*EPG*))
　　if (!$SCR.out \subseteq$ GET-LAST-LITERAL-SET(*EPG*)) **return** Ø
　　return *EPG*
end

The set of *SCR* inputs denoted by L_0 represents the initial state of the *EPG*, which is then iteratively expanded, until one of the following two stopping conditions is satisfied: (*i*) the graph reaches a level for which the set of literals contains all the user required output parameters, (*ii*) the graph reaches a fixed point level where $(A_{i+1} \equiv A_i)$ and $(L_{i+1} \equiv L_i)$ holds. For each layer $i > 0$, new services are discovered (**ALGORITHM _2**) from a global service repository R, based on the semantic matching (see formula (3)) between the input parameters of the services and the set of literals on the previous layer i-1. The discovered services are organized in clusters of services. In case a newly discovered service cannot be associated to an existing cluster, a new cluster of services is created (CREATE-NEW-CLUSTER). The output parameters of the discovered services are added to an existing cluster of literals of L_i. In case there is no suitable cluster of literals in L_i, a new one is created and associated to the considered output parameter (see BUILD-LITERALS-SET in **ALGORITHM _1**). For choosing the suitable cluster of literals the *F_Measure* (formula (4)) is used.

ALGORITHM _2. WEB-SERVICE-DISCOVERY

Input: L_i – the literals set on layer i of the *EPG*; R – repository of available services;
Output: $S = \{ (sc_1, L_{i1}),...(sc_m, L_{im}) \mid L_{ij} \subseteq L_i \}$ – a set of tuples containing the discovered service clusters and subsets of literals from L_i;
Comments: sc_i is a service cluster; L_{ij} is the subset of literals from L_i representing the input parameters of the services contained in sc_i; R is a repository of semantic Web services;

```
begin
  S = Ø; flag = false
  foreach s in R do
    begin
      foreach (sc_j, L_ij) tuple in S do
        begin
          Select a service s' from sc_i
          if (( F_Measure(s.functionality, s'.functionality ) > 0) && (simS(s.in, L_ij) > 0 )) then
          begin
            sc_j = sc_j ∪ s; flag = true; R = R \ {s};
          end
        end
      if ( ! flag ) then
        begin
          sc' = CREATE-NEW-CLUSTER(s, L_i); S = S ∪ {sc'}
        end
    end
  return S
end
```

If a cluster of services has not been previously added to the *EPG* (tested by invoking EXISTS), then for each service contained in the newly created cluster, a new entry in the *MSL* is created (**ALGORITHM _3**). The composition algorithm establishes semantic similarity links between the services on previous layers and the services on the current layer of the *EPG*. For each service s added to the current layer, the following steps are performed if the service does not have a MSL entry

(**ALGORITHM** _3): (1) the current matrix dimension n is incremented, (2) the service s is associated to the element $msl_{n+1, n+1}$, (3) the *simS* between the output parameters of every service s_i of row i in the *MSL* and the input parameters of service s is computed, (4) the semantic similarity link between the services s and s_i is created (CREATE-SIM-LINK) and stored in the *MSL*.

ALGORITHM _3: BUILD-MSL

Input: *MSL* – the Matrix of Semantic Links; s – a Web service;
Output: *MSL* – the updated *MSL*
Comments: n – the number of current *MSL* lines and columns; CHECK-SERVICE – checks if a Web service has an entry in *MSL*; GET-SERVICE - returns the Web service associated to a row and column in *MSL*; GET-DIMENSION – returns the current dimension of the *MSL*;

```
begin
   n = GET-DIMENSION (MSL)
   if ( ! CHECK-SERVICE(s) ) then
     begin
        n = n + 1
        for row = 0 to n do
          begin
             s' = GET-SERVICE(row, row)
             if (simS(s'.out, s.in) > 0 ) then MSL[row][n+1]=MSL[n+1][row]=CREATE-SIM-LINK(s',s)
             else MSL[row][n+1] = MSL[n+1][row] = Ø
          end
     end
   return MSL
end
```

---

6 The Immune-Inspired Selection Technique

For finding the optimal composition we adapted and enhanced a version of the CLONALG algorithm [7], which was proposed for optimization problems. We chose to adapt CLONALG to the problem of Web service composition because it better converges to the global optimum by iteratively introducing new candidate solutions that enlarge the search space (compared to genetic algorithms which may stagnate on local optima) [7]. Our immune-inspired solution uses the *EPG* and the *MSL* generated by the composition algorithm (see Section 5) as well as a multi-criteria function *QF* (see formula (7)) to find and rank the valid compositions according to *QoS* user preferences and semantic quality.

6.1 The Biological Immune System and Web Service Selection

This section overviews the clonal selection process of the biological immune system and identifies ways of mapping the biological immune concepts to Web service composition.

Clonal Selection in Biological Immune Systems. Clonal selection is one of the most important processes of the immune system. It is triggered when a B-cell has high affinity to an invading pathogen (antigen presenting cell), and as a result, the B-cell is stimulated to clone itself. Through cloning, identical copies of the B-cell are obtained. The number of copies is proportional to the affinity value. The clones are involved in an affinity maturation process which helps in improving their specificity to the invading pathogen by means of mutation. Mutation is inverse proportional to the affinity value, meaning that the clones having high affinity do not need to be mutated as much as the ones with low affinity. The affinity matured clones pass through new selection processes aiming at (*i*) keeping the clones having high affinity to the pathogen, and (*ii*) eliminating the clones with low affinity. The selected clones are then differentiated into memory cells and effector cells.

Mapping Web Service Composition to the Biological Clonal Selection Process. For the Web service composition, clonal selection is mapped as follows: (*i*) a B-cell (or antibody) is represented by a service composition solution, (*ii*) a pathogen (or antigen) is represented by a function *f* that evaluates the set of composition solutions in order to find the optimal one in terms of *QoS* attributes, and (*iii*) the affinity between an antibody and an antigen is represented by the value of the function *f* for a composition solution [2, 3].

In our approach, the antigen is represented by a multi-criteria function *QF* which evaluates the *QoS* and semantic quality of a Web service composition solution, *sol*. *QF* is formally defined as follows:

$$QF(sol) = \frac{w_{QoS} * QoS(sol) + w_{Sem} * Sem(sol)}{w_{QoS} + w_{Sem}} \tag{7}$$

where *QoS(sol)* represents the *QoS* score of *sol*; *Sem(sol)* represents the semantic quality score of *sol*; w_{QoS} and w_{Sem} represent the weights established according to user preferences related to the relevance of *QoS* and semantic quality during the evaluation of a composition solution.

The *QoS* score of a composition solution, *sol*, is computed using formula 8:

$$QoS(sol) = \frac{\sum_{i=1}^{n} w_i * qos_i(sol)}{\sum_{i=1}^{n} w_i} \tag{8}$$

where $qos_i(sol)$ represents the value of a *QoS* attribute computed for the composition solution *sol*, w_i is the weight established according to user preferences related to the relevance of the qos_i attribute and *n* is the total number of *QoS* attributes considered.

The semantic quality score of a solution *sol* is computed as follows:

$$Sem(sol) = \frac{\sum_{i=1}^{n} simS(s_{kl}^j.out', s_{qr}^p.in')}{n-1} \tag{9}$$

where s_{kl}^j is the service *l* in cluster *k* from layer *j*, s_{qr}^p is the service *r* in cluster *q* from layer *p*, s_{kl}^j, s_{qr}^p are part of the solution *sol*, *j* < *p* and *n* is the total number of services involved in the solution *sol*.

The objective of applying the clonal selection principle is to obtain the optimal solution sol_{opt} which maximizes the QF function. Thus, the affinity between the antibody and antigen is considered to be the value of the QF function for a solution sol. We use a binary alphabet to encode an antibody (a solution sol). As compared to [2] and [3], our encoding takes into consideration clusters of services. We represent an antibody as a set $\{[s_{01},...,s_{0m_0}],...[s_{01},...,s_{0m_n}]\}$, where s_{ij} is a Web service from cluster j of layer i, n is the number of layers in the planning graph, and m_i is the number of clusters on layer i. Each Web service is encoded as a binary string representing the identification number of the service within its cluster.

6.2 The Immune-Inspired Selection Algorithm

Our immune-inspired selection algorithm (**ALGORITHM _4**) determines the optimal solution sol_{opt} according to QF (see formula (7)), by considering the set of solutions resulted from the Web service composition algorithm (**AGORITHM _1**). Applying the selection algorithm for a triple (EPG, MSL, QF) requires the following initializations to be performed: (*i*) define a formula to compute n_c the number of clones to be generated for each solution, and (*ii*) define a function to compute m_r the rate of mutation, according to the affinity value.

ALGORITHM _4: IMMUNE-WEB-SERVICE-SELECTION

Input: EPG; MSL; QF; d;
Output: B
Comments: d – the number of solutions to be replaced; $B = \{(sol_1, QF(sol_1)), ..., (sol_n, QF(sol_n))\}$; $C_{sol} = \{c_{1sol}, ..., c_{nsol}\}$ – the set of clones of a solution sol; C_{sol}^* - the set of tuples $(sol_i^*, QF(sol_i^*))$ where sol_i^* represents an affinity matured clone corresponding to c_{jsol} and $QF(sol_i^*)$ represents the score of sol_i^*; $S = \{(sol_1, QF(sol_1)), ..., (sol_n, QF(sol_n))\}$.
begin
  B = GENERATE-SOLUTIONS (1, EPG, MSL, QF)
  while (! stopping_condition) **do**
    begin
      foreach $(sol_i, QF(sol_i))$ **in** B **do**
        begin
          C_{sol} = GENERATE-CLONES (sol_i)
          C_{sol}^* = AFFINITY-MATURATION (sol_i, C_{sol})
          $B = B \cup C_{sol}^*$
        end
      $B = B \setminus$ GET-LOW-AFFINITY-SOLUTIONS (B, d)
      S = GENERATE-SOLUTIONS (d, EPG, MSL, QF)
      $B = B \cup S$
    end
  return B
end

We choose to calculate the number of clones to be generated for each solution according to the formula indicated in [7]:

$$n_c = round(\beta * n) \qquad (10)$$

where β is a multiplying factor, and n is the total number of solutions.

We define the mutation rate of a solution as in formula 11:

$$m_r(sol) = round(\frac{\alpha * | sol |}{n - i + 1}) \qquad (11)$$

where α is a multiplying factor, $| sol |$ refers to the number of Web services contained in the solution sol, n is the number of solutions and i is the index corresponding to each solution ($i = 1$ corresponds to the highest affinity solution). The values of the multiplying factors α and β are specific to the problem being optimized and influence the speed by which the selection algorithm converges towards the optimal solution. In our approach we have considered that $\alpha = \beta = 1$.

The immune-inspired selection algorithm (**ALGORITHM _4**) iterates over a set B of Web service solutions until a stopping condition is satisfied. The stopping condition is considered the state in which no new solution can be generated. Initially, the set B contains a single pair $(sol, QF(sol))$ where sol is a randomly generated valid composition solution and $QF(sol)$ is the calculated affinity for the solution sol. Within each iteration, for each pair $(sol_i, QF(sol_i))$ of B, the following steps should be performed: (1) generation of the C_{soli} set of n_c clones, corresponding to a solution sol_i (GENERATE-CLONES); (2) for each solution sol_i its set of clones C_{soli} is submitted to an affinity maturation process (**ALGORITHM _5**) which returns the set of tuples $(sol_i*, QF(sol_i*))$ representing the matured solutions and their associated affinity scores; (3) the updating of the set B with the affinity matured clones, (4) the elimination of a number, d, of solutions having the lowest affinity in B (GET-LOW-AFFINITY-SOLUTIONS) and (5) the generation of a number, d, of new valid solutions based on the *EPG* and *MSL* which are added to B (GENERATE-SOLUTIONS). The affinity maturation process is of particular interest as it aims to improve a solution so that it converges towards the optimal one. The affinity maturation process involves a series of mutation steps to: (1) identify the set RS of Web services which minimize the affinity of sol (LOW-AFFINITY-SERVICES); (2) randomly replace the identified services with other services from the same cluster (RANDOM-REPLACE); (3) for each valid (VALID) matured $c*$ clone, its score is calculated and the pair $(c*, QF(c*))$ is added to the $C_{sol}*$ set. Affinity maturation is inverse proportional to the affinity of a solution, which means that the number of replaced Web services is low when the affinity of the solution is high. Through affinity maturation we obtain new solutions which increase the problem search space.

ALGORITHM _5: AFFINITY-MATURATION

Input: sol – a Web service composition solution; C_{sol} – set of sol clones;
Output: $C_{sol}*$ - set of tuples $(sol*, QF(sol*))$ where $sol*$ represents an affinity matured solution and $QF(sol*)$ represents $sol*$ score;

```
begin
  RS = LOW-AFFINITY-SERVICES (sol, m_i(sol))
  foreach c in C_sol do
    begin
      c* = RANDOM-REPLACE(RS)
      if VALID (c*) then C_sol* = C_sol* U (c*, QF(c*))
    end
  return C_sol*
end
```

The output of the immune-inspired selection algorithm is the set of valid solutions ranked according to their affinity to *QF*, the first solution being the optimal one, sol_{opt}.

The computational cost per generation of the selection algorithm in the worst case is $O(n_cL)$, where n_c represents the number of candidate solution clones and L represents the number of Web services involved in a composition solution [7]. The selection algorithm scales well to any number of available services by considering a strategy of determining in each iteration step a number d of low affinity solutions and replacing them with new, yet unexplored candidate solutions.

7 Experimental Results

We have experimented and evaluated our composition method on a set of scenarios from trip and social event attendance planning domains. We developed and used in our experiments a set of 110 semantic Web services from the two domains. The set of Web services was annotated according to the SAWSDL specification. To semantically describe the user requests and the services capabilities, we developed two ontologies, one for each considered domain. The ontology for planning a trip stores 200 concepts organized on 8 hierarchic levels.

This section presents the experimental results obtained by applying our composition method to the problem of making travel arrangements described in section 3. For the user request presented in Table 1, our composition algorithm has discovered a set of appropriate services (see a subset of these services in Tables 2-8), out of the repository of available services. In our experiments we have considered four *QoS* attributes: availability (*Av*), reliability (*Rel*), cost (*Ct*) and response time (*Rt*).

Table 1. User request expressed as inputs, outputs, *QoS* weights and semantic quality weight

in_1, in_2,...	out_1, out_2, ...	QoS weights	SemQ weight
SourceCity, DestinationCity, StartDate, EndDate, NumberOfPersons,NumberOfRooms, Hotel,MediterraneanFood	Vacation Price	Total QoS: 0.25; Av:0.15;Rel:0.25; Ct:0.45; Rt:0.15	0.75

Table 2. The set of Web services of cluster 1 on layer 1

WS code	WS operation	in_1, in_2,...	out_1, out_2,...	QoS
s_{111}	SearchHotel	DestinationCity, Hotel	HotelName	Ct: 4.0; Rel:2.5; Av:3.0; Rt:1.25
s_{112}	SearchExotic Hotel	EuropeanExoticDestination City, Accommodation	Mediterranean HotelName	Ct:2.0; Rel:1.0; Av: 3.5; Rt: 2.75
s_{113}	Search European ExoticHotel	EuropeanDestinationCity, Hotel	Luxury Mediterranean HotelName	Ct:4.5;Rel: 1.75; Av: 4.0; Rt: 2.0

Table 3. The set of Web services of cluster 2 on layer 1

WS code	WS operation	in₁, in₂,...	out₁, out₂,...	QoS
s_{121}	SearchFlight	SourceCity, DestinationCity, StartDate	FlightIdentifier	Ct:3.0;Rel: 3.0; Av: 4.0; Rt: 2.0
s_{122}	SearchFlight Online	SourceCity, DestinationCity, StartDate	Identifier	Ct:2; Rel: 0.75; Av: 0.5; Rt: 1.0
s_{123}	SearchFlight Online	EuropeanSourceCity, EuropeanDestinationCity	FlightIdentifier	Ct:3.0;Rel: 4.0; Av: 2.5; Rt: 3.5

Table 4. A subset of the Web services of cluster 3 on layer 1

WS code	WS operation	in₁, in₂,...	out₁, out₂,...	QoS
s_{131}	SearchCar RentalCompany Travel	DestinationCity	RentalCompany	Ct:5.0;Rel: 3.0; Av: 4.0; Rt: 1.0
s_{132}	SearchCar RentalCompany Travel	EuropeanDestinationCity	CarRental Company	Ct:3.0;Rel: 2.0; Av: 2.5; Rt: 1.5
s_{133}	SearchCar RentalCompany Travel	EuropeanDestinationCity	RentalCompany	Ct:2.0;Rel: 2.5; Av: 2.0; Rt: 1.0

Table 5. A subset of the Web services of cluster 1 on layer 2

WS code	WS operation	in₁, in₂,...	out₁, out₂,...	QoS
s_{211}	BookHotel	HotelName, StartDate, EndDate, Breakfast, NumberOfHotelRooms, NumberOfPersons,	HotelPrice	Ct:1.25;Rel:1; Av:0.5; Rt: 3.5
s_{212}	BookEuropean ExoticHotel	LuxuryMediterraneanHotel Name, StartDate, EndDate, NumberOfPersons	HotelPrice	Ct:2; Rel:3; Av:2.05; Rt:2.95
s_{213}	BookExotic Hotel	MediterraneanHotelName, StartDate, EndDate, NumberOfHotelRooms, NumberOfPersons, MediterraneanFood	HotelPrice	Ct:4.95;Rel:4; Av:3.05; Rt:1.0

Table 6. A subset of the Web services of cluster 2 on layer 2

WS code	WS operation	in₁, in₂,...	out₁, out₂,...	QoS
s_{221}	BookFlight Online	Identifier, NumberOfPersons, Date	Confirmation	Ct:1.95;Rel: 2.75; Av: 2.5; Rt: 3.0
s_{222}	BookFlight	EuropeanFlightIdentifier, NumberOfPersons, VacationStartDate	FlightPrice	Ct: 2.0; Rel: 0.95; Av: 1.25; Rt: 2.5
s_{225}	BookFlight Online	FlightIdentifier, NumberOfPersons	FlightPrice	Ct:3.0; Rel:2.0; Av:1.0; Rt:3.0

Table 7. The set of Web services of cluster 3 on layer 2

WS code	WS operation	in₁, in₂,...	out₁, out₂,...	QoS
s_{231}	BookCar	CarRentalCompany, StartDate, EndDate	CarRental Confirmation	Ct:2.5;Rel: 2.0; Av:1.25;Rt:1.05
s_{232}	BookRentalCar	CarRentalCompany, StartDate, EndDate	RentalCarPrice	Ct: 3.5; Rel: 4.0; Av: 3.95; Rt: 1.0
s_{233}	BookRentalCar	CarRentalCompany, StartDate, EndDate	CarRental Confirmation	Ct: 1.5; Rel: 1.0; Av: 0.75; Rt: 2.0

Table 8. A subset of the Web services of cluster 1 on layer 3

WS code	WS operation	in₁, in₂,...	out₁, out₂,...	QoS
s_{311}	TotalVacation Price	FlightPrice, CarPrice	VacationPrice	Ct:1.5;Rel: 2.0; Av:1.0;Rt: 1.25
s_{313}	TotalVacation Price	FlightPrice, HotelPrice, RentalCarPrice	VacationPrice	Ct:3.25;Rel:2; Av:1.75;Rt:0.95

Based on the user request and the set of services, the composition algorithm iteratively builds the *EPG* along with the *MSL*. In Table 9 we illustrate a set of the semantic similarity links between the outputs of a service s_i and the inputs of a service s_j for the considered example. These semantic similarity links are stored in the *MSL*.

Table 9. The semantic similarity links stored in the matrix of semantic links (partial)

s_i	s_j	Semantic similarity link between the outputs of s_i and the inputs of s_j
s_{111}	s_{211}	({(HotelName, HotelName)}, 1)
s_{112}	s_{211}	({(MediterraneanHotelName, HotelName)}, 0.79)
s_{122}	s_{222}	({(Identifier, EuropeanFlightIdentifier), 0.94})
s_{131}	s_{231}	({(RentalCompany, CarRentalCompany)}, 0.92)
s_{232}	s_{311}	({(RentalCarPrice, CarPrice)}, 0.96)
s_{225}	s_{311}	({(FlightPrice, FlightPrice)}, 1)

For the trip planning scenario we performed two experiments on the immune-inspired selection algorithm. In the first experiment we generated the entire set of valid composition solutions in order to identify the optimal composition solution which is $sol_{opt} = \{ [s_{111}, s_{121}, s_{131}] [s_{213}, s_{225}, s_{232}] [s_{313}] \}$ with an affinity of 9.645. Such an approach in which the entire search space is generated is infeasible when working with large sets of services and requires the definition of a proper stopping condition. This stopping condition should guarantee that the algorithm returns the optimal composition without generating the entire search space. In the next experiment we have considered a value Δ as a stopping condition for the immune-inspired selection algorithm. Δ refers to the difference between the best solution found so far and a new generated solution. More precisely, when this difference is equal to Δ the algorithm stops. We tested the immune-selection algorithm on Δ taking the following values: 0.1, 0.05, 0.025, 0.0125, 0.005 and 0.001. By analyzing the experimental results we have drawn the following conclusions: (i) for $\Delta = 0.005$ the optimal solution was almost always generated in a small number of iterations (see in Table 10 the identified composition solutions), (ii) the number of iterations in which the optimal solution is obtained is independent of the first solution's affinity if the affinity of the randomly generated solutions is greater than the local optimal solution.

Table 10. The high-affinity composition solutions

Affinity	QoS score	Semantic quality score	Solution
9.645	3.112	11.823	[s_{111}, s_{121}, s_{131}] [s_{213}, s_{225}, s_{232}] [s_{313}]
9.583	3.155	11.726	[s_{113}, s_{121}, s_{131}] [s_{213}, s_{225}, s_{232}] [s_{313}]
9.548	3.331	11.62	[s_{111}, s_{121}, s_{131}] [s_{213}, s_{223}, s_{232}] [s_{313}]
9.493	3.005	11.655	[s_{111}, s_{121}, s_{131}] [s_{213}, s_{222}, s_{232}] [s_{313}]

8   Conclusions and Future Work

In this paper, we have proposed a new method for the automatic Web service composition by combining an Enhanced Planning Graph (EPG) with an immune-inspired algorithm for finding the optimal composition solution. In our method, the services involved in composition are organized in service clusters according to their functionality and input parameters. We keep the semantic similarity links between the services in a Matrix of Semantic Links (MSL). The immune-inspired algorithm uses the *EPG* and the *MSL* to find the optimal composition solution according to user preferences. The composition and selection methods have been tested on a set of scenarios from the trip and social event attendance planning domains. The experimental results prove that the proposed composition and selection methods provide either the optimal composition solution (in the most cases) or a local optimum composition solution close to the global one. As future work we intend to test our composition approach on more complex scenarios and enhance the composition algorithm with error handling and compensation facilities.

References

1. Yan, Y., Zheng, X.: A Planning Graph Based Algorithm for Semantic Web Service Composition. In: Proc. of the 10th Conference on E-Commerce Technology and the Fifth Conference on Enterprise Computing, E-Commerce and E-Services, Washington DC, USA, pp. 339–342 (2008)
2. Gao, Y., et al.: Immune Algorithm for Selecting Optimum Services in Web Service Composition. Wuhan University Journal of Natural Sciences 11(1), 221–225 (2006)
3. Xu, J., Reiff-Marganiec, S.: Towards Heuristic Web Services Composition Using Immune Algorithm. In: Proc. of the International Conference on Web Services, Beijing, China, pp. 238–245 (2008)
4. Paolucci, M., et al.: Semantic Matching of Web Services Capabilities. In: Horrocks, I., Hendler, J. (eds.) ISWC 2002. LNCS, vol. 2342, pp. 333–347. Springer, Heidelberg (2002)

5. Skoutas, D., Simitsis, A., Sellis, T.: A Ranking Mechanism for Semantic Web Service Discovery. In: Proc. of the IEEE Congress on Services, Salt Lake City, UT, pp. 41–48 (2007)
6. Russell, S., Norvig, P.: Artificial Intelligence: A Modern Approach. Prentice Hall/Pearson Education, Upper Saddle River (2003)
7. Castro, L., von Zuben, F.: Learning and Optimization using the Clonal Selection Principle. Proc. of the IEEE Transactions on Evolutionary Computation, Special Issue on Artificial Immune Systems 6(3), 239–251 (2002)
8. McIlraith, S., Son, T.: Adapting Golog for Composition of Semantic Web Services. In: Proc. of the Eighth International Conference on Knowledge Representation and Reasoning (2002)

Web Database Schema Identification through Simple Query Interface*

Ling Lin and Lizhu Zhou

Department of Computer Science and Technology
Tsinghua University, Beijing 100084, China
linling03@mails.tsinghua.edu.cn, dcszlz@tsinghua.edu.cn

Abstract. Web databases provide different types of query interfaces to access the data records stored in the backend databases. While most existing works exploit a complex query interface with multiple input fields to perform schema identification of the Web databases, little attention has been paid on how to identify the schema of web databases by simple query interface (SQI), which has only one single query text input field. This paper proposes a new method of instance-based query probing to identify WDBs' interface and result schema for SQI. The interface schema identification problem is defined as generating the full-condition query of SQI and a novel query probing strategy is proposed. The result schema is also identified based on the result webpages of SQI's full-condition query, and an extended identification of the non-query attributes is proposed to improve the attribute recall rate. Experimental results on web databases of online shopping for book, movie and mobile phone show that our method is effective and efficient.

1 Introduction

Web databases (WDBs) are important Web resources which provide structured data records of high quality and quantity. The data records are usually hidden in the backend WDBs, and can be obtained by first submitting queries through the query interfaces and then extracting data records from the query result webpages. This process requires the understanding of two schemas of WDB, the interface schema and the result schemah [5,13]. For simplicity, this paper uses S_I to denote an instance of the interface schema, and S_R to denote an instance of the result schema respectively. S_I is the schema of an query interface, which indicates how the query interface should be used while inputting the keywords to query the WDBs. S_R is the schema of the data records in the result webpages, which helps to perform automatic data extraction from the result pages.

There are many notable works on schema identification of WDBs that mainly use complex query interfaces (CQIs) to perform query probing for the identification task. CQI has multiple text inputs, as shown in Fig. 1(a). Each input

---

* This work is supported by the National Natural Science Foundation of China (Grant No. 60833003).

Z. Lacroix (Ed.): RED 2009, LNCS 6162, pp. 18–34, 2010.

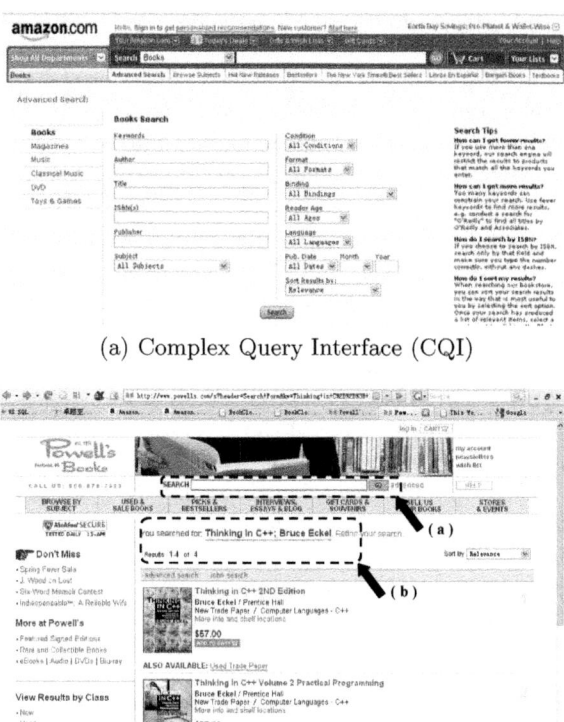

(a) Complex Query Interface (CQI)

(b) Simple Query Interface (SQI)

Fig. 1. Example Webpages of CQI and SQI

is labeled with an attribute name, indicating on which attribute column of the backend data table will the querying keyword in this input be searched. To understand S_I of CQI is to figure out which input box corresponds to which attribute. Existing works mainly exploit the information around the interface, the result of query probing and certain domain specific knowledge to do schema identification and matching [5,7,15,6,13].

In addition to CQI, there is another kind of query interface for WDBs, the simple query interface (SQI), as shown in the dashed rectangle (a) of Fig. 1(b). Compared to CQI, SQI is different in several ways. (1) SQI has only one text input field, usually labeled with simple words like "keywords" or "search", rather than the attribute names as in CQI. Therefore, little information around SQI can be exploited as in the situation of a CQI. (2) SQI can accept multiple query keywords of different attributes in its single input, while in CQI one input corresponds to one attribute column. (3) A query with multiple keywords is searched on the attribute columns (usually more than one columns) that have full text index in the backend database [4,10], which means that the keywords reappearing in the query results may not indicate the same attribute as it meant in the query. All the above shows that SQI has a very different mechanism of query submitting and processing from CQI's. Therefore, the probing method for SQI should be designed significantly different from that for CQI.

SQI is simple and flexible for users' queries and adopted by many WDBs. In fact, some websites only provide SQI for user query, such as the product search on www.360buy.com, the search of mobile phone, digital camera and other products on www.amazon.cn, and so on. However, few works could be found from the literature that address the schema identification problem when there is only SQI provided for query. In this paper, we address the problem of WDB schema identification through SQI. The task of S_I identification is defined as the problem of generating the full-condition query through SQI. The probing strategy is designed according to two aspects of the query, the hit rate of the query result and the reappearance word frequency of the query words. Additionally, an extended matching of non-query attribute values is proposed to improve the attribute recall rate of S_R of the WDB.

The rest of this paper is organized as follows. Section 2 introduces and defines the problem of WDB schema identification through SQI. Section 3 discusses the SQI probing strategy and the interface schema identification. Section 4 discusses the result schema identification through SQI. Section 5 reports the experimental results. Section 6 reviews the related works and Section 7 concludes this paper.

2   The Problem of Schema Identification through SQI

In a target application domain, there exists a common schema that gives an abstract description of the objects in the application, called **domain schema** S_G. The schema is viewed as a set of attributes $S = \{A_i | 1 \le i \le n\}$ [5,13], where A_i denotes an **attribute**. For the domain, S_G is predefined by users and it intentionally contains all the attributes that can well describe the target data. As mentioned before, S_I denotes the instance of the unknown **interface schema** of the target WDB, and S_R denotes the instance of the **result schema**. It is assumed that $S_I \subseteq S_G, S_R \subseteq S_G$. Conforming to S_G, we can instantiate a set of data instances $\{I\}$ that can be used for schema identification. The data record instance I is denoted as a set of attribute values $I = \{a_i | 1 \le i \le n\}$ where a_i denotes an **attribute value**. The target of WDB schema identification is to use S_G and $\{I\}$ to tell S_I and S_R of a given WDB. Instance-based query probing uses I to compose a **query** Q, which is a set of attribute values $Q = \{a_i^Q | a_i \in I\}$. Generally speaking, the keywords in Q are searched in the full text index which is built on the selected attribute columns of WDB [4,10]. The **query result** R_Q is analyzed to identify WDBs' unknown schemas according to S_G and Q. Information obtained from the query result pages includes the number of result records $|R_Q|$, the reappearance of the query words, etc. For convenience, Q is also expressed as a set of attributes $Q = \{A_i^Q\}$. An data instance I can refer to a data record in the WDB during the instance-based probing process.

2.1   Effective Query of Instance-Based Probing

This section discusses the key issue of instance-based probing through SQI, generating an effective query for query probing. First, two constraints that make a query to be effective are introduced. Based on the constraints, the quantitative metrics of generating the query, hit_Q and tf_Q, are also proposed and analyzed in the following section.

To identify S_I of SQI means to find a proper query method that can precisely retrieve the data from the backend WDB. Therefore, given a data instance, choosing a proper set of its attribute values to compose a query is important. Since the SQI has only one input, given an instance with n attribute values, the number of different queries composed from the instance can be as many as $\sum_{i=1}^{n} C_n^i = 2^n - 1$. Among all the possibilities, only one kind of query is useful for schema identification and regarded as effective query, which takes two requirements.

(1) The query result shows that there are matching data in the WDB, which means that the number of data records in the query result should be greater than zero.
(2) The query words' reappearance in R_Q should avoid semantic ambiguity. In the result webpage, the attribute values used in Q will reappear. Ideally, these reappearing query keywords should refer to the same attributes as what they are meant for in the query.

To obtain the reliable result webpage for analysis, a successful probing should aim at achieving the proper query Q^* that satisfies the above constraints. In this paper, the kind of query is called **Effective Query**, denoted as Q^*.

To satisfy the effective query constraint (1), Q should not include the attribute that is not contained by S_I. Otherwise, WDB will search the keywords only on the attribute columns that are contained in S_I, which will lead to zero matched data records. Since S_I is unknown, it is safe to use fewer attributes to form a query. On the other hand, using too few attributes to compose Q may do harm to satisfying constraint (2), because the query result of Q with fewer keywords has higher probability of semantic ambiguity as elaborated below.

1. Taking one query word for example, the reappearing word may be present in more than one kind of attribute position of the result record. For example, suppose $Q = $"*William Shakespeare*", when searching in the online book shopping WDB, it may appear as the author of books, and may also appear as the title of books. On the contrary, if $Q = $"*A Midsummer Night's Dream, William Shakespeare, Paperback*", it is explicit that "*William Shakespeare*" here refers to the author of a book.
2. The reappearing word may represent attribute values of different data object. For example, if $Q = $"*A Midsummer Night's Dream*", when querying a website that sells multiple kinds of products, the query result may contain other products besides books, such as movies or other audio/videos. On the contrary, if $Q = $"*A Midsummer Night's Dream, William Shakespeare, Paperback*", the query result will contain only books.

Consequently, by using more attribute values to compose a probing query, the possibility that *"William Shakespeare"* may reappear in both author and title positions of a result record is much reduced.

The above discussion shows that there exists a certain tradeoff between the number of result records and the semantic explicitness of the query words' reappearance, with respect to the **number of attributes in the query** $|Q|$. To better balance between the two aspects, the reasonable number and selection of the keywords should be decided to identify the target WDB's schemas effectively. Therefore, two metrics are proposed to represent the two aspects quantitatively, hit_Q and tf_Q.

2.2   The Full-Condition Query of the SQI

Definition 1. *Hit rate of Query* *describes the selective effect of a query Q generated by the same data instance I. It is denoted by*

$$ hit_Q = \frac{|R_Q|}{|R_G|}, $$

where $|R_G|$ is the number of result data records of a query Q_G, such that $|R_G|$ is maximum among all the query results generated by I.

$|R_G|$ normalizes the hit_Q value into the domain $[0, 1]$. The number of returned data records can be obtained from result webpages as shown in Fig. 1(b) dashed rectangle (b). WDB usually processes the multiple-keyword query using "AND" expression, which is the situation discussed in this paper. There are few WDBs using "OR" or other query processing strategy to process multiple keywords, which is ignored here and left to the future work.

Definition 2. *Reappearance of Query Keyword* *describes the word frequency per result record of the reappearing query keywords in the result webpage.*

$$ tf_Q = \begin{cases} \sum_{A_i \in Q} \frac{tf_{A_i}}{|R_Q|} & |R_Q| > 0 \\ 0 & |R_Q| = 0 \end{cases}, $$

where $tf_{A_i} = \frac{n_{A_i}}{\sum_k n_k}$, where n_{A_i} is the word count of query word A_i^Q in the query result, and $\sum_k n_k$ is the entire word count of the query result.

Apparently, $tf_Q \in [0, 1]$ increases as $|Q|$ increases. Note that $|R_Q|$ is used as the denominator, which makes tf_Q a better metric than $\frac{n_{A_i}}{\sum_k n_k}$ in evaluating the query's constraint and the semantic explicitness of the reappearing keywords.

Ideally, the effective query that is most helpful to the schema identification should contain as many attributes as possible while keeping the query result non-empty. With the above defined metrics, keeping query result non-empty means that $Q \subseteq S_I$ and $hit_Q > 0$, while containing as many attributes as possible means that tf_Q should be as large as possible. Therefore, the target of WDB's schema identification can be transformed into the problem of generating the full-condition query of SQI, to be defined as follows.

Definition 3. *Full-Condition Query of SQI*, *abbr. as FCQ, is an effective query which contains all the attributes that can be queried through the SQI.*

With above definition, the interface schema S_I identification problem is equal to the FCQ generation problem. The result schema S_R identification is equal to identifying the structure of the data from the result webpage of a FCQ.

2.3   The Three Phases of Effective Query Probing

To obtain the effective query that contains as many queriable attributes as possible, a straightforward strategy is to start from one single attribute and add more attributes one by one until the query result becomes zero or all attributes of the query instance are added. Based on the metrics of hit_Q and tf_Q, given one instance I, the process of generating a series of effective query by increasing the number of attribute values (the query keywords) can be characterized by 3 phases.

Taking the website www.powells.com for example, Fig. 2 shows the changing trend of hit_Q and tf_Q values in the probing process. $Q_1 - Q_6$ are the queries generated from the same book instance, in which the attribute values of title, author, publisher, format, publishing-date and page-number are added into Q one by one. The 3 phases are as follows. (1) $Q_1 - Q_3$. As the values of title, author and publisher are added gradually, the query conditions and query constraint become stronger. As a result, $|Q|$ increases and R_Q decreases, and this in turn makes hit_Q decrease and tf_Q increase. (2) $Q_3 - Q_4$. The format "Paperback" is added to form Q_4, but it doesn't actually strengthen the query constraint compared to Q_3. That means that SQI of this website can query on the attribute format, but for this probing instance the newly added attribute does not reduce the number of result records. Therefore, R_Q and hit_Q remains the same, and tf_Q increases. (3) $Q_5 - Q6$. The values of publishing-date and page-number are added. Because the two attributes can not be queried through SQI, hit_Q and tf_Q become 0. Therefore, Q_5 and Q_6 are not effective queries.

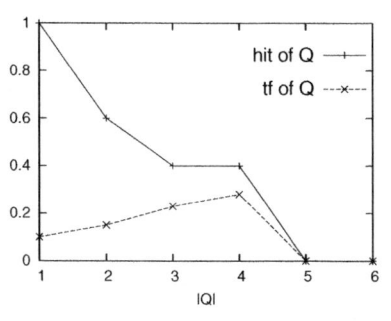

Q_1 = "A Midsummer Night's Dream"

Q_2 = "A Midsummer Night's Dream, William Shakespeare"

Q_3 = "A Midsummer Night's Dream, William Shakespeare, Arden Shakespeare"

Q_4 = "A Midsummer Night's Dream, William Shakespeare, Arden Shakespeare, Paperback"

Q_5 = "A Midsummer Night's Dream, William Shakespeare, Arden Shakespeare, Paperback, September 1979"

Q_6 = "A Midsummer Night's Dream, William Shakespeare, Arden Shakespeare, Paperback, September 1979, 320 pages"

Fig. 2. Example of SQI's 3-Phase Probing Process

From the above example, the 3 phases of SQI's probing process can be summarized as follows.

1. Higher hit_Q and lower tf_Q values. When Q contains fewer attribute, $|R_Q|$ is large, hit_Q is high and tf_Q is low; and hit_Q decreases as $|Q|$ increases.
2. Hit_Q values remains the same and tf_Q increases. When adding an attribute $A_{i+1}^Q \in S_I$ into Q, if it doesn't actually strengthen the query constraint, R_Q remains the same, hit_Q remains the same and tf_Q increases.
3. Both hit_Q and tf_Q values become zero. When newly added attribute $A_{i+1}^Q \notin S_I$, hit_Q and tf_Q values become 0, which makes Q become a non-effective query.

Note that the sequence of the attributes added into Q will affect the process of the 3 phases. For example, if the attributes $A \notin S_I$ are added into Q earlier than the attributes $A \in S_I$, phase 2 is shortened and the probing process goes into phase 3. This kind of attribute adding sequence should be avoided, because the probing of other attributes that haven't been added into the query $A^{\overline{Q}} \in S_I$ are shielded by the previously added attributes $A \notin S_I$, which makes them unable to be tested and identified in this situation. Therefore, our paper exploits two methods to avoid the early adding of $A \notin S_I$ into Q. The first one is to remove the candidate attributes whose single-attribute probing yields zero result, which will be further discussed in Algorithm *Candidate_Attr_Sort*. The other is to delete the latest added attribute from Q which makes $|R_Q| = 0$, which will be further discussed in Algorithm *SQI_Proing*.

Moreover, there are some special cases of the 3-phase query probing, which can be exploited to make probing process more efficient.

(1) In some domain, there exists some primary attributes of the data object, denoted as A_K. The "book title" attribute of the "book" object is a typical example. Usually A_K is the attribute that the Web users are most interested in, and most WDBs in the domain have them in their S_I and S_R (i.e. $A_K \in S_I, A_K \in S_R$). Therefore, in query probing, using A_K can help to faster decide whether WDB contains the instance or not, especially when the target WDB does not contain the probing instance. If $R_{A_K} = 0$ then WDB doesn't contain the instance; otherwise, more attribute values of this instance should be added to Q for further probing. For the situation that A_K has a strong filtering effect in query result, using A_K earlier in the probing process can help merge phases 1 and 2 and thus improve the efficiency.
(2) When SQI can support the query of all the attributes $A_i \in S_G$ for certain WDBs, phase 3 will not appear, i.e. the probing process may end at phase 2.

From the above discussion, in the 3-phase of the probing process, the full-condition query (FCQ) of SQI occurs at the end of query probing phase 2. Therefore, we propose two algorithms to perform this probing process and to get FCQ.

3 Full-Condition Query Generation through Instance-Bases Probing

This section introduces the two important algorithms proposed for instance-based probing through SQI, Algorithm 1 *SQI_Probing* and Algorithm 2 *Candidate_Attr_Sort*.

The probing process is implemented by Algorithm *SQI_Probing*, as shown in Algo. 1. The input of the algorithm includes the target SQI that is to be probed, the data instance set Ins used for probing and the domain schema S_G; the output is the generated full-condition query Q_I, indicating the attribute composition of S_I when it is not $\emptyset$. The algorithm contains mainly 2 steps.

1. Preprocessing for Q_I composing, line 2-6. In this step, $\overline{Q}_i$ and R_{Gi} of each instance I_i are obtained by the algorithm *Candidate_Attr_Sort*, which will be discussed later. Q_I will be generated using the I_i with the maximum $\overline{Q}_i$ and higher R_{Gi}.
2. The probing process with the selected instance I, line 7-20. Line 9 retrieves the head element in the queue $\overline{Q}$ and adds it into Q. Line 10-11 queries the WDB with newly generated Q and updates hit_Q and tf_Q according to the query result R_Q. Line 12-13 removes the latest added attribute from Q that yields zero result (when $hit_Q = 0$). Line 14-16 records the attribute into Q_I which is regarded as a member of S_I, and updates the larger tf_Q when $hit_Q > 0$ as defined before. The entire probing process stops when either of the two results is achieved. If $Q_I \neq \emptyset$, Q_I is the FCQ of given SQI, whose attributes compose the S_I of target WDB. Otherwise ($Q_I = \emptyset$), the WDB does not contain the instances given and new instances may be collected and used for further probing.

The major overhead of query probing is the network transferring and the minimum time interval to wait between two queries as required by the WDB, which cost much longer time than local computation and local data retrieval. Therefore, the number of queries submitted to WDB mainly determines the efficiency of probing process. The unit operation of the probing algorithm complexity is defined as one time of query submission and result page retrieve. Both algorithm complexity and empirical efficiency are analyzed on this base. The first part of probing complexity in the above step 1 will be discussed in Algo. 2. The second part in step 2 is $|\overline{Q}_i|$ which has a upper bound of $|S_i|$.

The key issue in step 1 of Algo. 1 is how to decide the sequence of the attributes added to Q. The number of probing queries is decided by the unknown size of the WDB schema S_I and the probing strategy. While the unknown S_I is fixed, the performance of the probing process can be improved by properly selecting the attributes in S_G to compose the query. As mentioned before, the number of all possible queries for a SQI is $\sum_{i=1}^{n} C_n^i = 2^n - 1$, which may overburden WDBs if using the exhaustive strategy. In order to balance the probing efficiency and the recall rate of the schema identification, a candidate attribute selection strategy is designed. The main idea is to earlier filter out the attributes that will cause zero query results.

Algorithm 1. $SQI\_Probing(S_G, Ins, SQI)$

Input : Golbal schema S_G, Sample instance set Ins, SQI

Output: Full-Condition Query Q_I

1 **begin**
2   **while** $Ins \neq \emptyset$ **do**
3   Select one instance I_i from Ins; $Ins \leftarrow Ins - I_i$
4   Record $\overline{Q}_i$ and $|R_{Gi}|$ for each I_i from
         $Candidate\_Attr\_Sort(S_G, I_i, SQI, \overline{Q}_i, |R_{Gi}|)$
5   **endw**
6   select I from $\{I_i\}$ and the related $\overline{Q}_i$ and $|R_{Gi}|$, such that I has the
      maximum $|\overline{Q}_i|$, or has larger $|R_{Gi}|$ when $|\overline{Q}_i|$ are equal; record the
      corresponding results as $|\overline{Q}|$ and $|R_G|$
7   **if** $\overline{Q} \neq \emptyset$ **then**
8        $Q_I \leftarrow \emptyset, TF_Q \leftarrow 0, Q \leftarrow \emptyset$
9        $A \leftarrow \overline{Q}.dequeue(), Q \leftarrow Q \cup \{A\}$
10       $R_Q \leftarrow Query(SQI, Q)$
11   Calculate hit_Q, tf_Q of R_Q with $|R_G|$
12   **if** $hit_Q = 0$ **then**
13          $Q \leftarrow Q - \{A\}$
14   **else if** $tf_Q > TF_Q$ **then**
15          $TF_Q \leftarrow tf_Q, Q_I \leftarrow Q$
16   **endif**
17   **return** Q_I
18   **else**
19   **return** $\emptyset$
20   **endif**
21 **end**

Algorithm *Candidate_Attr_Sort* implements the attributes sequence deciding process and records the R_G value as defined in Definition 1, as shown in Algo. 2. The candidate attributes of the given instance are enqueued according to the number of records in the result of each single-attribute query. There are mainly 3 steps in this algorithm. The algorithm complexity can be much reduced to $|A_K|$ if I does not exist in WDB and A_K is defined in S_G; otherwise the complexity is $|S_G|$. The input of the algorithm includes the domain schema S_G, current data instance I and the target SQI. The output of the algorithm includes the candidate attribute queue $\overline{Q}$ that will be used to compose the query Q in Algo. 1, and the maximum result number R_G of instance I.

1. Primary attribute probing and enqueuing, line 3-10. If the domain schema S_G contains any A_K, then use A_K for probing. If the result number is above zero, enqueue A_K and record R_K as R_G; otherwise, the WDB does not contain the given instance, return empty queue.
2. Other attributes' probing, line 11-13. For the remaining attributes in $\overline{Q}$, perform single-attribute query for each A_i and record the result R_i respectively.

3. Other attributes sorting and enqueuing, line 14-23. Sort A_i in $|R_i|$'s descending order, and inserted them into the candidate attribute queue $\overline{Q}$. The attributes with $|R_i| = 0$ are filtered, so that non-effective query can be avoided to improve probing efficiency. Update R_G when necessary. Note that when assigning the value of R_G, R_K is preferred than the maximum R_i of other attributes. It is because A_K is first tested and enqueued into $\overline{Q}$ than other attributes, if there is A_K defined in S_G.

Algorithm 2. *Candidate_Attr_Sort($S_G, I, SQI, \overline{Q}, |R_G|$)*

Input : Global schema S_G, Probing Instance $I = \{A_i | 0 \leq i \leq n\}$, SQI
Output: $\overline{Q}$ - candidate attributes queue in descending order of the
           number of records of each A_i's query result, $|R_G|$ - the maximum
           number of records among all the query results generated from I

1 **begin**
2      $\overline{Q} \leftarrow \emptyset, |R_G| \leftarrow 0$
3   **if** $\exists$ *primary attribute* $A_K \in S_G$ **then**
4          $R_K \leftarrow Query(SQI, A_K)$
5   **if** $|R_K| = 0$ **then**
6   **return**
7   **else**
8              $\overline{Q}.enqueue(A_K)$, $I \leftarrow I - \{A_K\}$, $|R_G| \leftarrow |R_K|$
9   **endif**
10   **endif**
11   **foreach** $A_i \in I$ **do**
12         $R_i \leftarrow Query(SQI, A_i)$
13   **endfch**
14   **foreach** $|R_i|$ *in descending order* **do**
15   **if** $|R_i| = 0$ **then**
16   **return**
17   **else**
18             $\overline{Q}.enqueue(A_i)$
19   **endif**
20   **endfch**
21   **if** *haven't assigned* $|R_K|$ *to* $|R_G|$ **then**
22         $|R_G| \leftarrow$ the maximum $|R_i|$
23   **return**
24 **end**

---

4   Result Schema Identification upon the Result of FCQ

Result schema identification is to discover the structure and semantic of the data objects from the query result webpage. The problem of S_R identification in the case of SQI is similar to the one in CQI, to identify the data objects from the data-intensive webpages. This paper exploits our previous work [9] for this

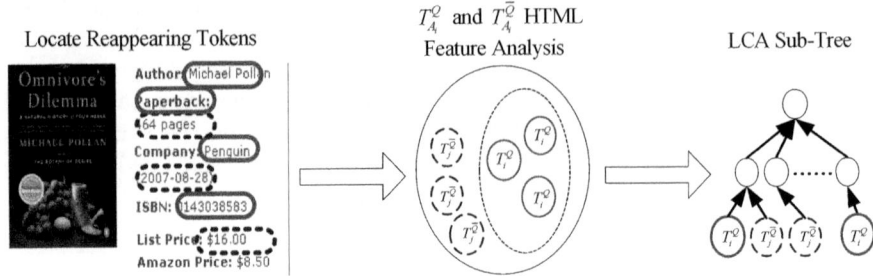

Fig. 3. Main Process of Extended Matching of Non-query Attribute Values

process. The details of the process are omitted here because they are beyond the focus of this paper.

One thing worth mentioning is that this paper improves the attribute recall rate of S_R identification by including the non-query attributes of the data instances through extended matching. The work of extended matching is worthwhile because of the observation that for certain WDBs, S_R may contain the attributes that are not included in S_I. These attributes usually appear together with the attributes used in the query and share certain similarity in HTML structure. This observation is exploited as heuristic rules to further identify the non-query attributes for S_R. For analysis, the result webpages are parsed into tokens and tree structure. The tokens of reappearing query keywords is denoted as T^Q, while the tokens of non-query attribute values are denoted as $T^{\overline{Q}}$. As shown in Fig. 3, two aspects of HTML features are exploited to assure the extended matching of the non-query keywords: (1) The similarity of outlook style of T^Q and $T^{\overline{Q}}$ tokens; (2) The closeness of the location of the T^Q and $T^{\overline{Q}}$ tokens, i.e. they usually reside in the same lowest common ancestor sub-tree (abbr. as LCA sub-tree). Experimental results show that the extended matching for non-query words $T^{\overline{Q}}$ improves the recall rate of attributes effectively.

5   Experiments

5.1   Data Sets and Experimental Settings

The experiments are performed on three online shopping domains, i.e. book, movie, and mobile phone. Table 1 shows the web databases probed in the experiment, including 20 book (English), 8 movie (English) and 7 mobile phone (Chinese) online shopping websites, all of which provide SQIs.

Table 2 shows the definition of the domain schemas, where the attributes in bold are designated as the primary attributes. Usually, the primary attributes of a web object are the ones which attract the most of user attention, and are always supported by the SQI query. Therefore, defining the primary attribute is helpful to improve the efficiency of query probing. It's noteworthy that primary attribute is not necessarily the key attribute of the corresponding database tables. For

Table 1. Domains and the Web Database Sites

Domains	WDB Sites	
Book (English)	www.a1books.com	www.abebook.com
	www.allbookstores.com	www.amazon.com
	www.barnesandnoble.com	www.bestbookdeal.com
	www.bestwebbuys.com	www.biggerbooks.com
	www.bookcloseouts.com	www.bookpool.com
	www.booksinc.net	www.bookstore.co.uk
	www.buy.com	www.chapters.indigo.ca
	www.christianbook.com	www.mysimon.com
	www.powells.com	www.randomhouse.com
	www.worldcat.org	shopping.yahoo.com
Movie (English)	www.amazon.co.uk	www.buy.com
	www.target.com	www.tower.com
	search.dooyoo.co.uk	shop.ebay.com/items
	shopping.yahoo.com	video.barnesandnoble.com
Phone (Chinese)	www.amazon.cn	search.360buy.com
	so.pcpop.com	search.yesky.com
	product.cnmo.com	mall.lusen.cn
	detail.zol.com.cn	

Table 2. Domains and the Global Schema

Domains	Global Schema
Book	**Title**, Author, Press, ISBN, Publish Date, Format, Pages
Movie	**Title**, **Director**, Starring, Year
Phone	**Brand**, **Type**, Network, Outlook, Monitor

example, book's ISBN uniquely identifies a book record, and thus is often selected as the key attribute of the book table. Whereas, not all of the query interfaces support to query by ISBN. On the other hand, querying by book title is a more natural choice for users, and supported by all of the related web databases. Thus, it makes more sense to select the book title as the primary attribute in online book shopping domain.

The experiments include two parts. The first part focuses on the query probing for interface schema and the efficiency analysis. The second part focuses on the result schema identifications with and without extended matching of non-query attributes.

5.2 SQI Probing and the Interface Schema Identification

Table. 3 shows the identified interface schema for half of the websites listed in Table. 1, and others are omitted for lack of space. Comparing different domains, the experiments also indicate that for the book and mobile phone domains, the

Table 3. Results of Interface Schema S_I Identification

WDB Sites	Attributes in S_I
WDBs of Book Domain	
www.a1books.com	title,author,publisher,isbn
www.abebook.com	title,author,publisher,format,publish date,isbn
www.allbookstores.com	title,author
www.amazon.com	title,author,publisher
www.barnesandnoble.com	title,author,publisher,format
www.bestbookdeal.com	title,author,format,isbn
www.bestbuy.com	title,author
www.bookcloseout.com	title,author,publisher,format,isbn
www.bookpool.com	title,author,publisher,publish date,pages,isbn
www.booksinc.com	title,author
WDBs of Movie Domain	
www.amazon.com	title,director,starring,year
www.barnesandnoble.com	title,director,starring,year
www.buy.com	title,director,starring
www.dooyoo.com	title,director,starring,year
WDBs of Mobile Phone Domain	
www.360buy.com	brand,type,network,outlook
www.amazon.com	brand,type
www.lusen.com	brand,type

query probing procedure will mostly go through phase 3, while for the movie domain, most of the probing process ends at the end of phase 2. This can be explained by the fact that the schema for movie domain is simpler than the other two domains.

The *SQI-Probing* algorithm proposed in the paper is also proved to be effective in generating *FCQ*. The experimental results show that the precision and recall rate of the interface schema identification based on *FCQ* are both 100%. The precision and recall are defined in the similar way as works [13,2], as shown in Equation 1 and 2. The encouraging result of S_I identification can be explained from the following aspects. (1) The single query input of SQI guarantees higher precision in S_I identification. (2) The *SQI-Probing* algorithm adopts the strategy of adding and trying all the candidate attributes in $\overline{Q}$ into Q one by one, which improves the recall rate effectively. Note that in this paper, we deliberately ignore the potential attributes outside the predefined domain schema S_G. In the future, the new concept discovery could be combined with this paper's framework to further improve the identification results.

$$Precision = \frac{\text{the Number of Correctly Identified Attributes}}{\text{the Number of All Identified Attributes}} \quad (1)$$

$$Recall = \frac{\text{the Number of Correctly Identified Attributes}}{\text{the Number of All Attributes in } S_I \text{ (or } S_R)} \quad (2)$$

Table 4. Domain Schema Scale and the Probing Efficiency

Domains	AttrN	SqiN	SinP	AveN	QueN
Book	7	4.740	0.500	4.300	11.416
Movie	4	3.810	0.571	2.286	9.048
Phone	5	3.121	0.500	2.000	8.245

The efficiency of the query probing through SQI is also analyzed. According to the instances used for probing, Table 4 records the number of attributes in the domain schema $AttrN$, the probability of single entry query result page $SinP$, the average entries in the first query result page $AveN$, the average number of probing queries per website $QueN$ and the average number of SQI schema attributes per website $SqiN$. Overall, the $QueN$ value is not high, which means that the required query probing times to a web database to identify the interface schema is not high. This result still holds even when the $SinP$ value exceeds 0.5, which means that the probability of single entry query result page is high and therefore it requires more probing instances for better result schema identification. Higher $SinP$ values and lower $AveN$ values mean better identification efficiency of SQI. The experimental data proves that the efficiency of the proposed SQI query probing procedure is generally acceptable. Looking at Table 4 more closely, the ratio $SqiN/AttrN$ is relatively low for the book and mobile phone domains. This indicates that for some non-primary attributes in these domains, e.g. the publishing date of a book, the SQI query support is not satisfactory. In such cases, it's important to employ extended identification based on non-query attribute values to better identify S_R. For the movie domain, since the number of attributes is less and most of them are important, SQI provides better query support to them, therefore the corresponding $SqiN/AttrN$ value is higher than the values in other domains.

5.3 Result Schema Identification and the Extended-Matching of Non-query Attributes

Table 5 shows the results for the result schema S_R identification, where the precision and recall rate are measured the same way as S_I. Note that before extended identification, the attribute recall rate is rather low. Further analysis shows that before the extended identification, the upper limit of attribute recall rate is the ratio of the number of attributes in the interface schema divided by the number of attributes in the result schema. Specifically, for the websites in the experiments, the attribute recall upper limit is 67.71% for book domain, 89.29% for movie domain and 66.67% for mobile phone domain.

This is not a new problem in this paper. Paper [13] also discusses the similar issue in the CQI context. In work [13], the experiments to 30 websites in book and second-hand car domains show that the average recall rate for the two domains are only 87% and 73% respectively. The reason is that the interface schema inherently constraint the attribute recall rate of the result schema to certain

Table 5. Experimental Results of Result Schema Identification

Domains	Before		Extended	
	Precision	Recall	Precision	Recall
Book	0.910	0.533	0.923	0.912
Movie	0.893	0.750	0.893	0.857
Phone	0.903	0.567	0.924	0.932

extent. Since the available attributes for query in SQI are generally less than those in CQI, the constraint is more significant in the SQI case. To address this problem, the extended identification based on non-query words is incorporated in this paper to improve the attribute recall rate for result schema. The data in Table 5 shows that the attribute recall rate is improved significantly after the extended identification. For example, in "Book" domain, the recall rate is increased from 0.53 to 0.91 after the extended identification. At the same time, the corresponding precision rate is kept at the same level, or even improved in the case of smaller attribute number in the schema. All these data prove the effectiveness of extended identification based on non-query words for SQI.

6 Related Works

Existing works mainly use CQI for WDB schema identification, which can be grouped into two categories, pre-query and post-query [11], or label-based and instance-based [13]. Pre-query and post-query methods are often used jointly to identify the WDB schema more efficiently. Pre-query methods exploit the information provided by the interface itself (the HTML codes that construct CQI), such as the attribute labels surrounding CQI's inputs, the value types of the attributes, the attribute value list in the drop-down menu, the users' tags, etc [5,7,16,6,1,3].

Post-query methods explore the data records stored in back-end databases by instanced-based query probing. Early works [8] exploit the length of the query results and the content of results [14] to judge which domain the WDBs belong to. They deal with text WDBs, but the similar result analyzing heuristics are also applicable for the structured database [13,12]. The result schema can be identified by exploiting the works on wrapper generation of data extraction. Work [13] uses the data instance to query the CQI, and exploit the query word reappearance information to do data extraction and labeling on the result webpage. Recent works exploit extractable instances in surface web [15,16] or user-generated tags [1] to better integrate hidden WDBs.

These works provide knowledge background for our work. The similarity between existing works and this paper is that we both use the instance-based query probing framework to identify WDB schema. The differences lie in several aspects. First, our work aims at the same target but uses another kind of query interface - SQI. Since there is little information that can be obtained from the interface itself, the proper way for SQI is to probe and analyze. Second, the probing strategy is quite different. The key issues related to SQI probing is to decrease the possibility of reappearance ambiguity in the result webpage while keeping the hit_Q rate of the query above zero. Moreover, in the result schema identification, extended matching method is proposed to improve the attribute-level recall rate of the result schema.

7   Conclusions

The paper proposes a method for systematic schema identification of Web databases with simple query interfaces (SQI). The method tries to identify the SQI interface schema by constructing effective full-condition query according to the characteristics of how SQI processes the query words. To construct the full-condition query efficiently, a probing strategy is carefully designed by analyzing the hit rate of the query words and the reappearance word frequency of the query words in the result webpages. Furthermore, the result pages returned from full-condition query are utilized to identify the result schemas. To improve the attribute recall in result schema identification, an extended identification based on non-query words is incorporated. The experimental results demonstrate that the proposed method is efficient to identify the interface and result schema for Web database with SQI.

As WDB is a kind of resource of large scale, our future work is to consider more complex query processing strategy of the SQI. For example, a small portion of WDBs exploit "OR" expressions to process multiple keyword query, or transfer to "OR" when the previously used "AND" expressions yielded zero results.

References

1. Ambite, J.-L., Gazen, B., Knoblock, C.A., Lerman, K., Russ, T.: Discovering and learning semantic models of online sources for information integration. In: IJCAI Workshop on Information Integration on the Web, Pasadena, CA (2009)
2. Arasu, A., Garcia-Molina, H.: Extracting structured data from web pages. In: ICDE, pp. 698 (2003)
3. Carman, M.J., Knoblock, C.A.: Learning semantic definitions of online information sources. J. Artif. Intell. Res (JAIR) 30, 1–50 (2007)
4. MySQL Conference Expo. Mysql conference expo. sphinx: High performance full text search for mysql
5. He, B., Chang, K.C.-C.: Statistical schema matching across web query interfaces. In: SIGMOD 2003: Proceedings of the 2003 ACM SIGMOD international conference on Management of data, pp. 217–228. ACM, New York (2003)
6. He, H., Meng, W., Lu, Y., Yu, C., Wu, Z., Meng, P.W.: Towards deeper understanding of the search interfaces of the deep web. In: World Wide Web (2007)
7. He, H., Meng, W., Yu, C.T., Wu, Z.: Wise-integrator: An automatic integrator of web search interfaces for e-commerce. In: VLDB 2003: Proceedings of the 29th international conference on Very large data bases, pp. 357–368 (2003)
8. Ipeirotis, P., Gravano, L., Sahami, M.: Probe, count and classify: categorizing hidden web databases. SIGMOD Rec. 30(2), 67–78 (2001)

9. Lin, L., Zhou, L.: Leveraging webpage classification for data object recognition. In: Web Intelligence, pp. 667–670 (2007)
10. MicroSoft. Querying sql server using full-text search
11. Ru, Y., Horowitz, E.: Indexing the invisible web: a survey. Online Information Review 29(3), 249–265 (2005)
12. Wang, J., Lochovsky, F.H.: Data extraction and label assignment for web databases. In: WWW, pp. 187–196 (2003)
13. Wang, J., Wen, J.-R., Lochovsky, F.H., Ma, W.-Y.: Instance-based schema matching for web databases by domain-specific query probing. In: VLDB 2004: Proceedings of the 30th international conference on Very large data bases, VLDB, pp. 408–419 (2004)
14. Wang, W., Meng, W., Yu, C.T.: Concept hierarchical based text database categorization in a metasearch engine environment. In: WISE 2000, Proceedings of the First International Conference on Web Information Systems Engineering, pp. 283–290 (2000)
15. Wu, W., Doan, A., Yu, C.: Webiq: Learning from the web to match deep-web query interfaces. In: International Conference on Data Engineering, p. 44 (2006)
16. Wu, W., Yu, C.T., Doan, A., Meng, W.: An interactive clustering-based approach to integrating source query interfaces on the deep web. In: SIGMOD Conference, pp. 95–106 (2004)

Semantic Interoperability and Dynamic Resource Discovery in P2P Systems

Devis Bianchini, Valeria De Antonellis, and Michele Melchiori

University of Brescia,
Dipartimento di Elettronica per l'Automazione, via Branze, 38
25123 Brescia - Italy
{bianchin,deantone,melchior}@ing.unibs.it

Abstract. Service-oriented architectures and Semantic Web technologies are widely recognized as strategic means to enable effective search and access to data and services in P2P systems. In this paper we present SERVANT, a reference architecture to support SERVice-based semANTic search, by means of a semantic distributed service registry. Specifically, SERVANT supports the automatic discovery of services, available in the P2P network, apt to satisfy user's requests for information searches. The SERVANT architecture is based on: a distributed service registry, DSR, composed of semantic-enriched peer registries and semantic links between peer registries holding similar services; a Service Knowledge Evolution Manager, to update peer knowledge; a Semantic Search Assistant, to find services satisfying a user's request, to suggest possible alternative services and to propose possible related services for composition. The proposed architecture allows for efficient semantic search based on service discovery throughout the network and is able to manage P2P network evolution.

1 Introduction

Service-oriented architectures and Semantic Web technologies are widely recognized as strategic means to enable effective search and access to data and services in P2P systems. Organization systems acting as peers can use semantic Web Services to expose and access distributed resources (i.e., data and services). In this way, platform independency is obtained and the possibility of integrating different organization systems over the Web is augmented. In P2P systems, the highly dynamicity and the absence of a common resource conceptualization pose strong requirements for semantic interoperability and dynamic change management.

In this paper, we present SERVANT, a reference architecture to support SERVice-based semANTic search in unstructured P2P systems. Specifically, SERVANT supports the automatic discovery of services, available in the P2P network, apt to satisfy user's requests for information searches. The SERVANT architecture is based on a distributed service registry, DSR, composed of semantic-enriched peer registries and semantic links between peer registries holding similar services. Moreover, each peer registry is equipped with: (i) a *Service Knowledge*

Z. Lacroix (Ed.): RED 2009, LNCS 6162, pp. 35–48, 2010.

Evolution Manager, apt to update peer local knowledge (when new services are locally added) and peer network knowledge (establishing new semantic links when new peers join the network or new similar services are published); (ii) a *Semantic Search Assistant*, apt to find services satisfying a user's request, to suggest alternative services, to propose related services for possible composition. These components are based on semantic-driven service matchmaking techniques. These techniques have been applied on a centralized service registry in [4]. In [5] we have then considered service discovery in P2P environments, where advantages of building and maintaining a semantic overlay on top of unstructured P2P networks for efficient service requests propagation have been analyzed and preliminary experiments have been presented.

In this paper, we integrate our previous work on semantic-driven service matchmaking and P2P service discovery in the SERVANT architecture. In particular, the SERVANT DSR is organized into two layers: a *logical layer*, in which single registries are connected as peers in a P2P network and services are registered on them; a *semantic layer*, where semantic service descriptions are added to the peer registries and the semantic overlay is built. Moreover, semantic-driven service matchmaking techniques are applied here to setup different kinds of inter-peer semantic links. Semantic links are exploited to guide the request propagation on the network towards peers that are likely to provide services matching the request, leading to an efficient and effective resource discovery in P2P networks without affecting network overload.

Generally speaking, our approach gives a contribution to scalable service discovery in P2P network without assuming the presence of centralized structures/coordinators nor a priory agreements on shared conceptualization among peers. This is obtained by defining a semantic overlay over the P2P network as result of interactions between neighboring peers and suitable optimization policies for service discovery that exploit it.

This paper is organized as follows: in Section 2, we introduce a reference example that supports the presentation of our approach; in Section 3, we describe the knowledge organization of the semantic-enriched distributed service registry; in Section 4, we explain how evolution of peer network knowledge is managed; in Section 5 the Semantic Search Assistant is presented. In Section 6 experimental results are discussed. In Section 7 a comparison with existing approaches in literature is given. Finally, Section 8 closes the paper.

2   Reference Example

As a reference example, let us consider the classical case of a traveller who wants to organize a week holiday in one of the European cities and is searching for a low-cost flight. He/she has not chosen the destination yet and his/her constraints regard the cost of the holiday and the departure and return dates. Firstly, he/she looks for available low-cost flights and, on the basis of the collected offers, decides which city to visit. Secondly, he/she has to find a cheap accommodation for the final destination of the journey. To support this kind of searches, the

SERVANT system helps the traveller to discover suitable search services, to find flight reservations and hotel booking facilities and display search results ordered by price. For example (see Fig. 1), service `AirLow` on peer R_X is a flight reservation service that provides the price and arrival city of a low-cost flight, given the departure and return dates, the departure city and the admitted flexibility with respect to the specified dates. Service `HotelSearching` on peer registry R_Z (to which peer registry R_X is connected in the P2P network) is an hotel booking service and provides the name, cost and stars of hotels in a specified city, given the required room type, the check-in and the check-out dates.

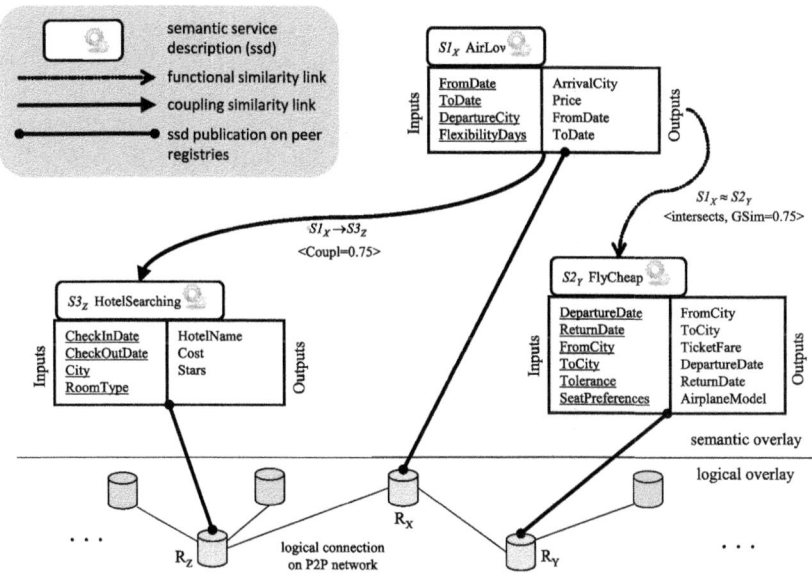

Fig. 1. Distributed service registry

In our example, the user's search can be supported by SERVANT in two ways: (i) given a low-cost-flight search submitted on peer registry R_X, the system is able to suggest not only local services (e.g., `AirLow`), but also similar services, in the same category, registered on different registries (e.g., service `FlyCheap` on R_Y); (ii) once the user selects a service for low-cost-flight search, say `AirLow`, the system is able to suggest possible related services (accepting as INPUT what is OUTPUT of `AirLow`), such as hotel booking facilities (e.g., service `HotelSearching` on R_Z). In our proposed system, the first requirement is implemented by establishing semantic links between similar services (*functional similarity links*). The second requirement is implemented by establishing semantic links between services that can be coupled for composition (*coupling similarity links*). In the following sections, SERVANT architecture components are described.

3   DSR Knowledge Organization

In the SERVANT architecture, a peer is equipped with an UDDI Registry[1], where each registered search service is associated to its *semantic service description*, expressed according to recently proposed languages for semantic annotation of service functional interface (e.g., WSDL-S [1]). Each peer is also equipped with an OWL-DL *peer ontology*, that provides concepts and semantic relationships used for annotation of service I/O parameters in the WSDL-S document. The set of semantic service descriptions constitutes the peer local knowledge.

Since we do not constrain nodes in the DSR to adopt a common shared conceptualization, different peer ontologies can be used on different nodes in the DSR. Different peer ontologies could refer to the same concept using different terms, that can be synonyms or related by other terminological relationships (e.g., broader/narrower terms). To bridge the gap between slightly different terminologies, peer ontologies are extended with a thesaurus built from WordNet[2]. A detailed explanation of how the thesaurus is built and used has been presented in [4]. Finally, according to the UDDI standard, registered services are associated to categories from the UNSPSC standard taxonomy[3].

Besides local knowledge about its own services, each peer maintains network knowledge in terms of semantic links to other registries in the DSR, containing similar services. Local and network knowledge constitute a semantic overlay built and maintained over the underlying P2P network. Semantic links are maintained between similar services to the purpose of extending the search results and optimizing the distributed discovery in the DSR. In particular, we distinguish between *functional similarity links*, denoted with $S_1 \approx S_2$, that relate similar semantic service descriptions, (e.g., services AirLow and FlyCheap), and *coupling similarity links*, denoted with $S_1 \longrightarrow S_2$, to denote that outputs of S_1 are related to the inputs of S_2 (e.g., outputs of services AirLow and inputs of HotelSearching). Semantic links are set by the Service Knowledge Evolution Manager and labeled with matching information between linked services obtained by applying semantic-driven service matchmaking techniques, as presented in the following section. In Fig. 1, the overall structure of DSR is shown: in the *logical overlay* peer registries are connected through the P2P network and in the *semantic overlay* semantic links labeled with matching information are established between semantic service descriptions.

In a peer registry, each published service is associated through the tModel mechanism (made available by the UDDI standard) to the WSDL-S document containing the semantic service description and to an XML document containing the network knowledge related to that service (i.e., the semantic links starting from it). The association of services to their categories is obtained through the

---

[1] http://www.uddi.org
[2] http://wordnet.princeton.edu
[3] The United Nations Standard Products and Services Code:
http://www.unspsc.org/

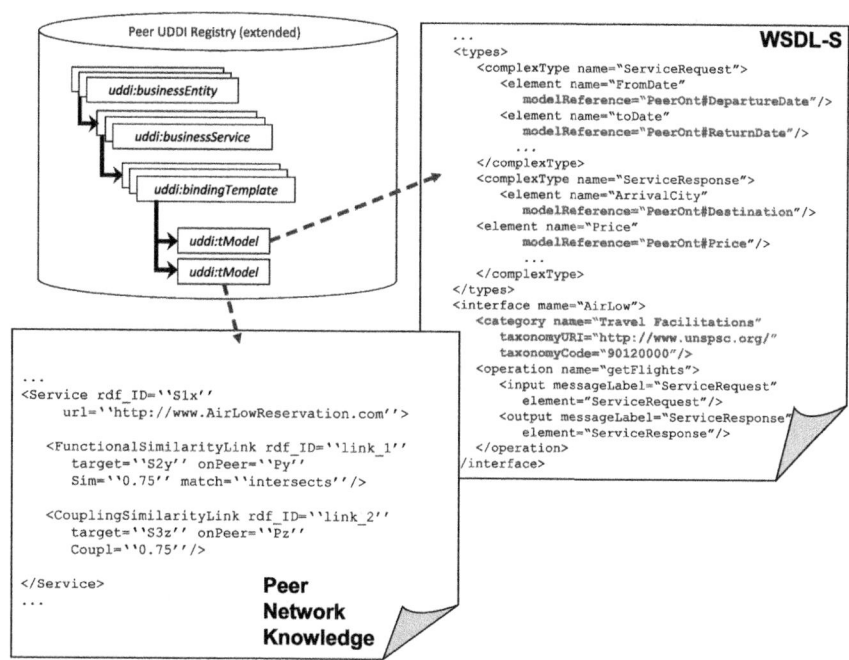

Fig. 2. Peer local and network knowledge in the semantic-enriched distributed service registry

`CategoryBag` structure provided within the `tModel`. In Fig. 2, the semantic service description and the network knowledge related to the `AirLow` service on peer R_X are shown. In the next sections, we will explain how semantic links are established, maintained and exploited for discovery purposes.

4 Service Knowledge Evolution Manager

The Service Knowledge Evolution Manager is the SERVANT component that is in charge of updating the peer local knowledge (when new services are registered) and the peer network knowledge, by establishing new semantic links. We will focus on peer network knowledge evolution. In particular, for establishing semantic links, semantic service descriptions in different peer registries have to be compared by applying semantic-driven service matchmaking techniques. Periodically, the Knowledge Evolution Manager starts a knowledge harvesting process to possibly establishing new semantic links.

Semantic link definition. In [4] we proposed an hybrid matchmaking model to compare semantic service descriptions based on peer ontologies and terminological knowledge (thesaurus). Matchmaking techniques have been defined to: (i) evaluate the degree of matching between services, to the purpose of establishing functional similarity links; (ii) evaluate the degree of interdependency between services, to the purpose of establishing coupling similarity links. Matchmaking techniques work on the basis of the OWL-DL peer ontology.

The *functional similarity link* is defined as a 4-uple:

$$\langle S_1, S_2, \texttt{MatchType}, Sim_{IO} \rangle \tag{1}$$

while the *coupling similarity link* is defined as a 3-uple:

$$\langle S_1, S_2, Coupl_{IO} \rangle \tag{2}$$

where S_1 is the (local) source of the link, S_2 is the (remote) target of the link. Semantic links are labelled with matching information to *qualify* the kind of match (S_2 MatchType S_1) and to *quantify* the degree of similarity between similar ($Sim_{IO}(S_1, S_2)$) or coupled ($Coupl_{IO}(S_1, S_2)$) services. The possible kinds of match are:

S_2 EXACT S_1, to denote that S_1 and S_2 have the same capabilities;
S_2 EXTENDS S_1, to denote that S_2 offers at least the same capabilities of S_1; the inverse kind of match is denoted as S_2 RESTRICTS S_1;
S_2 INTERSECTS S_1, to denote that S_1 and S_2 have some common capabilities;
S_2 MISMATCH S_1, otherwise.

The degree of match $Sim_{IO}(S_1, S_2)$ between semantic service descriptions is defined as:

$$Sim_{IO}(S_1, S_2) = \frac{\sum_{i,j} NA(in_i, in_j)}{|IN(S_1)| + |IN(S_2)|} + \frac{\sum_{h,k} NA(out_h, out_k)}{|OUT(S_1)| + |OUT(S_2)|} \in [0, 1] \tag{3}$$

where: $in_i \in IN(S_1)$, $in_j \in IN(S_2)$, $out_h \in OUT(S_1)$, $out_k \in OUT(S_2)$; $NA(t_1, t_2)$ is a coefficient evaluating the name affinity between terms t_1 and t_2. To compute the NA coefficient, we apply the formula defined in [4], based on the combined use of the thesaurus and the peer ontology. Note that $Sim_{IO}(S_1, S_2) = Sim_{IO}(S_2, S_1)$, but symmetry property does not hold for the kind of match. Finally, the degree of coupling $Coupl_{IO}(S_1, S_2) \in [0, 1]$ is measured on the basis of the number of output parameters in the first service that can be recognized to have semantic correspondences with the input ones of the second service:

$$Coupl_{IO}(S_1, S_2) = \left[2 \cdot \frac{\sum_{i,j} NA(out_i, in_j)}{|OUT(S_1)| + |IN(S_2)|} \right] \in [0, 1]$$

Note that $Coupl_{IO}(S_1, S_2) \neq Coupl_{IO}(S_2, S_1)$. Functional and coupling similarity links are established during the network knowledge harvesting phase explained in the following.

Network Knowledge Harvesting. Since in SERVANT no central coordination mechanisms or structures are defined, each registry is autonomous and has the ability of identifying similar services registered on different nodes by means of a process of network knowledge harvesting. Specifically, at predefined time intervals, a peer R_X sends a probe request for each locally available service S_1 that is not yet source of a semantic link. The probe request contains the semantic description of the service. A peer R_Y, receiving the request from R_X, applies the semantic-driven service matchmaking techniques between the probe request S_1 and each local semantic service description S_2 and, for each matching service, sends back an answer to R_X, that sets its local service S_1 as source of the link as explained in the following. Firstly, functional similarity links are checked. The kind of match between S_1 and S_2 is evaluated. In case of partial match (S_2 RESTRICTS|INTERSECTS S_1), the $Sim_{IO}(S_1, S_2)$ coefficient is computed. EXACT and EXTENDS matches correspond to $Sim_{IO}(S_1, S_2) = 1.0$, while MISMATCH corresponds to $Sim_{IO}(S_1, S_2) = 0.0$.

S_1 and S_2 are recognized as matching if the kind of match is not MISMATCH and Sim_{IO} is equal or greater than a threshold δ. The best value of δ is chosen through a training phase. The threshold δ is set to an initial value (i.e., $\delta = 0.7$) that is increased or decreased until a satisfactory trade-off between recall and precision is obtained on a training set of service requests and advertisements. Service categories are initially exploited to filter out not matching services: if there is not at least a category for S_1 that is semantically related in the UNSPSC taxonomy to a category for S_2, or viceversa, the kind of match is directly set to MISMATCH and $Sim_{IO}(S_1, S_2) = 0.0$. If a match between S_1 and S_2 is not recognized, then $Coupl_{IO}(S_1, S_2)$ is computed. The combined use of MatchType and Sim_{IO} enables a more flexible service comparison: not only EXACT matches are considered (that is a very strong condition), but also partial matches given a degree of match equals or greater than the threshold δ.

If $Coupl_{IO}(S_1, S_2)$ is equal or greater than a threshold α, where α is set to filter out not relevant coupling values, a coupling similarity link between S_1 and S_2 is established. The choice of actual values of α is determined by a training phase similar to the one performed for threshold δ. For each identified similar or coupled service, a reply is sent back from R_Y to R_X containing: (i) a reference to the matching service, (ii) if a functional or a coupling similarity link must be established, and (iii) the corresponding matching information. A similarity link is then set from S_1 on R_X to S_2 on R_Y.

If a semantic service description is removed, the similarity links starting from it are removed without the need of any propagation of messages on the network. Disconnection of a registry from the network is managed as follows: R_X recognizes that a semantic neighbor R_Y is disconnected if it has not been answering the service requests sent by R_X for more than a given period of time. In this case the similarity links towards semantic service descriptions published on R_Y are removed from R_X. If R_Y is unavailable for a shorter period, the similarity links are not removed to avoid to loose this kind of information in case of temporary disconnections.

Example. Services $S1_X$ and $S2_Y$ in the running example have at least an INTER-SECT match since there are some semantic correspondences among their I/O parameters (e.g., flexibilityDays – tolerance, fromCity – departureCity, `fromDate - departureDate, ...`). However, the match is not EXACT nor EX-TENDS since input `SeatPreferences` of $S2_Y$ does not corresponds to any input of $S1_X$. On the other hand, $S2_Y$ provides outputs `FromCity` and `AirplaneModel` that are not provided by $S1_X$ and therefore RESTRICTS match does not hold too. As a consequence, the match type is INTERSECT.

5   Semantic Search Assistant

The knowledge collected and organized during the harvesting phase is exploited during the semantic search process. When a new service request S_R is submitted to a registry R_X, similar services must be identified throughout the DSR. The service discovery task is performed according to the following steps.

Selection of semantic neighbors. The service request S_R submitted to the local registry R_X is matched against the local semantic service descriptions and a list $MS(S_R)$ of matching results is obtained. The request S_R is then forwarded to the other nodes of the DSR. To prune the set of registries to be investigated, thus avoiding time-consuming service search and P2P network overload, registries that are related to services $Si_X \in MS(S_R)$ through functional similarity links are selected as request recipients. Moreover, candidate request recipients can be filtered according to different forwarding policies, that are based on the matching information labeling the functional similarity links.

According to a minimal policy, search over the network stops when matching services which fully satisfy the request have been found. Formally, if $\exists Si_X \in MS(S_R)$ such that Si_X EXACT | EXTENDS S_R, it is not necessary to forward the service request to the semantic neighbors of P_X, since Si_X already satisfies the request. Otherwise, the list of request recipients is investigated to find remote services that potentially offer additional functionalities with respect to local services. A request recipient p is considered for service request forwarding if the functional similarity link set towards p is not labeled with RESTRICTS or EXACT. Otherwise, this means that p does not provide services with additional functionalities with respect to those already provided by service $Si_X \in MS(S_R)$ on peer R_X.

Exhaustive policies can be applied following the same rules, but the search does not stop when matching services that fully satisfy the request are found, in order to find other services that could present, for example, better non functional features (e.g., QoS, contextual information, service peer reliability). In [5] a detailed presentation of different forwarding rules based on functional similarity links is provided. Note that without the organization of services through semantic links, the discovery process would rely on conventional P2P infrastructures and associated routing protocols for request propagation in the network (e.g., flooding). Exploiting the semantic links, it is possible to enforce request forwarding according to content similarities rather than to the mere network topology.

Request forwarding and collection of search results. Once the request recipients have been selected, the service request S_R is forwarded towards them in order to obtain required search results on the DSR. Each registry R_Y receiving the request checks for locally available matching services: if matches have been found, R_Y replies to the registry R_X, from which the request started. Moreover, R_Y repeats the forwarding procedure based on its network knowledge. Search results are collected and ranked according to the similarity value. The forwarding action is performed by applying a TTL (Time-To-Live) mechanism to further decrease network overload. Each time a registry finds local results, it decreases the TTL value by one and then forwards the service request.

Extending the search results through coupling similarity links. Once the user selects one of the search results, coupling similarity links are exploited to propose to the user additional results collecting those services, whose inputs are related to the outputs of the selected services.

In the running example, if $\mathcal{S}1_X$ is selected, the system exploits the coupling similarity link $(\mathcal{S}1_X \longrightarrow \mathcal{S}3_Z)$ to propose the $\mathcal{S}3_Z$ service to the user.

6   Experimental Results

A simulator has been designed to evaluate the effectiveness of the forwarding policies over the semantic service overlay. To this aim, we extended the Neurogrid P2P simulator[4]. The simulator operates as follows. Firstly, it generates a P2P network: a set of nodes is instantiated and logical connections are randomly established, given a maximum number of outgoing edges for each node. The number of peers and the maximum number of connections for each node are parameters that can be set in a simulation run. The simulations have been performed on a network with 500 peers and a maximum number of logical connections between peers set to 5. Secondly, services are randomly assigned to nodes in the P2P network. A test set of WSDL-S documents[5] has been considered: it consists of 894 semantic Web services from 7 domains (education, medical care, food, travel, communication, economy, weapons) and 26 service requests. Matching information are pre-computed and stored in a data set. Such a data set is exploited by the simulator to decide when to establish a semantic link, when a service positively matches a request and when to forward a request to another peer. Each index representing a service is then randomly assigned to one or more peers. In other words, matching evaluation in the simulator is performed by accessing the pre-computed results in the data set without invoking the matchmaker. The choice of using precomputed matching results instead of run time computation involving the matchmaker is motivated by our purpose of evaluating the behavior of forwarding policies rather than DSR performances in terms of response time. An experimental evaluation concerning the adopted service matchmaker has been described in [4].

Fig. 3 shows the comparison between the implemented forwarding policies with the well known Gnutella P2P protocol both in terms of efficiency and

---

[4] http://www.neurogrid.net
[5] http://projects.semwebcentral.org/projects/sawsdl-tc/

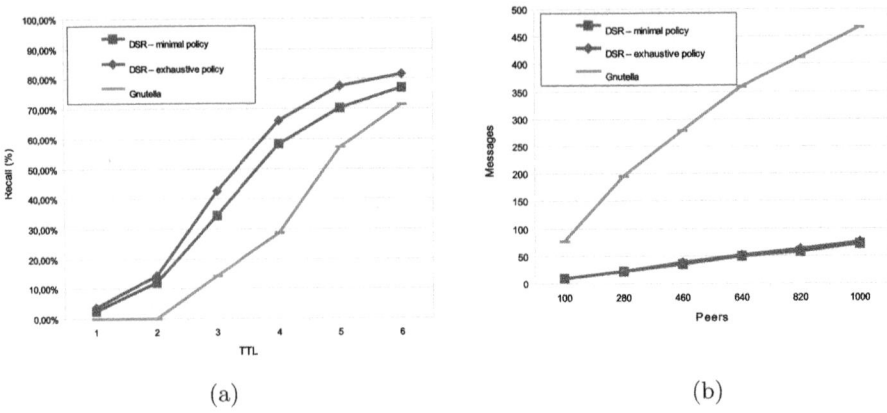

Fig. 3. Comparison between SERVANT and Gnutella for: (a) recall, (b) generated traffic

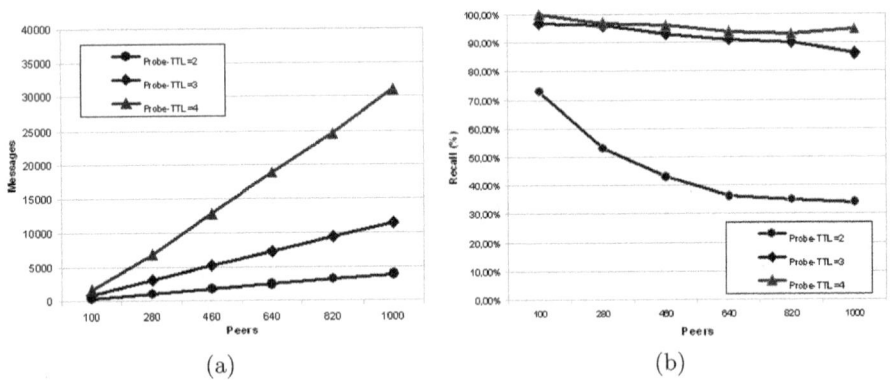

Fig. 4. Evaluation of semantic overlay setup: (a) generated traffic, (b) recall

scalability. Actually, Gnutella is oriented to document discovery, but we have implemented in the simulations a service discovery process exploiting the Gnutella forwarding policy, that is based on a flooding strategy relying on logical connections between peers. Gnutella forwarding policy is well-known and it is frequently considered as a reference example. In Fig. 3(a) we report the results of recall evaluation. The recall is defined with respect to a service request and is measured as the ratio between the number of services actually retrieved by the Semantic Search Assistant with respect to all the services relevant to the request. To establish the number of the services relevant to a request R, the simulator just counts the number of services that match with R in the pre-computed data set. SERVANT works better than Gnutella, but Gnutella tends to get good performances as TTL becomes high. This is due to the fact that in the considered network configuration the simulations work with 500 peers and about 5 connections for peer. In such a configuration, with TTL = 6, Gnutella is prone to flood the network reaching an high percentage of the peers and thus retrieving most of the services relevant to the request. Fig. 3(b) plots the average number of messages produced and forwarded on the network after submitting a request to a peer. We note the good results obtained by both the SERVANT forwarding policies with respect to Gnutella. However, generated traffic due to the creation of the semantic overlay must be also considered for SERVANT forwarding policies (see Fig. 4). This overhead is due to the propagation of probe requests, one for each shared service. Probe messages are forwarded to other peers according to a flooding strategy, since semantic links are not set in this phase yet. To keep low the number of generated messages, probe requests are sent with a low TTL value (2 or 3). If no answer is received, probe requests are sent again with an incremented TTL. In Fig. 4(a) the total number of probe messages generated in the simulations are plotted. In Fig. 4(b) is shown how the recall value change as the number of nodes increases, if different TTLs are used for probe messages. The higher the value of probe TTL, the higher the number of semantic links established by each peer and this fact biases positively the recall.

7   Related Work

Semantic service discovery on P2P architectures has been an important issue for the Semantic Web and several approaches have dealt with this problem. Semantic-driven service discovery on a P2P network has been addressed in [10], where each peer provides its own service, described using DAML-S service ontology, and the Gnutella protocol is used to forward service requests on the network according to a flooding-based mechanism, thus avoiding the use of a centralized service registry. No semantic links are maintained between peers, while in SERVANT a semantic layer is built on top of the P2P infrastructure. Other approaches use distributed architectures constituted by several UDDI registries properly organized to make more efficient request propagation. In METEOR-S [13] service descriptions are kept in UDDI Registries semantically enhanced with local domain ontologies, while a centralized registries ontology is adopted to classify peer registries. During the discovery process, registries ontology is browsed to find the proper node to which the request must be forwarded. A three-layer distributed UDDI registry, called ad-UDDI, has been also proposed in [6]. Each ad-UDDI registry is associated to one or more categories from a standard classification. All ad-UDDI registries are registered in a centralized server. Neighboring relationships between two ad-UDDI registries are established if they share at least one category. With respect to these approaches, SERVANT does not rely on a centralized structure for managing registries classification, for adding or removing a registry or for managing neighboring relationships, thus avoiding a system bottleneck and a single point of failure. Centralized components have been avoided also adopting structured P2P solutions [2,9,12], that organize peers or shared services through fixed structures, like DHT (Distributed Hash Tables), which require more maintenance efforts and a common conceptualization or ontology to describe the resources at hand. With respect to these attempts, SERVANT does not assume a priori semantic agreement among peers and does not constrain to the adoption of fixed structures to organize resources. Approaches like the ones described in [3,11] organize peers into semantic communities and request forwarding is performed inside the borders of the communities or between semantically related communities. In [3] a P2P-based system to support efficient access to e-catalogs resident data is provided, where scalability issues are solved by organizing information space in communities. Each community is associated to a reference ontology and is related to other communities through semantic links, defined as mappings between ontologies. A query rewriting algorithm is used to determine which part of a request submitted to a community can be answered locally and which part requires to be forwarded to other communities. Forwarding policies are defined at community level, while in SERVANT different forwarding policies exploit semantic links at service level and associated matching information. An approach for service discovery based on a semantic overlay is proposed in [11], where offered services are semantically described according to peer local ontologies. Peers with similar ontologies are supposed to offer services in the same domain and are clustered to form *SemSets*. In each *SemSet*, a coordinator peer is elected. Coordinators of semantically related communities (e.g., Rental and Transport) are related through semantic relationships that are exploited for query routing between *SemSets*. With respect to SERVANT, this approach relies on *SemSet* coordinators (that is, a form of super-peers) for service discovery and adopts a coarse-grained routing among communities rather than among peers. OntSum [8] is an attempt to completely decentralize resource discovery that shares with SERVANT the assumption of peers endorsed with local ontology and an effective, semantic-based, request forwarding, but is not involved with service discovery. In the RS2D approach [7] for semantic service discovery in P2P networks, each peer first determines the set of local services matching a request by using an OWL-S matchmaker, then forwards the request to a selected set of neighbor peers from which it is expected to receive semantically relevant services and, at the same time, minimizing the network traffic, evaluated according to a Bayesian model.

8   Conclusions

In this paper, we presented the two-layer SERVANT reference architecture for scalable semantic searching in P2P systems, that integrates in a comprehensive environment our previous works on semantic-driven service matchmaking techniques [4] and P2P service discovery [5]. In SERVANT each peer registry is endorsed with a knowledge infrastructure for semantic description of locally available services and semantic links towards similar/coupled services registered on different registries. The proposed architecture allows for efficient semantic search based on service discovery throughout the P2P network and is able to manage DSR evolution. SERVANT design aims at obtaining a trade-off between recall and generated traffic over the P2P network. Quality issues have not been addressed in this paper, but we are taking them into account in context of the

Italian national research project TEKNE (http://www.tekne-project.it/), where a more general DSR architecture is being developed. In this architecture, selected web services are used to build collaborative business processes and monitor their quality by defining performance indicators. Web services are characterized by functional and non functional aspects in terms of quality attributes that are mapped into performance indicators at process level. The quality aspects will be considered to select at runtime the services collected through our discovery mechanism with the purpose of maximizing the process performance indicators. Future work will also be devoted to properly validate the resulting application in real case scenarios.

Acknowledgements

This work has been partially supported by the TEKNE (Towards Evolving Knowledge-based internetworked Enterprise) FIRB Project (http://www.tekneproject.it/), founded by the Italian Ministry of Education, University and Research.

References

1. Akkiraju, R., Farrell, J., Miller, J., Nagarajan, M., Schmidt, M., Sheth, A., Verma, K.: Web Service Semantics - WSDL-S. A joint UGA-IBM Technical Note, version 1.0 (2005), http://lsdis.cs.uga.edu/Projects/METEOR-S/WSDL-S
2. Arabshian, K., Schulzrinne, H.: An Ontology-based Hierarchical Peer-to-Peer Global Service Discovery System. Journal of Ubiquitous Computing and Intelligence 1(2), 133–144 (2007)
3. Benatallah, B., Hacid, M.S., Paik, H.Y., Rey, C., Toumani, F.: Towards semantic-driven, flexible and scalable framework for peering and querying e-catalog communities. Information Systems 31(4-5), 266–294 (2008)
4. Bianchini, D., De Antonellis, V., Melchiori, M.: Flexible Semantic-based Service Matchmaking and Discovery. World Wide Web Journal 11(2), 227–251 (2008)
5. Bianchini, D., De Antonellis, V., Melchiori, M., Salvi, D.: A Semantic Overlay for Service Discovery Across Web Information Systems. In: Bailey, J., Maier, D., Schewe, K.-D., Thalheim, B., Wang, X.S. (eds.) WISE 2008. LNCS, vol. 5175, pp. 292–306. Springer, Heidelberg (2008)
6. Du, Z., Huai, J., Liu, Y.: ad-UDDI: An Active and Distributed Service Registry. In: Bussler, C.J., Shan, M.-C. (eds.) TES 2005. LNCS, vol. 3811, pp. 58–71. Springer, Heidelberg (2006)
7. Basters, U., Klusch, M.: RS2D: Fast Adaptive Search for Semantic Web Services in Unstructured P2P Networks. In: Cruz, I., Decker, S., Allemang, D., Preist, C., Schwabe, D., Mika, P., Uschold, M., Aroyo, L.M. (eds.) ISWC 2006. LNCS, vol. 4273, pp. 87–100. Springer, Heidelberg (2006)
8. Li, J., Vuong, S.: OntSum: A Semantic Query Routing Scheme in P2P Networks Based on Concise Ontology Indexing. In: Proc. of International Conference on Advanced Information Networking and Applications (AINA 2007), Los Alamitos, CA, USA, pp. 94–101 (2007)

9. Liu, J., Zhuge, H.: A semantic-based P2P resource organization model R-Chord. Journal of Systems and Software 79, 1619–1631 (2006)
10. Paolucci, M., Sycara, K.P., Nishimura, T., Srinivasan, N.: Using DAML-S for P2P Discovery. In: Proceedings of the Int. Conference on Web Services, ICWS 2003, pp. 203–207 (2003)
11. Sapkota, B., Nazir, S., Vitvar, T., Toma, I., Vasiliu, L., Hauswirth, M.: Semantic overlay for scalable service discovery. In: Proc. of International Conference on Collaborative Computing: Networking, Applications and Worksharing, Los Alamitos, CA, USA, pp. 387–391 (2007)
12. Skoutas, D., Sacharidis, D., Kantere, V., Sellis, T.: Efficient Semantic Web Service Discovery in Centralized and P2P Environments. In: Sheth, A.P., Staab, S., Dean, M., Paolucci, M., Maynard, D., Finin, T., Thirunarayan, K. (eds.) ISWC 2008. LNCS, vol. 5318, pp. 583–598. Springer, Heidelberg (2008)
13. Verma, K., Sivashanmugam, K., Sheth, A., Patil, A., Oundhakar, S., Miller, J.: METEOR-S WSDI: A Scalable Infrastructure of Registries for Semantic Publication and Discovery of Web Services. Journal of Information Technology and Management, Special Issue on Universal Global Integration 6(1), 17–39 (2005)

Data Source Management and Selection for Dynamic Data Integration

Martin Husemann and Norbert Ritter

University of Hamburg, Information Systems,
Vogt-Kölln-Straße 30, 22527 Hamburg, Germany
{husemann,ritter}@informatik.uni-hamburg.de
http://vsis-www.informatik.uni-hamburg.de

Abstract. Selection-dynamic data integration employs a set of known data sources attached to an integration system. For answering a given query, suitable sources are selected from this set and dynamically integrated. This procedure requires a method to determine the degree of suitability of the individual data sources within a short timeframe, eliminating conventional schema matching approaches. We developed a registry component for our DynaGrid virtual data source which analyzes data sources upon registration and constructs a catalog of schema fragments grouped by content and cohesion. Given a concrete query, it provides a ranked list of data sources capable of contributing to answering the query. In this paper, we first give an overview of dynamic data integration and the DynaGrid virtual data source. We then present the design and the functionality of the registry component and illustrate its task in the overall process of selection-dynamic data integration.

Keywords: virtual data source; dynamic data integration; source selection; data source catalog.

1 Introduction

In general, interacting with an original data source containing structured data allows posing direct and precise queries and delivers direct result data. A user, however, first has to find a data source with suitable content, learn about its specific structure to pose a precise query, and accept the result data in the given form. If the scope of a data source is limited, several data sources with differing structures may have to be found and queried, and the individual results need to be aggregated by the user.

On the other hand, search engines are typically versatile to use and disregard concrete content. A user can thus pose queries regarding any content to one and the same search engine, whose interface is plain and well known. Those queries, however, cannot be as specific or precise as with original data sources, but are limited to keywords. Search engines do not return direct result data, but only lists of sources which contain the query keywords. The user has to evaluate these sources manually and usually has to access sources found suitable directly to retrieve actual result data.

Z. Lacroix (Ed.): RED 2009, LNCS 6162, pp. 49–65, 2010.

In practice, these two approaches are used in combination. As a first step, a relatively simple keyword query to a search engine is used to find data sources potentially suitable for a given need for information. In a second step, the actual detailed queries are posed to the sources listed by the search engine. For users, search engines thus present a tool for the discovery of data sources. However, the overall process to acquire concrete data for a given demand is tedious and has to be executed mostly manually: Initial keywords need to be deduced, the list of potential sources needs to be reviewed, individual sources need to be made acquainted and queried, and their individual results need to be aggregated.

Our research interest is the transparently integrated use of distributed data sources from a user's point of view. In order to fully leverage the content of data sources connected to the Internet, comprehensive, well-defined query interfaces are only a first step. Such interfaces facilitate technical aspects of data access, but still force users to adapt to each single data source. In order to directly provide users with data according to their demands, special data provision services are required that bridge the gap between individual demands and existing data sources. We designed the DynaGrid virtual data source as a prototype of such a service. It can be used as a single place to address queries to and processes data from original data sources into the form required by the user.

Demand-oriented data provision should combine aspects of search engines and direct data source access as well as additional functionality to reduce manual work as far as possible. We identified six concrete requirements in this context, two of which concern the way users approach data sources:

S1. Single point of contact;
       abstraction from the location of data
S2. Single (uniform) interface;
       abstraction from the native structure of data

Search engines comply with requirement S1 by providing a single, well-known access point to their index of data sources, which contains information on where to find the original data. This is actually more of an indirection step than an abstraction, but it still relieves users of finding original data sources on their own. Technically, the *discovery* of data sources takes place, i. e., the first acquaintance is made, during the construction of the index, with the help of crawlers that basically stumble upon new sources by following links from already known sources. The acquisition of data sources for satisfying a concrete demand, however, is done by the user while evaluating the results of the keyword query to the search engine.

Requirement S2 is implemented by providing the keyword query interface to the data source index. However the structure of an original data source is, its content is flattened into the index and can subsequently be queried uniformly. This flattening causes a loss of query precision, though: Keyword queries are less precise than structured queries. For precise queries and results, the user still has to interact with original data sources directly.

A demand-oriented data provision service should overcome these deficiencies by providing an actual abstraction from the location and the native structure of data. This especially concerns the acquisition of data sources for satisfying a concrete demand (i. e., answering a given query), which should be performed automatically. The decisive point here is not discovering a data source and making it acquainted with the data provision service, but choosing the data sources best suitable for answering a query from a set of sources that may have been discovered previously.

We gave an overview of the DynaGrid virtual data source in previous work [1]. In this paper, we elaborate on the DynaGrid Registry, the registry component of the DynaGrid virtual data source. Its task is to accept registrations of data sources and perform analyses of thus newly acquainted data sources in order to make them usable to the virtual data source. To that end, a specialized catalog of data source contents is built and maintained by the Registry. We explain the specific organization of the data source catalog, the procedure of data source analysis, and the process of selecting data sources from the catalog for answering a given user query.

In order to illustrate the background, Section 2 summarizes our concept of dynamic data integration and Section 3 discusses related work. Section 4 then gives an overview of the DynaGrid virtual data source while Section 5 elaborates on the DynaGrid Registry. Section 6 concludes the paper.

2   Dynamic Data Integration

The most common approaches to integration of structured data are centered on the creation of a *global schema* which comprises the schemas of the participating data sources and allows accessing the distributed data as if it was contained in a single data source. Integration systems that implement such an approach and transform the queries to the global schema into queries to the original data sources are called *mediators* [2]. Mediation comprises the selection of participating data sources, the construction of the global schema, and the creation of integration directives for the schemas of the participating data sources toward the global schema, i. e., the rules for merging the sources' schemas into the global schema or for mapping queries to the global schema onto the sources' schemas.

In order to provide a clearly defined set of terms, we devised a taxonomy of approaches to data integration, which is depicted in Figure 1. At the first level of the taxonomy, data integration is distinguished into *fixed integration*, where mediation takes place at the design-time of an integration system only, and *adaptive integration*, where mediation can also be performed at run-time of an integration system. Only adaptive integration systems support changes in their original data base, i. e., in the participating data sources, at run-time.

At the second level of the taxonomy, adaptive data integration is distinguished into *static integration* and *dynamic integration*. In static integration systems, mediation is performed before a query can be posed. In dynamic integration systems, mediation is performed depending on and specifically catering for the current query. Static integration systems with automatic mediation can support changes of the global schema (i. e., changing demands) and changes to their

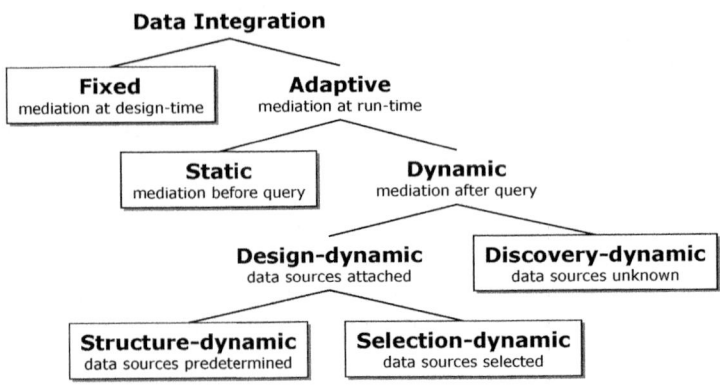

Fig. 1. Taxonomy of approaches to data integration

data base (i. e., changing supply) by repeating the mediation process. Despite this adaptivity, however, they are still static towards individual queries, which have to meet the current global schema. As at any given time there is only one global schema, the construction of a suitable global schema becomes increasingly awkward with growing frequency of the changes of queries. A wide variance of queries posed in parallel cannot be supported.

We therefore propose *dynamic integration* as a new type of integration where mediation is performed directly between the query and the original data sources instead of predefining a global schema. Posing the query is the first step in the integration process. Since there is no predefined global schema, the query can be posed freely as an expression of the user's data demands (requirement S2). In contrast to search engines, however, queries are not limited to keywords, but can be precise queries with the same expressiveness as direct queries to the original data sources.

From the information contained in the query, a *query schema* is built as a virtual global schema to which the query can be directly posed, i. e., compared to static integration, the order of defining the global schema and posing a query is reversed. This procedure eliminates the need of manually and explicitly defining a global schema.

After suitable data sources to support the query schema have been selected and the appropriate integration directives have been created, the data sources are accessed and their individual results are integrated. These steps are performed automatically and are transparent to the user, who thus does not need to interact with the original data sources directly (requirement S1), but is provided with direct and current results.

As depicted in Figure 1, we identified three kinds of dynamic data integration. With *discovery-dynamic integration*, there are no predetermined data sources attached to the integration system. Data sources suitable for answering the current query therefore need to be discovered in a previously unexplored search space during the integration process. These data sources are then used to answer the query and afterward detached. While this approach theoretically offers maximum currency and specificity for the selection of data sources, it is impracticable for practical application since exploring a search space at a large scale is of incalculable complexity.

With *design-dynamic integration*, dynamic mediation is limited to designing the integration directives over a given data base depending on the current query. In case of *structure-dynamic integration*, the set of data sources taking part in query answering is a predetermined subset of the data sources attached to the integration system. This subset may change between queries, but is independent of the current query and remains static during its processing. Dynamic mediation performs the creation of the integration directives from the data sources in the subset toward the query; differing queries may thus result in differing integration directives. In case of *selection-dynamic integration*, the definition of the query-answering subset is part of dynamic mediation, i.e., the data sources taking part in answering a query are dynamically selected from the larger set of data sources attached to the integration system depending on the query. The integration directives are then created the same way as with structure-dynamic integration.

The approach of dynamic data integration obviously implies several serious challenges. Most importantly, after the query has been posed, all the process steps must be performed automatically. Automatic integration within a closely limited time foreseeably leads to a decreased result quality compared to careful integration with manual optimizations. Dynamic integration therefore has a delimited field of application in scenarios where the requirements for flexible support of changing queries outweigh the requirements for precise results. Such scenarios typically have exploratory characteristics, e.g. the search for information (similar to amateur usage of Web search engines) or the initial analysis of data source content prior to static integration (as a tool for database professionals). Result quality and practical benefit can also be increased by limiting the content scope of the integration system to a specific domain, which leads to more uniform data source content and thus better match quality.

3   Related Work

Data integration has been an active research topic in the field of information management for many years. At the core of the integration process, the elements of the participating data sources need to be mapped to each other or to a common global schema. Suitable mappings are usually determined through a process of matching schema elements, and a lot of research has been focused at automating this process [3,4]. When structured data is considered, the most prominent types of sources are relational and XML databases. Data from both types of sources can be subsumed in a hierarchical data model, thus some approaches can be applied to both XML and relational data while other approaches are specific to one of the models. In any case, all the approaches are directed at one-time schema matching during the design of an integrated data source; they do not take into account the possibility of harnessing the automation to conduct schema matching specific to user queries at run-time.

Several integration systems which can automatically integrate data sources at run-time have been proposed [5,6,7,8]. While some approaches in this context mention a notion of dynamic integration or dynamic attachment of data sources, this does not refer to data integration depending on the current query, but merely to the integration of new or changed data sources into the running integration system. The mediation between a given query and the data sources in these cases is still static in terms of its independence of the query.

BioNavigation pursues goals similar to those of DynaGrid in so far as it aims at making a greater set of data resources available to the user without forcing the user to locate and analyze the resources manually [9]. The set of resources attached to the system can be browsed and resource-independent queries can be formulated. The system then generates all possible evaluation paths on the resources. Support of browsing and querying is based on an ontology onto which resource contents are mapped.

The DynaGrid approach deliberately avoids employing a common ontology or a global schema as this would effectively result in static integration of the attached sources' schemas into a predefined target schema. Instead, the data source catalog is gradually constructed as data sources are registered, i.e., its content and organization depend on the particular data sources. The procedure for building the catalog also abstracts from the precise structures in the data sources by generalizing element relationships.

ProtocolDB has been developed to remedy limitations of the BioMOBY format by representing resources on dedicated syntactic and semantic levels [10,11]. It is intended to support resource discovery and selection via semantics rather than syntax. BiOnMap enhances ProtocolDB with a logic-based method to infer previously unknown properties of resources from those properties which are stored in the resource metadata catalog, allowing to retrieve more resources fitting a given user query compared to just matching the query to the known resource properties [12].

All of these three approaches employ catalogs or repositories in which resources are categorized with the use of ontologies. While the use of semantics is a very feasible way to improve resource categorization and retrieval, it was dismissed in the DynaGrid approach. In the context of dynamic integration, the organization of the catalog needs to avoid complex structures and time-consuming reasoning to facilitate an efficient and speedy retrieval of data sources. A similar requirement for speedy processing exists in service selection and composition. In both scenarios, moving as much of the associated complexity to some point before query processing is an obvious procedure, and approaches to achieve this with logic-based reasoning have been proposed [13]. However, as there is no predefined common ontology in DynaGrid, the catalog ontology would have to be built automatically from the registered data sources. This is not feasible, especially in view of the fact that structured data sources are typically not semantically annotated.

4   The DynaGrid Virtual Data Source

In order to investigate demand-oriented data provision through virtual data sources, we developed a prototype of a virtual data source in our *DynaGrid* project [1]. Its architecture is shown in Figure 2. The DynaGrid virtual data source has been designed as a group of Grid services, which are currently implemented with the Globus Toolkit [14]. Original data sources are autonomously run by data source operators under locally individual conditions and connected to the Grid via OGSA-DAI *Grid Data Services* [15]. At the moment, the development of DynaGrid is focused on relational databases as sources of structured data and emphasizes the study of the specific challenges related to dynamic data integration. Nonetheless, the basic concepts could be extended to other types of structured data sources such as XML databases.

Due to the impracticability of discovery-dynamic integration, we chose to investigate selection-dynamic integration, which we consider the most useful and most interesting approach. The Registry component thus maintains a *catalog* of original data sources known to the virtual data source. Data sources are registered through a *registration* interface. A newly registered data source is analyzed by the Registry with regard to its content and structures in order to be cataloged. The catalog allows *content-based lookups* of data sources, which sets the Registry apart from common directory services such as the original OGSA-DAI Service Group Registry which only allow name-based lookups [16]. Content-based lookups enable the dynamic selection of data sources depending on a given query. Details of the Registry are given in Section 5.

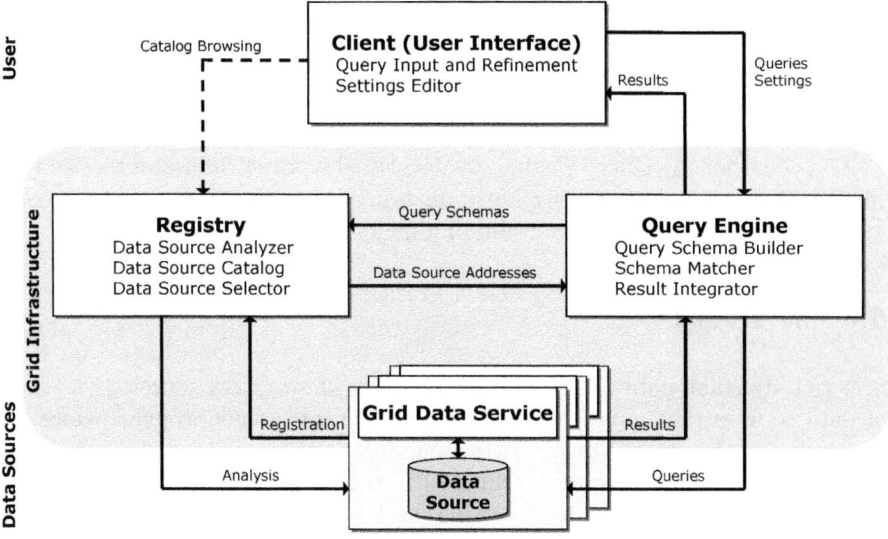

Fig. 2. Architecture of the DynaGrid virtual data source

The Query Engine component comprises the functionality for the processing of user queries. It accepts conjunctive queries posed in a variant of SQL, i. e., typically Select-Where statements with an optional OrderBy clause. A query specifies *result entities* and their attributes about which information is demanded. In SQL, this translates to table and column names in the Select clause. Constraints on the attribute values are defined in the Where clause. The query schema is built from the information on entities, their attributes, and their relationships contained in the query. Since entities may possess more attributes than those mentioned in the query, we refer to the query schema as the *partial virtual global schema* (PVGS). There are many potential *actual global schemas* that contain the section specified by the PVGS, which alleviates the creation of the integration directives.

The query schema is sent to the Registry, which selects candidate sources for further processing. The candidate sources' addresses are sent to the Query Engine as a ranked list sorted by the data sources' coverage of the query schema. Details of the selection process are given in Section 5.3.

The Query Engine performs an *iterative matching* of the query schema and the candidate sources' schemas, i. e., the query schema is matched with the schema of the top-ranked source, then this intermediate result is matched with the schema of the second-ranked source, and so on. The integration directives are created based on the match results following a modified Local-as-View (LAV) approach [17], with the PVGS as a starting point for the global schema. If a source schema cannot be expressed as a view over the global schema because of missing elements, *auxiliary elements* are added to the global schema. In order to facilitate a straightforward view definition, an auxiliary element is constructed basically by carrying over the respective element from the data source currently being integrated. Matching high-ranked sources first serves for creating the initial auxiliary elements from sources with a high similarity to the PVGS. This way, the actual global schema is created as a superset of the PVGS. The query is then executed on the data sources using the MiniCon algorithm [18], and the results are delivered to the client.

As a client for the Query Engine, we developed a graphical user interface with special emphasis on supporting both amateur and experienced users in posing and refining queries as well as evaluating query results.

5   The Registry

Selection-dynamic data integration operates on known data sources, i. e., a set of data sources that have been attached to the integration system before the processing of the current query. Attaching a data source means making the integration system in some way acquainted with technical and content-related aspects of this source so that it can be used for query answering at short notice. Technical aspects comprise any information needed to access the data, e. g. the location of the data source, downtime phases, login data, usage costs, interface descriptions, and necessary drivers. Content-related aspects are e. g. the contained data and its structures, various types of quality attributed to the source, and the source's reputation.

Identifying such information about data sources beforehand limits the integration system's *data base* and thus the search space for suitable data sources to the known sources, which in principle poses a restraint of the fundamental idea of dynamic integration. However, the ability to decide on the sources to answer a query by *selecting* suitable sources from a set of known sources instead of having to *find* such sources from scratch is an essential step to facilitate dynamic integration in a tolerable time frame. Source discovery for answering a concrete query can be regarded as a two-phase process: building up knowledge about available data sources and matching the available sources with the query. Decoupling the basic analysis of data sources, which yields information that is not specific to a certain query, from the processing of individual queries shifts complexity from the critical time of query answering to comparatively time-uncritical tasks which can be delegated to a dedicated component.

As functionality directly related to query answering is off-loaded into separate components, the influence of these components on the query results grows. The construction and organization of the data source catalog and the implementation of the source selection decisively affect the overall quality of the query results; they practically become integral parts of the query processing. We bundled these tasks in the Registry component of the DynaGrid virtual data source which is therefore of equal importance to the overall system as the Query Engine component, although its operations are transparent to users.

Interfaces and Functionality. As depicted in Figure 2, the Registry provides three main interfaces. The *Browsing Interface* can be used to browse the data source catalog. This interface is the only way through which users interact directly with the Registry. By browsing the catalog, they can get an overview of the domain covered by the Virtual Data Source and the various terms used in the data sources, which alleviates formulating precise queries.

The *Registration Interface* is used for registration, deregistration, and updates of data sources, i. e., for operations related to catalog construction and maintenance. In its current form, data sources are explicitly registered by their respective operators or by other authorized parties such as the operator of the Virtual Data Source. Automated methods of source discovery, e. g. based on crawlers, could also be used. When the Registry has become acquainted with a new or updated data source, missing information about this source is gathered through an import and analysis of metadata, which is explained in Section 5.2.

The *Query Interface* is used by the Query Engine to request data sources suitable for answering queries that conform to a given query schema. The Registry then provides a list of candidate sources based on coverage of the query schema. In contrast to the common name-based lookups of values, our Registry offers *content-based lookups*. The user and also the Query Engine can this way abstract from the names or locations of data sources and focus on the query content. The process of source selection is covered in Section 5.3.

5.1 Organization of the Data Source Catalog

As the precise integration of sources is done by the Query Engine, the Registry's task is to provide in a prefixed step a set of *candidate sources* for the integration out of the larger set of attached sources. This allows for simplified data structures and operations in favor of smaller processing times of queries in the Registry. The data source catalog is consequently built on a coarse data model and the processing of data sources' information performs several generalizations to achieve a manageable catalog size. While a consideration of instance data offers advantages for the selection process, it also implies generating huge index structures which can easily outgrow the content of the data sources themselves and are therefore infeasible for use in the data source catalog [19]. The catalog is thus built on normalized schema data.

Normalization of Terms. In order to reduce the syntactic heterogeneity in the catalog, names of relations and attributes are mapped to *concepts*. A concept comprises a set of *terms* which are closely related and can (roughly) be regarded as synonyms. This approach is similar to the *synsets* used in WordNet [20], and the current implementation of DynaGrid uses WordNet for term normalization, i. e., for grouping terms into concepts. As depicted in Figure 3, a concept has a unique identifier by which it is handled internally. All of the terms mapped to a concept are considered equally relevant, i. e., there is no main term associated with a concept. Consequently, two terms are regarded as equal when they are mapped to the same concept. A concept can be related to other concepts through generalization/specialization ("is-a") and aggregation/disaggregation ("part-of") associations. Associations are transitive.

Automatically normalizing terms into concepts is imprecise and may miss mapping synonyms to the same concept as well as distinguishing homonyms

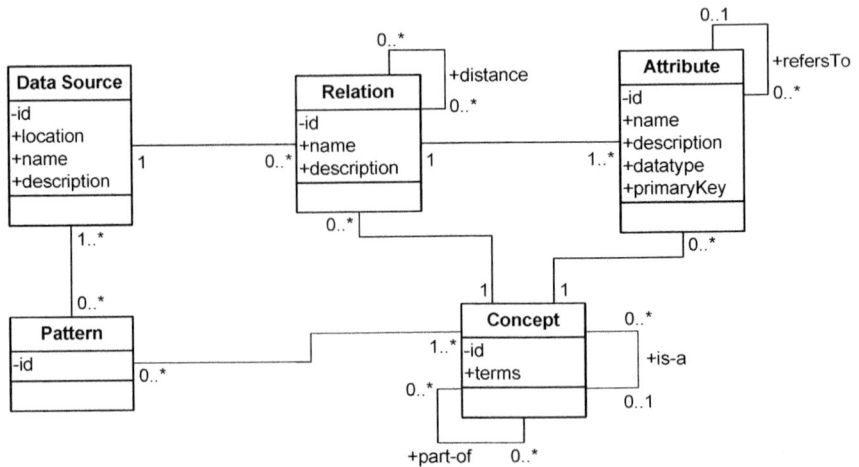

Fig. 3. Coarse data model of the Registry

into separate concepts. Limiting the scope of a virtual data source to a specific application domain reduces this effect. Imprecision and false mappings, however, are inherent to any linguistic matching. Although this is not the focus of our research, the DynaGrid architecture allows exchanging the method of normalization, and we will investigate more sophisticated alternatives in the future.

Concepts and their associations are stored in a *Concept Repository* located in the Registry. The Concept Repository thus holds information about the application domain, not concrete data sources, and is intended to evolve with the registration of new data sources. It is therefore not designed as a domain ontology with predefined elements and associations, but as a loose taxonomy of concepts. Providing a domain ontology for a changing set of data sources would imply creating a form of a universal "domain schema" to which data sources would be mapped. While this would ideally shift all of the complexity associated with integrating the sources to the time of registration, it would practically create a static integration system, which is not our goal. Normalizing identifying terms to concepts during registration, however, shifts complexity from the query processing time to an uncritical "maintenance time" between queries without creating rigid structures in the data source catalog.

The Concept Repository offers basic operations to add, update, and remove terms, concepts, and associations. Given a term, it provides the concept to which this term is mapped (i. e., the actual normalization). Given two terms or two concept identifiers, it provides the association between them if it exists.

Data Structures and Operations. The coarse data model of the catalog is depicted in Figure 3. Each of the stored elements has a unique *identifier* which is assigned by the Registry and used for internal handling.

- *Data sources* are stored with their *name* and a *description* as well as their *location*, which in a Grid environment is a portType.
- A data source contains a set of *relations*, which are also stored with their *name* and *description*. Each relation has a map of *distances* to other relations of the same data source which is determined during registration.
- A relation contains a set of *attributes*, stored with their *name* and *description* as well as their *datatype*. An attribute may be part of the *primary key* of the respective relation and *refer to* another attribute in some relation of the data source as a foreign key.
- Relations and attributes are mapped to *concepts*. A concept holds a set of *terms* which are subsumed by it. It may refer to a more general concept (*is-a*) and to one or more concepts it constitutes a part of (*part-of*).
- *Patterns* are collections of coherent concepts. A pattern refers to the set of concepts it comprises and to the data sources which contain relations that have been mapped to these concepts, i. e., which hold data matching the pattern. Patterns are created during the registration of data sources and map to sets of coherent relations.

A central concept of the catalog is the *fragmentation* of data sources' schemas. Decomposing large schemas into fragments has been recognized to alleviate general schema matching [21]. Query schemas are usually far smaller than data source schemas, i. e., they comprise only a few relations. Matching such query schemas directly to monolithic data source schemas at the time of query processing would be a highly complex procedure with low result quality. Therefore, data source schemas are partitioned into *fragments* according to associations between their elements. As the normalization of terms, fragmenting data source schemas during registration shifts complexity from the query processing time to an uncritical maintenance time. In the current implementation, fragmentation is based on foreign key associations between relations, i. e., a fragment consists of relations which are coherently connected by referential constraints, and the smallest possible fragment consists of one relation without incoming or outgoing referential constraints.

The schema S of a data source D can be regarded as an undirected graph $G_S = (V_S, E_S)$ with a set of vertices $v \in V_S$ and a set of edges $e \in E_S$, such that for every relation $R_i \in S$ there is a $v_i \in V_S$ and for every referential constraint between two relations $R_i, R_j \in S$ there is an $e_i = (v_i, v_j) \in E_S$. Such a graph is called a *schema graph*. A *fragment graph* $G_{SF} = (V_{SF}, E_{SF})$ with a set of vertices $v \in V_{SF}$ and a set of edges $e_i^{SF} \in E_{SF}$ is calculated as the transitive closure of a schema graph G_S, i. e.,

$V_{SF} = V_S$ and
$E_{SF} = \{e_i^{SF} = (v_i, v_j) | P(v_i, ..., v_j)$ is the shortest path from v_i to v_j in $G_S\}$.

The set F_S of *fragments* of S is then given as the set of cliques in G_{SF}.

The edges of a schema graph are weighted with a weight of 1. The edges of a fragment graph are weighted with the length of the path between the two vertices in the schema graph. We define the following sets and functions:

- $T = \{$'NUMERIC','TEXT','DATE'$\}$ denotes the set of data types used in the catalog. Data sources' attribute data types are mapped to this set during registration to simplify schema matching during integration later on.
- C denotes the set of concepts in the Concept Repository.
- L denotes the set of locations of the data sources attached to the integration system.
- A_S denotes the set of attributes in the relations of S.
- $attribute : V_S \rightarrow \mathcal{P}(A_S)$ provides the attributes of a relation.
- $datatype : A_S \rightarrow T$ provides the data type of an attribute.
- $concept : \{V_S \cup A_S\} \rightarrow C$ maps a relation or an attribute to a concept.
- $distance : V_S \times V_S \rightarrow \{\mathbb{N} \cup \infty\}$ provides the length of the path between two vertices of G_S. This is the weight of the edge e^{SF} between those vertices or ∞ if no such edge exists.
- $source : F_S \rightarrow L$ provides the data source which contains a fragment.
- $cardinality : F_S \rightarrow \mathbb{N}$ provides the cardinality of a fragment, which is defined as the number of vertices in the fragment.
- $expansion : F_S \rightarrow \mathbb{N}$ provides the length of the longest path between those vertices in G_S which are contained in a fragment, which is equal to the highest edge weight in this fragment.

5.2   Registration and Analysis of Data Sources

In order to register a data source, at least the location of the source needs to be given. OGSA-DAI Grid Data Services support querying basic metadata about the schema of the underlying database. From this metadata, the names of the relations as well as the names, data types, primary key flags, and referential constraints of the attributes can be gathered. The name of the data source and the various descriptions are optional information and not required for the operations of the registry. In cases of highly specific or unusual relation and attribute names, which might hinder the mapping to concepts, the descriptions can be used to provide alternative identifying terms. The distances between relations are calculated with the transitive closure of the schema graph using the Floyd-Warshall algorithm [22] and stored in separate maps for each relation.

The fragmentation process yields groups of connected relations as fragments. We chose relations as the granularity of fragments since the query schema derived from a user query also consists of one or more connected relations and determines the form of the final output of the virtual data source, i. e., the results provided by the virtual data source always consists of at least one complete relation.

A pattern stored in the catalog represents fragments with the same *content* in one or more of the attached data sources. The exact *structure* of these fragments, i. e., the individual connections of the contained relations via referential constraints, may differ. For example, data sources D1 and D4 shown in Figure 4 both hold fragments containing the concepts {1, 2, 3}, but their schema subgraphs differ in the connections of the respective relations. Both fragments are represented by a single pattern in the catalog; in the example, this is pattern A as shown in Table 2. The generalization of fragments into patterns alleviates the selection process because registry queries need to be evaluated only against the patterns, not against the individual fragments. A pattern in the catalog is created when the first data source containing an according fragment is registered; it holds a reference to this data source. If another source containing a fragment with the same content is registered, the reference to that source is added to the existing pattern.

The procedure for the registration of a data source is given as follows:

1. Create the schema graph, calculate the fragment graph and the distances, and determine the fragments.
2. Map the names of relations and attributes to concepts.
3. Store the information about the data source, the relations, and the attributes in the catalog.
4. Store the fragments as patterns.

Example. Table 1 shows exemplary data sources D1 to D4, which are registered in ascending order, together with the fragments that have been calculated from their schemas. The content of the fragments has been normalized and is represented through concept identifiers. This is the situation after step 2.

Table 2 shows the patterns stored in the catalog after the registration of data sources D1 to D4 with their pattern identifier, the contained concepts, and the

Table 1. Normalized exemplary data sources and their fragments

Data Source	Fragments
D1	{1, 2, 3} {4, 5}
D2	{1, 2} {6, 7}
D3	{1, 2, 3, 4} {8, 9}
D4	{1, 2, 3} {6, 8}

Table 2. Patterns gathered from the exemplary data sources

Pattern	Concepts	Data Sources
A	{1, 2, 3}	D1, D4
B	{4, 5}	D1
C	{1, 2}	D2
D	{6, 7}	D2
E	{1, 2, 3, 4}	D3
F	{8, 9}	D3
G	{6, 8}	D4

data sources which contain relations that map to the respective pattern. This is the situation after step 4.

5.3   Query-Dependent Selection of Data Sources

In order to select data sources to answer a given user query, the query schema built from the user query is used as a *registry query* by the Query Engine. It conveys the structure of the results desired by the user. From the Registry's point of view, it can be handled similarly to data source schemas. In contrast to data source schemas, the schema graphs created from query schemas are considered to be coherent, i.e., a query schema is always processed as one single fragment. Query schemas contain no referential constraints due to their origin, but it is feasible to assume that all the entities specified in a user query are meant to be interlinked.

The Registry determines the coverage of the registry query by the various patterns in the catalog and creates a ranked list of the data sources which are referenced by those patterns with a coverage greater than zero.

The *query coverage* of a pattern is defined as $\frac{|P \cap RQ|}{|RQ|}$, with P being the set of concepts contained in the pattern and RQ being the set of concepts contained in the registry query. The query coverage ranges from 0 (if no concepts of the registry query are contained in the pattern) to 1 (if all concepts of the registry query are contained in the pattern).

The *cohesion* of a fragment in a data source with respect to a registry query is defined as $\frac{|f_S \cap RQ|}{expansion(f_S \cap RQ)}$ for fragments with a cardinality of ≥ 2, with f_S being the set of concepts contained in the fragment, $f_S \cap RQ$ being the subset of concepts in the fragment which are contained in the registry query, and

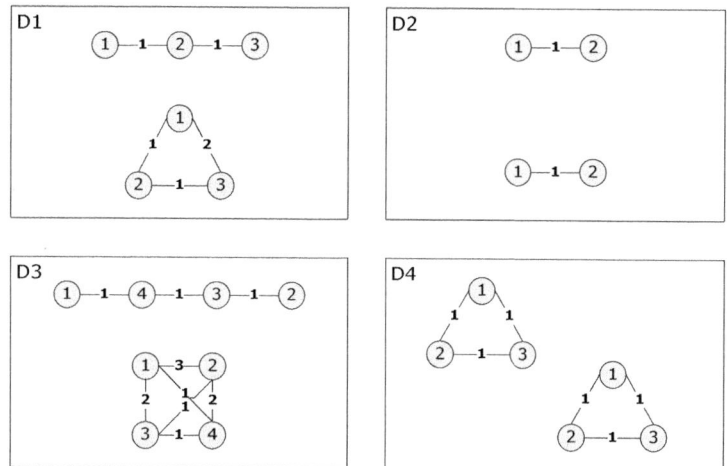

Fig. 4. Relevant schema subgraphs and fragments of the exemplary sources

$expansion(f_S \cap RQ)$ being the length of the longest path between the respective vertices in G_S. The cohesion is a number in $\mathbb{Q}^{\geq 0}$; for fragments with a cardinality of 1 it is defined as 1, provided that $f_S \cap RQ \neq \emptyset$. It states how closely those relations in the data source which are relevant to the query are connected to each other; a closer connection (i. e., a greater cohesion) indicates a tighter relationship of the relations' contents and thus a better suitability of the data source for answering the query.

The procedure for the selection of data sources is given as follows:

1. Create the schema graph and calculate the fragment graph of the query schema. (The fragment graph consists of exactly one fragment.)
2. Map the names of relations and attributes to concepts.
3. Determine the query coverage of the patterns in the catalog. Sort the patterns into descending classes according to their query coverage, discarding patterns with a query coverage of 0.
4. Determine the data sources referenced by each pattern.
5. Within each coverage class, sort the data sources by the cohesion of their relevant fragments with respect to the registry query.

Example continued. Table 3 shows the result of intersecting an exemplary registry query which has been normalized to the set of concepts $RQ = \{1, 2, 3\}$ with the patterns from Table 2. While the query coverage of patterns B, D, F, and G is 0, patterns A, E, and C provide a query coverage >0. They are sorted into two coverage classes CC1=$\{$A, E$\}$ and CC2=$\{$C$\}$. The data sources referenced by these patterns are the sources D1 to D4 from Table 1.

The relevant schema subgraphs and the associated fragments of sources D1 to D4 are depicted in Figure 4. For each source, the upper graph is the schema subgraph from which the fragment shown as the lower graph is derived. Note that the

Table 3. Exemplary registry query intersected with the patterns from Table 2

Pattern	Intersection	Query Coverage	Pattern	Intersection
$A \cap RQ$	$\{1, 2, 3\}$	1	$B \cap RQ$	$\emptyset$
$E \cap RQ$	$\{1, 2, 3\}$	1	$D \cap RQ$	$\emptyset$
$C \cap RQ$	$\{1, 2\}$	$\frac{2}{3}$	$F \cap RQ$	$\emptyset$
			$G \cap RQ$	$\emptyset$

Table 4. Cohesions of the exemplary data sources w. r. t. RQ

Coverage Class	Data Source	$|f_S \cap RQ|$	$expansion(f_S \cap RQ)$	Cohesion
CC1	D4	3	1	3
	D1	3	2	1.5
	D3	3	3	1
CC2	D2	2	1	2

differing subgraph structures of sources D1 and D4 lead to differing expansions, visible as the differing highest edge weights in the respective fragments.

Table 4 shows the cohesions of the sources with respect to the registry query and the final ranking of data sources by coverage and cohesion. The selected data sources are provided to the Query Engine in a list sorted by their ranking. Each list entry contains the location of the data source and its coverage and cohesion with respect to the registry query.

6   Conclusion and Future Work

In this paper, we presented a registry service for selection-dynamic data integration which provides suitable data sources for answering a given user query. After giving an overview of the concept of dynamic data integration and our Dyna-Grid virtual data source, we introduced the functionality and the interfaces of the Registry component. We elaborated on the design of the data source catalog and the methods for registering and selecting data sources. The core feature of the DynaGrid Registry is its capability of content-based lookups, which provide data sources based on their content-related suitability for user queries.

In forthcoming research, we plan to extend the existing client with a registry browsing interface. We will also perform evaluations regarding query processing performance and result quality in various application contexts. Based on the results, we will fine-tune the Registry's data model and operations, investigating e. g. intra-relation fragmentation and filtering of nonrelevant attributes.

References

1. Husemann, M., Ritter, N.: A Virtual Data Source for Service Grids. In: Second Int. Conf. on Data Management in Grid and P2P Systems, September 2009, pp. 24–35 (2009)

2. Wiederhold, G.: Mediators in the Architecture of Future Information Systems. IEEE Computer 25(3), 38–49 (1992)
3. Shvaiko, P., Euzenat, J.: A Survey of Schema-Based Matching Approaches. In: Spaccapietra, S. (ed.) Journal on Data Semantics IV. LNCS, vol. 3730, pp. 146–171. Springer, Heidelberg (2005)
4. Rahm, E., Bernstein, P.A.: A survey of approaches to automatic schema matching. VLDB J. 10(4), 334–350 (2001)
5. Gounaris, A., Sakellariou, R., Comito, C., Talia, D.: Service Choreography for Data Integration on the Grid. In: Knowledge and Data Management in GRIDs, February 2007, pp. 19–33. Springer, Heidelberg (2007)
6. Gorton, I., Almquist, J., Dorow, K., et al.: An Architecture for Dynamic Data Source Integration. In: 38th Hawaii Int. Conf. on System Sciences (January 2005)
7. Chang, K.C.C., He, B., Zhang, Z.: Toward Large Scale Integration: Building a MetaQuerier over Databases on the Web. In: CIDR, January 2005, pp. 44–55 (2005)
8. Al-Hussaini, L., Viglas, S., Atkinson, M.: A Service-based Approach to Schema Federation of Distributed Databases. Technical Report EES-2006-01, University of Edinburgh (November 2005)
9. Lacroix, Z., Parekh, K., Vidal, M.E., et al.: BioNavigation: Selecting Optimum Paths Through Biological Resources to Evaluate Ontological Navigational Queries. In: Ludäscher, B., Raschid, L. (eds.) DILS 2005. LNCS (LNBI), vol. 3615, pp. 275–283. Springer, Heidelberg (2005)
10. Aziz, M., Lacroix, Z.: ProtocolDB: Classifying Resources with a Domain Ontology to Support Discovery. In: 10th Int. Conf. on Information Integration and Web-based Applications Services, November 2008, pp. 462–469 (2008)
11. Wilkinson, M.D., Links, M.: BioMOBY: An Open Source Biological Web Services Proposal. Briefings in Bioinformatics 3(4), 331–341 (2002)
12. Ayadi, N.Y., Lacroix, Z., Vidal, M.E.: BiOnMap: A Deductive Approach for Resource Discovery. In: 10th Int. Conf. on Information Integration and Web-based Applications Services, November 2008, pp. 477–482 (2008)
13. Li, J., Ma, D., Zhao, Z., et al.: An Efficient Semantic Web Services Matching Mechanism. In: Second Int. Workshop on Resource Discovery (August 2009)
14. Foster, I.T.: Globus Toolkit Version 4: Software for Service-Oriented Systems. In: IFIP Int. Conf. on Network and Parallel Computing, November 2005, pp. 2–13 (2005)
15. Antonioletti, M., Atkinson, M.P., Baxter, R., et al.: The design and implementation of Grid database services in OGSA-DAI. Concurrency - Practice and Experience 17(2-4), 357–376 (2005)
16. Antonioletti, M., Atkinson, M., Baxter, R., et al.: OGSA-DAI: Two Years On. In: The Future of Grid Data Environments Workshop, GGF10 (March 2004)
17. Lenzerini, M.: Data Integration: A Theoretical Perspective. In: PODS, June 2002, pp. 233–246 (2002)
18. Pottinger, R., Halevy, A.Y.: MiniCon: A scalable algorithm for answering queries using views. VLDB J. 10(2-3), 182–198 (2001)
19. Yu, B., Li, G., Sollins, K.R., Tung, A.K.H.: Effective keyword-based selection of relational databases. In: SIGMOD, June 2007, pp. 139–150 (2007)
20. Fellbaum, C. (ed.): WordNet - An Electronic Lexical Database, May 1998. MIT Press, Cambridge (1998), http://wordnet.princeton.edu
21. Rahm, E., Do, H.H., Maßmann, S.: Matching Large XML Schemas. SIGMOD Record 33(4), 26–31 (2004)
22. Floyd, R.W.: Algorithm 97: Shortest path. ACM Commun. 5(6), 345 (1962)

A Provenance-Based Approach to Resource Discovery in Distributed Molecular Dynamics Workflows

Sérgio Manuel Serra da Cruz[1], Patricia M. Barros[1,3], Paulo M. Bisch[3],
Maria Luiza M. Campos[2], and Marta Mattoso[1]

[1] PESC – COPPE/UFRJ, [2] PPGI – IM-NCE/UFRJ, [3] IBCCF – UFRJ
Federal University of Rio de Janeiro (UFRJ)
P.O. Box: 68511, Rio de Janeiro, RJ, 21941-972, Brazil
{serra,pmbarros,marta}@cos.ufrj.br, mluiza@nce.ufrj.br,
pmbisch@biof.ufrj.br

Abstract. The major challenge of *in silico* experiments consists in exploiting the amount of data generated by scientific apparatus. Scientific data, programs and workflows are resources to be exchanged among scientists but difficult to be efficiently used due to their heterogeneous and distributed nature. Provenance metadata can ease the discovery of these resources. However, keeping track of the execution of experiments and capturing provenance among distributed resources are not simple tasks. Thus, discovering scientific resources in distributed environments is still a challenge. This work presents an architecture to help the execution of scientific experiments in distributed environments. Additionally, it captures and stores provenance of the workflow execution in a repository. To validate the proposed architecture, a bioinformatics workflow has been defined for the execution of a real molecular dynamics simulation experiment, called GromDFlow. The experiment highlights the advantages of this architecture, which is available and is being used for several simulations.

Keywords: provenance, scientific workflows, resource discovery, metadata.

1 Introduction

Since at least Newton's laws of motion three centuries ago, scientists have recognized theoretical and experimental science as the basic research paradigms for understanding nature. Recently, computer simulations, also known as *in silico* experiments, have become a new paradigm for scientists to explore domains that are inaccessible to traditional experiment [14], such as the predicting climate change, earthquake simulations and molecular dynamics. *In silico* experiments are increasingly demanding high performance computing (HPC), grid and cloud environments, spanning organizational and spatiotemporal boundaries and managing huge amounts of data. As information technology is deployed in scientific communities, the development of novel tools and new techniques is required to support and manage these distributed processes, so that the datasets associated with generated scientific knowledge can be used as effectively as possible.

Z. Lacroix (Ed.): RED 2009, LNCS 6162, pp. 66–80, 2010.

Broadly speaking, a scientific experiment is strictly associated to a set of controlled actions, which can be understood as variations of tests, where their products are usually compared to each other to accept or refute a hypothesis. *In silico* experiment, in the Molecular Dynamics (MD) domain, involves a computational study simulating in detail the interatomic interactions in proteins. There is a well-founded relationship between the amino acid sequence and 3D structure, which is a major goal of theoretical molecular biology [23]. The process and dynamics from sequence to 3D structure is helpful and important in understanding diseases, protein design and nanotechnology. With the improvements in software providing a powerful computational platform, the atomistic protein folding simulations are being heavily used by biologists.

Like in many other fields of science like: engineering, astronomy, high energy physics and bioinformatics. MD experiments involve dozens of long running simulations, so that they usually require the use of both distributed computing and data intensive techniques. Users often find difficulties when managing data between data sources and applications. In most cases there is no standard solution for workflow design and execution with tailored scripting mechanisms are being implemented in a case by case basis. In order to assist the users in building and managing computational processes, several researchers have investigated the use of scientific workflows enacted by Scientific Workflow Management Systems (SWfMS) that often are designed for the definition, execution and monitoring of complex processes in a fairly stable manner. Thus, to aid users to reduce burden of managing data resources and shrink the time spent to prepare MD simulations, we have coded a distributed scientific workflow named GromDFlow [10].

Traditionally, MD requires several executions of a workflow specification with different inputs. The set of the trials, also named essays, represent distinct workflow executions of one scientific experiment. Resource selection may affect the outcome of a scientific experiment. It is a fundamental step among the essays of the experiment. Thus, resource discovery plays an important role in workflow composition, for example, in finding an adequate activity for the flow. However, this is only part of the problem. Combining activities and datasets that can be chained along the workflow is not simple. The success of workflow reuse depends on the quality, completeness and effectiveness of scientific resource discovery. Provenance data repositories can effectively help this resource discovery, since they store all executed activities of the workflow.

Most SWfMS are exporting their workflow provenance data, including specification, in the common OPM (Open Provenance Model). OPM [19] is a joint effort to represent provenance uniformly and promote interoperability between SWfMS. OPM is designed to meet requirements, such as: to allow provenance information to be exchanged between systems, by means of a compatibility layer based on a shared provenance model; to allow for developers to build and share tools that operate on such provenance model; to define provenance in a precise, technology-agnostic manner, allowing multiple levels of description to co-exist; and, finally, to define a core set of rules that identify the valid inferences that can be made on provenance representation. In essence, OPM consists of three kinds of nodes: *artifact, process* and *agent.* OPM based provenance repositories aim to store heterogeneous workflow specifications, results and descriptors, based on a shared provenance model, supporting a wide range of queries.

Monitoring of scientific workflows is important for many purposes including status tracking, recording provenance, or performance improvement. Resource discovery is an indispensable phase in these scenarios. But resource discovery is broader than this; it is the process of identifying, locating and accessing resources that have a particular property to implement a single task [2]. A SWfMS consists of not only the workflow engine but also auxiliary services. These services encompass many of the non-control-flow aspects of script-based orchestration, including resource discovery for accessing data and data provenance recording [32]. For example, a particular challenge in workflows is integration of resources. Locating remote datasets and codes, handling faults appropriately, cataloging large volumes of data produced by the system, and managing complex resource mappings of workflow stages onto distributed environments require scientific workflow stages to access a host of auxiliary workflow services.

Resource discovery for choosing workflows from a workflow database can take advantage of queries like "what workflows use these two programs". However, current solutions fail to answer such queries like "what essays enacted by researcher X have used 10 nodes of the cluster Y" or "what are the concrete workflows that were generated from the specification of abstract workflow Z that use the program P". In this paper, we address the emerging problem of scientific resource discovery with the support of provenance metadata. We focus on how provenance gathered along the whole execution of a distributed workflow would help to enable the linkage between data and resources. We present a provenance metadata schema to represent relevant workflow execution data in HPC environments. The use of provenance information on remote parallel execution is evenly explored, improving resource discovery through provenance querying and also helping scientists to fine tune the definition of these scientific experiments. This provenance metadata can be seen as OPM compatible in the context of HPC. In [10] we presented services to gather provenance from scientific experiments enacted as distributed workflows, but this gathering was restricted to remote executions with a very simple provenance model. In this work, we present an architecture that extends these services, modeling provenance metadata from parallel executions, capturing and storing provenance metadata generated during the whole experiment lifecycle. Such approach is a step towards the above-mentioned challenges on independent distributed workflow execution and provenance gathering. This paper is organized as follows. Section 2 discusses some related work and distributed provenance gathering issues. Section 3 presents a layered approach used to ease resource discovery through provenance queries. Section 4 provides an overview of a real molecular dynamics simulation experiment, called GromDFlow. Section 5 describe the GromDExp Portal and discusses provenance queries for resource discovery. Finally, section 6 concludes the paper.

2 Provenance Gathering and Resource Discovery

In this section, we discuss the problems of having to collect provenance metadata from distributed workflows, like GromDFlow, when moving from one workflow execution engine to another engine to execute remote activities of the same scientific workflow. We stress that provenance metadata, gathered during the composition and execution, may help scientists to discover hidden resources, enabling the reuse and repurpose of workflows of scientific experiments like, for instance, MD. Provenance metadata management catalyzes the existing demand behind information resources on distributed environments, which can be used as a base for the assessment of information quality, improving the contextual information behind the generation, transformation and publishing of scientific data on the Web. Scientists, in their daily duties, frequently deal with large flows of data much larger than they can quickly analyze. Thus, they often use distributed and heterogeneous environments like high performance computing clusters, grids or clouds to execute their distributed workflows. But, to take advantage of these environments, scientists face issues like: (i) choosing which activities are independent of the others to be executed in the distributed environment; (ii) modeling abstract and concrete (distributed) workflows; (iii) submitting activities to the distributed environment; (iv) detecting performance bottlenecks; (v) monitoring processes status; and (vi) gathering provenance. These issues are hard to be controlled by a single SWfMS, as they require the combination of provenance metadata from distributed environments to ease querying and analysis on the scientific data flows.

2.1 Metadata, Provenance Metadata and Experiment Lifecycle

Metadata are not the only information needed to ascertain the quality of the data when the data are generated as the result of a variety of scientific processing, it is important to know exactly how the data was obtained, which input datasets. Metadata offer metrics that may be used to predict the outcome of the execution of a scientific experiment on selected resources [4]. Experiment´s metadata provide resource characterization that allows their comparison with similar resources, thus addressing the need of combining multiple complementary resources to implement completely a single task. Finally, experiment´s metadata play a decisive role in data analysis, in particular to track experiments through provenance data.

Provenance, which was initially focused on the lineage or historical trail of a resource [6], can be described in various terms, depending on the domain where it is applied [20], [25], [26]. For instance, the provenance of a data product contains descriptions about the process and datasets used to derive it. In this paper, we consider provenance metadata as the semi- or automatically and systematically captured and recorded information that helps users or computing systems to determine the derivation history of a data product, starting on its original sources and ending at a given repository.

The provenance metadata required to support resource discovery may come from a variety of sources including human inputs, direct reporting from applications and annotations from observations of human and system activities that evolve over time. It provides important documentation that is essential to preserve the data, to determine its quality and the authorship of a scientific investigation, to reproduce it as well as to interpret and validate the associated scientific results.

We share Mattoso *et al.* [13] view of an experiment lifecycle, which relies on gathering distinct subjects of provenance during all its stages [9]. We believe that such approach may aid scientists not only to have more control on the scientific experiment tests but also to increase knowledge reuse and sharing between distinct research teams. For example, by relating models to algorithms which are associated to programs and finally to executions, more expressive and high-level resource discovery queries can be answered, instead of the ones which are solely based on data about the execution of workflows. As described in our previous work [9] [13], the major stages of a scientific experiment lifecycle generates different kinds of provenance metadata. The stages are identified as: *Composition, Execution* and *Analysis*. Each stage has an independent cycle, taking place at distinct moments of the experiment, and handling explicit provenance metadata. For instance, the *composition* is responsible for setting up the experiment activities. It includes the specification and modeling of scientific experiments in different levels of abstraction and the registering of workflow variations in the context of the experiment. The *execution* phase encapsulates the infrastructure activities that must be accomplished when running a scientific workflow modeled by a set of software components (*e.g.*, local or remote programs, web services, and grid services). In other words, the execution phase is responsible for retrieving a concrete workflow definition, somehow executing this definition in an appropriate engine, and producing results to be analyzed in the following phase of the life cycle. Once the scientific experiment is completely executed, scientists must select measurement data and *analyze* them to verify if their hypothesis is confirmed or refuted and draw conclusions about the scientific experiment. Provenance can be fine-grained or coarse-grained. The description of fine grained (*e.g.* dataset at execution stage) or coarse grained (*i.e.* annotations at composition stage) information resources.

2.2 Gathering Provenance Resources in Distributed Workflows

SWfMS have been designed as having distributed or centralized execution control. Distributed SWfMS like Swift [33], Askalon [31] and Triana [8], focus on high performance and resource scheduling of the Execution stage. On the other hand, centralized SWfMS (*e.g.* Taverna, [19], VisTrails [7], [24], Kepler [18]) are do not fully support all stages of provenance gathering. However, centralized SWfMS support the execution stage by having a single workflow execution engine, enacting locally the whole execution of a given scientific workflow. For instance, VisTrails provides visualization facilities and provenance gathering of the whole composition process, capturing the evolution of a workflow. Despite of these facilities, VisTrails, in its current public version, lacks support to connections to distributed environments, and, consequently, cannot collect provenance on these environments. Kepler has some of these facilities; however, if a sub-workflow needs to be executed under a HPC, these activities will need a Kepler's HPC execution engine.

If scientists need to change from one environment to another, from local execution to a distributed environment like HPC, grid, or cloud, they may send activities of a sub-workflow to be remotely executed one by one. In this way, they can keep the local SWfMS in charge of the execution control, although this can severely deteriorate performance. Another option is to specify the sub-workflow with the distributed SWfMS language, so that it will execute under the remote SWfMS and take advantage of the remote resources without coming back and forth to the local SWfMS.

In this scenario, a typical scientific workflow may want to have its provenance recorded by a centralized SWfMS but still taking advantage of high performance environments. We aim at showing that having an independent provenance gathering mechanism gives flexibility to help in moving from one SWfMS to another in a distributed environment. Such approach can be used to record provenance remotely using the same representation model as the local SWfMS, allowing scientists to identify and locate existing resources that have a particular property. For instance, resources can be organized with respect to provenance metadata that characterizes their content, semantics, characteristics, performance and quality of the scientific experiment. Thus, a resource discovery system integrated with the SWfMS may allow the expression of provenance queries to identify and locate resources that implement a specific stage of the scientific experimentation.

In summary, there are several tasks not supported or handled individually by SWfMS. These tasks are not represented in relationships to the provenance metadata that describes the experiment, such as: monitoring the execution of scientific tasks on distributed environments; supporting scientists to reuse and share abstract workflows; and querying provenance metadata resources gathered from distinct stages of the scientific experiment lifecycle. In order to meet these needs, new frameworks, models, theories, and techniques supporting a broader experiment lifecycle must be investigated. One area where SWfMS and provenance management can be particularly useful is resource discovery in the context of scientific data generated by collaborative scientific investigations.

3   Resource Discovery through Provenance Metadata

Resource discovery is the process of identifying, locating and accessing resources that have a particular property to implement a single task [2]. It typically relies on a repository produced with the voluntary registration of resources by providers and users or with automated searching and classification of resources on the Web, P2P or grids [1]. Resource discovery may assist users in the identification and localization of resources that have a particular property. There are several approaches that address the problem of classifying resources on the Web or on grid environments [3], others support queries against metadata stored in resource repositories [27] but few explore provenance metadata generated by distinct execution environments, particularly HPC ones.

Resources may have a syntactic description or a semantic description. Resource discovery systems can use syntactical description to support the discovery of resources accepting a particular data format rather than the discovery of resources that capture a conceptual task regardless of their input and output format. According to Ayadi, Lacroix and Vidal [1], a resource metadata can be associated to its content (for data sources), its semantics (in terms of relationships or ontological classes), and its quality (curation, reliability, trust). This last characteristic is directly related to provenance metadata. We present our approach to provide independent provenance gathering capacity to scientific experiments.

3.1   A Resource Discovery Layered Approach

We advocate that both the qualitative and quantitative measures associated to an experiment may be vastly improved through the analysis of provenance metadata. We propose a multi-layer approach to enable provenance metadata gathering along all stages of a scientific experiment lifecycle. Its main advantages are the simplicity, flexibility, ease of integration while keeping the independence of SWfMS. The layers are: *interface, application, provenance services* and *persistence*.

Through the *interface layer*, the scientist may choose the abstract workflow that will be executed, set its parameters, select input type, make annotations and define experiments' variables to be used in the scientific experiment. These data and metadata are stored in a database at the persistence layer. The interface layer reduces scientists' concerns with the SWfMS details, activity distribution policy or operational configurations on the distributed environment which are being used to execute the workflow. The main functionality of the layer is to collect provenance data at the composition stage, because it is hard to be collected at workflow run-time. Additionally, the layer can also be used to help scientists to monitor the progress of the execution of distributed activities that are running in a remote environment, and also to query provenance metadata resources. The interface layer is represented through a Web Portal, to be further discussed in section 5.

The *application layer* abstracts underlying heterogeneous data into data products, services and legacy software into workflows tasks and provides efficient management for data products, workflows tasks and provenance metadata. The layer consists of individual workflows specifications; it is responsible for the execution of the concrete scientific workflows. This layer allows the use of a local SWfMS as transparent as possible, encapsulating the SWfMS functionalities. The *provenance services layer* contains a set of modules to collect provenance metadata from the interface layer and from the distributed environment, storing it at the persistence layer. These modules will be discussed in subsection 3.2.

Finally, the *persistence layer* is one of the principal components of the architecture. It can store data generated at three distinct stages of the experiment lifecycle. It has interfaces to store relevant data to help composing a workflow or metadata produced by a given scientific experiment.

3.2 Provenance Services

In order to help scientists to collect provenance metadata generated at the execution stage of an experiment lifecycle we have adopted Matrioshka [10], which consists of a set of services that can be coupled to a SWfMS to provide distributed provenance support to a workflow application (Figure 1). The arrows mean the possible data flow between the services.

Matrioshka has been conceived: (i) to operate over heterogeneous HPC or grid environments; (ii) to be independent of the SWfMS used for workflow execution and of the underlying data storage system; (iii) to be able to handle heterogeneous dataset representations; (iv) to support different levels of provenance data granularity; and (v) not to interfere in the workflow performance [11].

The *Provenance Broker* provides the underpinning to a flexible provenance repository generation; it is a mediator Web service located among three peers: a SWfMS, a heterogeneous information source (a distributed service provider) and the provenance consumers (*e.g.* scientists that execute queries through a Web interface to discover resources). It aims to accomplish three main roles: (i) to gather provenance metadata through "event notifications"; (ii) to provide metadata transformations; (iii) to route gathered metadata.

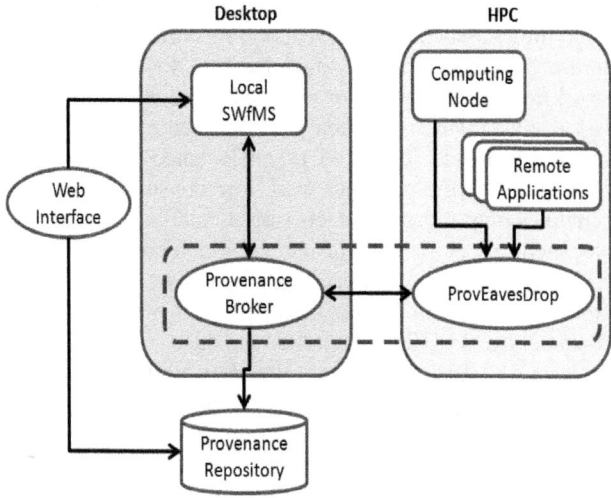

Fig. 1. Matrioshka services overview, adapted from Cruz *et al.* [10]

The first role is associated to communication between a given workflow enactment engine and remote event listeners (*ProvEavesdrop*), running in distributed environments. The broker gathers and tags data products from both local and remote workflows, also controlling messages throughout the system. It can listen to logging message streams generated from ProvEavesdrop services. The second role classifies messages according to a set of rules previously defined by the scientist for a given experiment. Experiment rules can encompass the duration of the experiment, annotations and data transformations. Finally, the third role dispatches all well-structured data collections defined by integrated uniform meta schemas to provenance repositories and organizes them as personal collections so that data provenance queries and statistics are easily retrieved or browsed by scientists.

The *ProvEavesdrop service* instance generates "event notifications" that provide details about the data being staged, the execution status of the remote application, the location of the intermediary and final output results, execution times, security warnings, error messages and so on. Each instance acts as a service mediator that runs in the background, rather than under the direct control of a user; it is usually initiated as a process by the SWfMS through the firing of a monitoring message.

Due to OPM initiative, it is possible to map and register the distinct kinds of provenance metadata generated during the distinct stages of the scientific experiment or the one gathered on distributed and heterogeneous environments. Thus, to evaluate the feasibility of the provenance services, we conceived a simple conceptual model OPM-compliant to register metadata of parallel execution of essays of a scientific experiment. Figure 2 shows only part of the conceptual data model (using crow's foot notation) of the provenance and resources repository, currently implemented in Matrioshka. It describes the provenance metadata also considering the remote environment and data about scientific experiments stages.

Briefly, according to our proposed model, the class *user* represents the different kinds of users that can access the portal. An experiment is specified using an abstract workflow (represented at the *abstract workflow* class) and defined as a flow of tasks and data (with no direct association to execution resources). This class is not detailed here but it represents the workflow as modeled by OPM, only at the abstract level. This abstract workflow may have one or many concrete workflows (represented at the *concrete workflow* class) which, on their turn, may be executed several times (each execution is an essay and is registered as an instance of the *execution* class). In addition, the execution of the concrete workflow consumes existing input data resources and generates output data products (represented at the *resource* class as input and output associated to specific code resources, which consume computing resources - for example, the number of processors used to execute an HPC activity). The class *computing resource* contains details of the operations performed and computational resources consumed by the HPC environment, such as nodes, queues and jobs. The class *code resource* contains details of the software used as workflows tasks and *data resource* contains descriptors to data consumed or produced by the workflow processing.

Through the use of the provenance repository represented according to the model of Figure 2, it is possible to correlate a scientific experiment to the distinct executions of its workflows, *i.e.* to make a correlation among the experiment, the workflows and the successive executions with distinct parameters and resources allocated. Despite of not being conceived to register provenance metadata at this extension, the OPM standard also can be used to support it. For instance, in the current schema, the OPM nodes are registered, *i.e.* an OPM-*artifact* can be represent as the class data an OPM-*process* is represented at the classes concrete workflow, experiment, and resource. the OPM-*agent* is represented at the class user.

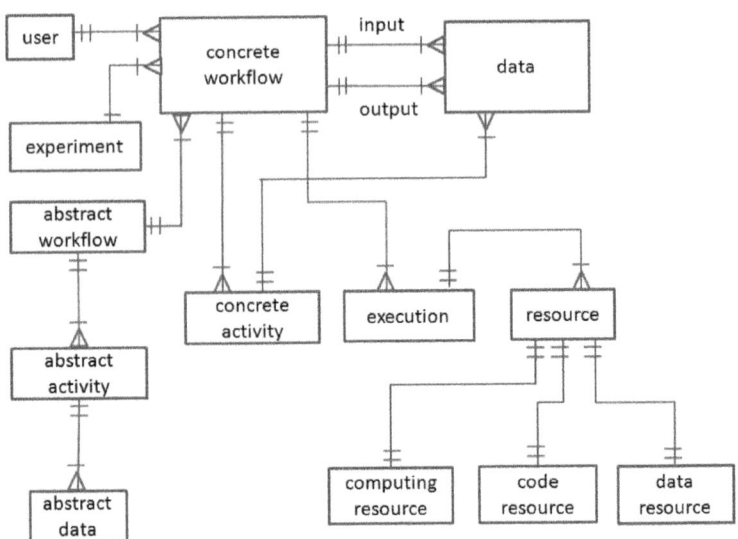

Fig. 2. An excerpt of the conceptual model for storing provenance and resources metadata (the attributes and keys are not shown, crow's foot notation was adopted)

As an example, let us consider there were seven executions with variations of the same abstract workflow, performed during a single experiment. Variations may include different parameters and input data sets and different computing resources. From these seven executions, three were related to protein *Ptn1* and four to protein *Ptn2*. These seven executions are typically registered as seven "isolated" concrete workflow executions, rather than seven trials of one experiment. Without capturing this relationship, the executions could be considered distinct, corresponding to separate experiments. Thus, resource discovery could lead to unrealistic conclusions.

4 The Molecular Dynamics Distributed Scientific Workflow

In this section, we discuss the characteristics of a distributed workflow named GromDFlow to run experiments of Molecular Dynamics (MD) in HPC environments.

MD simulations evaluate the motion of particles in a molecular system; they use classical potential energy to describe the system [23] [30]. Usually, to start simulations, an energy minimization is performed to calculate the coordinates that minimize the potential energy of the system. MD simulation uses GROMACS package [29]. To perform MD simulations it is necessary to: (i) use a PDB file which can be found in the PDB database [21], an archive of experimentally determined 3D structures of biological macromolecules; alternatively, one can use PDB files from model structures; (ii) configure a set of applications of GROMACS package to perform the calculations; and (iii) generate and distribute the jobs over a HPC facility. In order to reduce the time spent to prepare MD simulations, we have coded a workflow named GromDFlow [10].

GromDFlow has been defined. It has been implemented in Kepler SWfMS. The workflow has been divided in two sub-workflows. The first one, called *LocalGRO-MACS*, runs programs locally, *i.e.*, in the same machine that the SWfMS has been configured. The second one, called *RemoteGROMACS*, run programs in a distributed environment, which can be a cluster or a grid.

To make distribution clearer, the *GromDFlow* was designed as a hierarchy of composite actors. The Connection actor initiates a SSH connection from a local workstation to a HPC cluster; the *LocalGROMACS* controls execution of local activities and invokes the provenance broker service. *RemoteGROMACS* uses the connection to invoke the remote execution of the distributed activities, which include the initializations of the DBMS and the ProvEavesDrop remote service in the HPC environment.

There is a correlation between the workflows' actors and the resource discovery layers. For instance, the Connection actor opens a connection to the machines involved with the execution of the workflows. It is related with the interface layer and the Web Portal application. The *LocalGROMACS* allows the execution of some local GROMACS applications, preparing intermediary files to be used in the HPC environment; it is related with the application layer. The *RemoteGROMACS* runs the molecular dynamics simulation in the HPC environment, which takes long computational time and requires remote parallel execution capacity. It is related to the application layer and due to the capacity to collect provenance data from distributed environment it is also associated with provenance services and persistence layers. The provenance collected at this layer allows scientists to execute provenance queries about the experiment that aid them to reveal hidden resources.

5 Querying Provenance Metadata Resources

In this section, we present a Web portal named *GromDExp*, which offers a graphical query interface that allows scientists to set parameters for the parallel execution of the MD workflows. The portal also simplifies resource discovery and suggests to the scientist the possibility to get a deeper comprehension of distinct executions of the same *in silico* experiment. This goal can be achieved through the queries of provenance metadata previously stored at the provenance repositories.

5.1 The GromDExp Portal

The GromDExp portal supports submission and execution of MD simulations, based on GromDFlow distributed workflow, through a HPC computing platform. However, we could not cover all possibilities of GROMACS package utilization. Thus, in order to help unskilled users we had to delimit GROMACS options based on our experience to facilitate its use. The GromDFlow allows the submission of parallel jobs to a HPC machine that runs under Scientific Linux 4. The HPC has 12 nodes, each node with 4 cores Intel Xeon 2.33GHz dual-core processors, totaling 96 cores with 8 GB of RAM using Gigabit Ethernet.

Fig. 3. Interface with query result about the remote environment (the arrow points to a new window, depicting the data, collect by Matriohska, related to an essay)

The portal layout was conceived to be as easily accessible as possible (to access the portal services, the user must first register, accepting the Conditions of Use.Once logged in, (s)he will be able to use the MD workflow in the following manner: (i) by submitting any PDB file, containing amino acids residues; (ii) by configuring the number of steps to calculate the molecular dynamics; (iii) by configuring the number of processors to be used at HPC; (iv) by querying provenance metadata about a given experiment; (v) by monitoring his(her) jobs, cancelling or removing them from HPC, also being able to download result files, with logs, trajectories, energies.

5.2   Queries through GromDExp

The provenance queries are triggered by scientists through the Portal, which also allows them to examine and compare the history concerning each individual *in silico* experiment. Through the portal, scientists can get new insights on MD experiments that are unable to be seen without provenance support. For instance, they can compare two different executions of the same experiment, and evaluate how they affect the 3D structure of a protein. Provenance metadata may also help scientists to be aware of what has happened during the execution of a workflow or to determine trust and authority of authors.

The query interface offers centralized access to all provenance metadata and data about the experiments, such as input files used and the output files generated in the distributed environment. At this time, the provenance queries are pre-defined based on the database schema presented in section 3.2.

GromDExp enables scientists to query all the concrete workflows that were executed, represented on a list that contains: workflow name, workflow description, date of creation, input data (parameters and files defined by the user) and execution output data (data generated during the execution in the distributed environment). The provenance repository may support the discovery of resources that are loosely equivalent to an implementation of a workflow. Some simple queries can be extracted from the model. Such as, how many successful parallel executions of a concrete workflow *cwf1* associated with an abstract workflow *awf1* of experiment *exp1* have been performed on the queue *q1* of cluster *c1*. Another simple example enabled the provenance repository is what is the amount of executions of the concrete workflows *cwf1* of experiment *exp1* where enacted with more than 32 cores. Another one is which research team member enacted the concrete workflow *cwf1* which produce the output data file *df1* with less than *m* minutes on queue *q2*.To evaluate the history of an experiment, scientists have to evaluate one, or more, provenance queries. Besides, since provenance usually captures intricate relationships between data items and processes, the corresponding provenance queries that need to be evaluated are often quite complex.

To perform a query, a request is sent to a provenance query engine (in this case a DBMS) by a querying actor at the Portal and the result is returned to GromDExp. To leverage the MD scientist from SQL we have predefined typical provenance queries that may aid scientists to discover resources. For instance, Figure 3 presents the interface with query results showing the number of processors of the remote environment that were used on the execution of a given workflow. Through the interface it is also possible to save all intermediary results and download the MD simulations output files.

Such example illustrates a scenario where the scientist may evaluate the result of the experiment based on the provenance collected throughout the experiment lifecycle.

6   Conclusion

Modeling provenance data from scientific experiments is an open issue, despite the efforts of current SWfMS and OPM. One of the contributions of this work is to improve provenance research by pointing out entities that should be represented to play an important role in provenance queries and resource discovery. This was done on our conceptual model for the first time in the literature. There are several new concepts there, such as the notion of experiment and the relationships between experiment, abstract and concrete workflows with execution resources. The services and resource discovery are showing a first step towards workflow reuse, workflow analysis and several other features such as modeling a high level experiment which has not been shown before. In this paper we presented a release of an architecture that is able to capture and store into a repository the distinct kinds of provenance metadata generated during the stages of experiments lifecycle. One of the goals of the architecture is to ease the discovery of hidden scientific resources while reducing the complexity of parallel execution of *in silico* scientific experiments. To evaluate it, we have developed a distributed scientific workflow on Kepler SWfMS to execute MD simulations based on GROMACS package, called GromDFlow. We also developed a portal prototype named GromDExp that helps querying provenance information from the whole experiment lifecycle. GromDExp, differently from workflow portals (like WHIP [14], BioWep[22] and P-Grade[31]), provides a single point of access, with a consistent look and feel interface, to a variety of content and core services, such as: configuration of MD *in silico* experiments, submission of workflows to remote environments, monitoring the execution of the experiment and also offering built-in queries on the provenance metadata through the Web. GromDExp is being used in a production environment at FISBIO Laboratory at IBCCF/UFRJ, helping researchers in the study of MD experiments, such as the project that involves the Shethna protein [6].

As future work, we are going to refine the provenance schema and the queries to interoperate with the OPM [19]. Besides, we are examining the development and use of ontologies to improve the representation of provenance metadata of all stages of scientific experiments. The ontology captures various elements of the provenance of scientific experiments as described in our taxonomy [9] including the "who", "what", "why", "where", "when" and "how" of the experiments. We believe that the development of the provenance metamodel and the deployment of Matriohska can significantly reduce effort in creating and managing provenance metadata. It can also help to improve the quality and accuracy of the metadata by eliminating possible human mistakes.

Acknowledgments

This work was partially funded by FAPERJ, CNPq and CAPES. We also thank UFRJ/FISBIO Laboratory (http://www.biof.ufrj.br/fisbio/).

References

1. Ayadi, N.Y., Lacroix, Z., Vidal, M.E.: BiOnMap: a deductive approach for resource discovery. In: 10th International Conference on Information Integration and Web-Based Applications & Services, pp. 477–482. ACM, New York (2008)
2. Azis, M., Lacroix, Z.: ProtocolDB: classifying resources with a domain ontology to support discovery. In: 10th International Conference on Information Integration and Web-Based Applications & Services, pp. 462–469. ACM, New York (2008)
3. Barbosa, L., Tandon, S., Freire, J.: Automatically Constructing a Directory of Molecular Biology Databases. In: Cohen-Boulakia, S., Tannen, V. (eds.) DILS 2007. LNCS (LNBI), vol. 4544, pp. 6–16. Springer, Heidelberg (2007)
4. Berners-Lee, T., Fielding, R.T., Masinter, L.: Uniform Resource Identifier (URI): Generic syntax. RFC3986, The Internet Society (2005), http://tools.ietf.org/html/rfc3986
5. Bitar, M., Santos, L.M.L., Bisch, P.M., Costa, M.G.S.: Molecular Modeling Studies of Nitrogenase's Conformational Protection Mechanisms. In: Gluconacetobacter Diazotrophicus and Azotobacter Vinelandii. XXXVIII SBBq, São Paulo, Brazil (2009)
6. Braun, U., Shinnar, A., Seltzer, M.: Securing Provenance. In: 3rd Conference on Hot Topics in Security, pp. 1–5. Usenix Association, California (2008)
7. Callahan, S.P., Freire, J., Santos, E., Scheidegger, C.E., Silva, C.T., Vo, H.T.: VisTrails: Visualization Meets Data Management. In: ACM SIGMOD International Conference on Management of Data, pp. 745–747. ACM, New York (2006)
8. Churches, D., Gombas, G., Harrison, A., Maassen, J., Robinson, C., Shields, M., Taylor, I., Wang, I.: Programming Scientific and Distributed Workflow with Triana Services. Concurr. Comput.: Pract. Exper. 18(10), 1021–1037 (2006)
9. Cruz, S.M.S., Campos, M.L.M., Mattoso, M.: Towards a Taxonomy of Provenance in Scientific Workflow Management Systems. In: Congress on Services - I. SERVICES, pp. 259–266. IEEE Computer Society, Washington (2009)
10. Cruz, S.M., Barros, P.M., Bisch, P.M., Campos, M.L., Mattoso, M.: Provenance Services for Distributed Workflows. In: 8th IEEE International Symposium on Cluster Computing and the Grid, pp. 526–533. IEEE Computer Society, Washington (2008)
11. Erl, T.: SOA: Principles of service design. Prentice Hall, Englewood Cliffs (2007)
12. Freire, J., Koop, D., Santos, E., Silva, C.T.: Provenance for Computational Tasks: A Survey. Computing in Science and Engineering 10(3), 11–21 (2008)
13. GExp: Supporting Large Scale Management of Scientific Experiments, http://gexp.nacad.ufrj.br/
14. Harrison, A., Taylor, I.: Enabling Desktop Workflow Applications. In: 4th Workshop on Workflows in Support of Large-Scale Science, pp. 1–9. ACM, New York (2009)
15. Hey, T., Tansley, S., Toll, K. (eds.): The Fourth Paradigm: Data-Intensive Scientific Discovery, Microsoft Research (2009)
16. Lacroix, Z., Legendre, C.R.L., Tuzmen, S.: Congress on Services - I. SERVICES, pp. 306–313. IEEE Computer Society, Washington (2009)
17. Lacroix, Z., Kothari, C.R., Mork, P., Wilkinson, M., Cohen-Boulakia, S.: Biological Metadata Management. In: Liu, L., Tamer Özsu, M. (eds.) Encyclopedia of Database Systems, pp. 215–219. Springer, US (2009)
18. Ludäscher, B., Altintas, I., Berkley, C., Higgins, D., Jaeger, E., Jones, M., Lee, E.A., Tao, J., Zhao, Y.: Scientific Workflow Management and the Kepler System. Concurr. Comput.: Pract. Exper. 18(10), 1039–1065 (2006)

19. Moreau (Editor), L., Plale, B., Miles, S., Goble, C., Missier, P., Barga, R., Simmhan, Y., Futrelle, J., McGrath, R., Myers, J., Paulson, P., Bowers, S., Ludaescher, B., Kwasnikowska, N., Van den Bussche, J., Ellkvist, T., Freire, J. Groth, P.: The Open Provenance Model (v1.01), Technical Report, University of Southampton (2008)
20. myExperiment, http://www.myexperiment.org
21. Protein Data Bank, http://www.pdb.org
22. Romano, P., Bartocci, E., Bertolini, G., De Paoli, F., Marra, D., Mauri, G., Merelli, E., Milanesi, L.: Biowep: a workflow enactment portal for bioinformatics applications. BMC Bioinformatics 8(Suppl. 1), S19 (2007)
23. Rossle, S.C.S., Carvalho, P.C., Dardenne, L.E., Bisch, P.M.: Development of a Computational Environment for Protein Structure Prediction and Functional Analysis. In: 2nd Brazilian Workshop on Bioinformatics, Macaé, RJ, Brazil, pp. 57–63 (2003)
24. Scheidegger, C., Koop, D., Santos, E., Vo, H., Callahan, S., Freire, J., Silva, C.: Tackling the Provenance Challenge One Layer at a Time. Concurr. Comput.: Pract. Exper. 20(5), 473–483 (2007)
25. Simmhan, Y., Plale, B., Gannon, D.: A Survey of Data Provenance in e-Science. SIGMOD Record 34(3), 31–36 (2005)
26. Srivastava, D., Velegrakis, Y.: Intentional Associations between Data and Metadata. In: ACM SIGMOD, pp. 401–412 (2007)
27. Tuffery, P., Lacroix, Z., Menager, H.: Semantic Map of Services for Structural Bioinformatics. In: 18th IEEE International Conference on Scientific and Statistical Database Management, pp. 217–224. IEEE Press, Los Alamitos (2006)
28. UKOLN. Choosing a Metadata Standard for Resource Discovery, http://www.ukoln.ac.uk/qa-focus/documents/briefings/briefing-63/html
29. Gromacs User Manual - Version 3.3, http://www.gromacs.org
30. Scott, W.R.P., Hunenberger, P.H., Tironi, G., Mark, A.E., Billeter, S.R., Fennen, J., Torda, A.E., Huber, T., Kruger, P., van Gunsteren, W.F.: The GROMOS Biomolecular Simulation Program Package. J. Phys. Chem. A 103(19), 3596–3607 (1999)
31. Wieczorek, M., Prodan, R., Fahringer, T.: Scheduling of Scientific Workflows in the Askalon Grid Environment. In: ACM SIGMOD, pp. 56–62 (2005)
32. Woollard, D., Medvidovic, N., Gil, Y., Mattmann, C.A.: Scientific Software as Workflows: From Discovery to Distribution. IEEE Software 4(25), 37–43 (2008)
33. Zhao, Y., Hategan, M., Clifford, B., Foster, I., von Laszewski, G., Raicu, I., Stef-Praun, T., Wilde, M.: Swift: Fast, Reliable, Loosely Coupled Parallel Computation. In: Congress on Services - I. SERVICES, pp. 199–206. IEEE Computer Society, Washington (2007)

On Building a Search Interface Discovery System

Denis Shestakov*

Department of Media Technology
Aalto University, Espoo, Finland-02150
`firstname.lastname@tkk.fi`

Abstract. A huge portion of the Web known as the deep Web is accessible via search interfaces to myriads of databases on the Web. While relatively good approaches for querying the contents of web databases have been recently proposed, one cannot fully utilize them having most search interfaces unlocated. Thus, the automatic recognition of search interfaces to online databases is crucial for any application accessing the deep Web. This paper describes the architecture of the I-Crawler, a system for finding and classifying search interfaces. The I-Crawler is intentionally designed to be used in the deep web characterization surveys and for constructing directories of deep web resources.

1 Introduction

Since current-day web search engines do not crawl and index a significant portion of the Web, web users relying on search engines only are unable to discover and access a large amount of information from the non-indexable part of the Web. Specifically, dynamic pages generated based on parameters provided by a user via web search forms (or search interfaces) are poorly indexed by major searchers and, therefore, are scarcely presented in searchers' results. Such search interfaces provide users with an access to myriads of databases which content comprise a huge part of the Web known as the deep Web [20].

Due to the huge volume of information in the deep Web, there has been a significant interest to approaches that allow users and computer applications to leverage this information. For example, works [3,17,21,26] discuss how to query the contents of web databases via their search interfaces that, as assumed, have been already discovered. However, the large scale of the deep Web makes this assumption unrealistic. In fact, even national [22,23] or specific community-oriented (e.g., bioinformatics community) parts of the deep Web are too large to be fully discovered. Manually created collections, such as the one for the Molecular Biology domain [9], are of great help to corresponding communities, but, because of the size of the deep Web, they uncover just the top of the iceberg of all community-specific resources. Similarly, existing directories of deep web resources (i.e., directories that classify web databases in some taxonomies) have extremely low coverage for online databases. For example, `Completeplanet.com`,

---

* Work done while at University of Turku.

Z. Lacroix (Ed.): RED 2009, LNCS 6162, pp. 81–93, 2010.

the largest of such directories, with around 70,000 databases covered only 15.6% of the total 450,000 web databases as of April 2004 [6]. Clearly, currently existing lists of online databases do not correspond to the scale of the deep Web. Besides, a technique for automatic finding search interfaces is of great interest to the people involved in such directories' building and maintaining.

The dynamism of the Web, when new sources being added all the time and old sources modified or removed completely, is another challenge that requires the automation of the search interface discovery process. One of the problems here is that search interfaces are very sparsely distributed over the Web, even within specific domains. For example, it was shown in [19] that only one of 38 (in average) web sites has at least one web search form, or, according to [5], approximately one of thousand web pages related to movies contains a movie search form.

To summarize, while relatively good approaches for querying the contents of web databases are now available, one cannot fully utilize them as most search interfaces are undiscovered. Thus, the ability to automatically locate search interfaces to web databases is crucial for any application accessing the deep Web. In this paper, we describe a system for the automatic detection of search interfaces and identifying database domains accessible via these interfaces. The proposed system called *I-Crawler* is specifically designed to be used in the deep web characterization studies as well as for automatic building of web databases' directories.

Our first contribution is an efficient recognition of non-HTML (i.e., interfaces implemented as Java applets or in Flash) and JavaScript-rich search interfaces. Such interfaces are beginning to prevail on the Web and, hence, handling them is crucial for any search interface discovery system. Additionally, we suggest to divide all forms into two groups based on the number of visible form controls and demonstrate that such separation improves the system accuracy. Our second contribution is an approach combining pre-query and post-query techniques for web database classification.

The rest of the paper is organized as follows. Section 2 discusses related work. In Section 3, we present our motivation and challenges. Section 4 describes our approach on search interface discovery. Section 5 presents the architecture of the I-Crawler system. In Section 6, we report our experiments with the I-Crawler and some preliminary results. Finally, Section 7 concludes the paper.

2   Related Work

Surprisingly, finding of search interfaces to web databases is a challenging problem in itself. Indeed, since several hundred thousands of databases are available on the Web [6], even an expert in a highly specialized domain cannot be aware of most relevant databases.

There are two classes of approaches to identify search interfaces to online databases: pre-query and post-query approaches. Pre-query approaches identify searchable forms on web sites by analyzing the features of web forms. Post-query techniques identify searchable forms by submitting the probing queries to forms and analyzing the result pages.

Bergholz and Chidlovskii [3] gave an example of the post-query approach for the automated discovery of search interfaces. They implemented a domain-specific crawler that starts on indexable pages and detects forms relevant to a given domain. Next, the Query Prober submits some domain-specific phrases (called "positive" queries) and some nonsense words ("negative" queries) to detected forms and then assesses whether a form is searchable or not by comparing the resulting pages for the positive and negative queries. Cope et al. [7] proposed a pre-query approach that uses automatically generated features to describe candidate forms and uses the decision tree learning algorithm to classify them based on the generated set of features.

The state-of-the-art approach to automatically locate web databases can be found in the works of Barbosa and Freire [1,2]. They built a form-focused crawler that uses three classifiers: the page classifier (classifies pages as belonging to topics in taxonomy), the link classifier (identifies links that likely lead to the pages with search interfaces in one or more steps), and the form classifier. The form classifier is a domain-independent binary classifier that uses a decision tree to determine whether a web form is searchable or non-searchable (e.g., forms for login, registration, site search, navigation, subscription, purchasing, commenting, polling, posting, chatting, etc.). Unlike the form crawler presented in [1,2], the I-Crawler can handle non-HTML and JavaScript-rich forms. Besides it has two different strategies for form analysis (see Section 4). The preliminary results (see Section 6) demonstrated that such separation of forms into two classes is meaningful. In addition, the I-Crawler classifies searchable forms using the combination of pre-query and post-query techniques.

Jayapandian and Jagadish [12] presented a framework for generating forms in an automatic and principled way, given a database and a sample query workload. The proposed formal representation of a form, specifically the expressivity of a form, could give an insight about form's structural features to be used for form classification purposes.

In [15], Madhavan et al. described a large-scale system for surfacing deep Web content, i.e., automatic filling out forms with precomputed inputs and adding result pages into a search engine's index. Interestingly, the system does not separate searchable forms from non-searchable ones, and is able to handle only get forms (post forms, non-HTML and JavaScript-rich forms, forms requiring any kind of personal information, and those with textarea fields are ignored) found in the Google index. The work is relevant to ours as it describes a robust and web-scalable post-query technique.

3 Motivation and Challenges

The problem of automatic identifying search interfaces arose during our characterization studies [23,22]. Basically, given a web site we crawled it to a certain depth and then analyzed all downloaded site's content to identify pages with

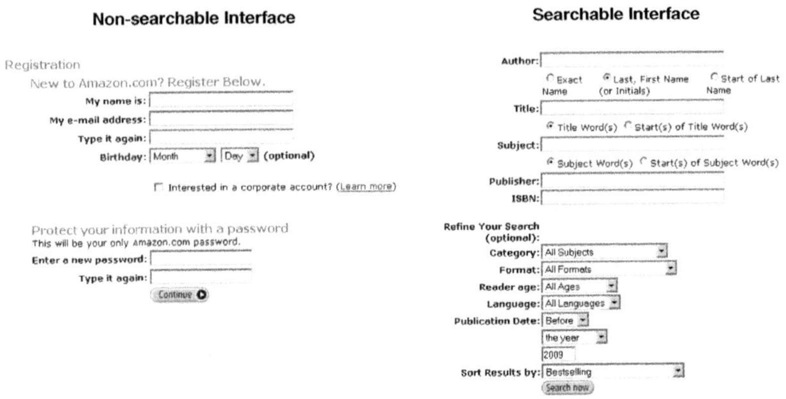

Non-searchable Interface

Searchable Interface

Registration

New to Amazon.com? Register Below.

My name is:

My e-mail address:

Type it again:

Birthday: Month ▾ Day ▾ (optional)

☐ Interested in a corporate account? (Learn more)

Protect your information with a password
This will be your only Amazon.com password.

Enter a new password:

Type it again:

Continue ➲

Author:

○ Exact ◉ Last, First Name ○ Start of Last
   Name   (or Initials)   Name

Title:

◉ Title Word(s) ○ Start(s) of Title Word(s)

Subject:

◉ Subject Word(s) ○ Start(s) of Subject Word(s)

Publisher:

ISBN:

Refine Your Search (optional):

Category: All Subjects ▾

Format: All Formats ▾

Reader age: All Ages ▾

Language: All Languages ▾

Publication Date: Before ▾

the year ▾

2009

Sort Results by: Bestselling ▾

Search now

Fig. 1. Non-searchable and searchable interfaces at Amazon.com

search forms. For instance, two forms on the Amazon.com depicted in Figure 1 have to be identified as non-searchable (the form for registration on the left) and searchable (the form for advanced book search on the right).

When analyzing a web page we (as well as Chang et el. in their characterization study [6]) used a semi-automatic approach – we automatically filtered out all pages without web forms and pages with those forms that are not search interfaces to web databases (e.g., forms for login, registration, etc.). At the filtering stage, searchable forms were distinguished from non-searchable ones using a set of heuristic rules obtained by manual reviewing of around 120 searchable and non-searchable forms (similar but more simplified heuristics was used in [14]). For instance, forms with password or file upload fields are non-searchable[1]. The goal of the filtering performed automatically was to filter out as many non-searchable forms as possible and, more importantly, to not filter out any searchable interfaces since, otherwise, we could not consider our estimates for the total number of deep web sites as reliable. In other words, we preferred to use a simple set of rules filtering out only a part of non-searchable forms but none of searchable forms than more advanced heuristics that filter out most non-searchable forms together with a few searchable ones. After the filtering, we manually inspected the rest of pages and identified searchable interfaces. In average, only one out of six forms was identified as searchable at this step. The manual inspection was, in fact, a bottleneck of our characterization studies. We were unable to enlarge the sample size and, hence, increase the accuracy of our estimates because of the restriction on the number of pages to be inspected within a given amount of time. Therefore, the automatic approach to identify search interfaces can significantly improve the accuracy of the estimates in web characterization studies.

Constructing directories of deep web resources like the one described in [9] is another application, where the automated identification of search interfaces

---

[1] Note that forms with upload controls may still be interfaces to databases: e.g., an image search based on an uploaded image.

could be very helpful. Such resource directories then can be utilized by conventional search engines. In particular, many transactional queries (i.e., find a site where further interaction will happen [4]) could be answered better if results of such queries contain links to pages with search interfaces via which a user can eventually get the required information. To make this a reality, a search engine should have a directory of web databases (more exactly, directory of links to pages with search interfaces to databases), where databases are classified into subject hierarchies, plus a certain mapping associating query terms with related databases. For instance, a user who issued a car-related query might be suggested to extend his/her search using web forms for car search. In this way, directories of web databases can improve the support of transactional queries by search engines.

We can divide the problem of constructing directory of deep web resources into three parts:

1. *Finding web pages with search interfaces.* The problem is that search interfaces are very sparsely distributed over the Web, even within specific domains. For example, as we already mentioned in Section 1, a regularly-crawled web page most likely contains no search form. Therefore, a strategy for visiting web pages which more likely have a search interface could be useful.

2. *Recognizing searchable forms in automatic way.* The task can be formulated as follows: given a page with a form, identify automatically if a form is searchable (a search interface to a database) or non-searchable. A great variety in the structure and vocabulary of forms makes this a challenging task. Moreover, even within a well-known domain (e.g., car classifieds) there is no common schema that accurately describes most search interfaces of the domain.

3. *Classifying searchable forms into subject hierarchy.* Given a search interface (identified at the previous step) to a web database and a hierarchical classification scheme (e.g., Yahoo!-like directory at http://dir.yahoo.com), which is a set of categories, define categories related to a database. There are several issues that complicate multi-class classification of searchable forms. First, existing data sets of searchable interfaces to be used as training sets are not large enough for multi-classification tasks. Second, many search interfaces belong to more than one different domains (see example in the next section). Third, certain search interfaces (with a few visible fields) are hard to classify reliably as the textual content of such interfaces provide us with little or no information related to the subject of underlying databases.

4   Our Approach: Interface Crawler

Our main goal is to develop a system able to detect efficiently and automatically whether a particular web form is searchable or non-searchable and then to identify a main subject of a database accessible via a given searchable form. The first step described in the previous section, namely, building an effective crawler that trained to follow links that are likely to lead to pages with search interfaces, is just partially considered. One particular application for our system is to use it in the deep web characterization studies and, thus, main concern is how to avoid missing searchable forms rather than how to increase the ratio of pages with search interfaces to all pages visited by a crawler. Anyhow, we performed several experiments (see Section 6) on possible crawling strategies.

Since we want to detect all search interfaces located on a set of pages it is crucially important to recognize both HTML and non-HTML search interfaces (i.e., interfaces implemented as Java applets or in Flash). Though nowadays most search interfaces are HTML forms, more and more non-HTML forms appear on the Web. In addition, the client-side scripts (mainly in JavaScript [8]) embedded within an HTML page technically complicate processing of a web page: to extract the structural and textual content of such interface an application has to not only retrieve a page but also process a page content by a layout engine[2]. Without rendering by a layout engine JavaScript-rich forms are likely to be not detected at all. Note that almost all known to us approaches to the deep Web do not consider client-side scripts and, hence, ignore forms with the embedded client-side code.

After the form detection, the next task is to recognize a form as searchable (a search interface to a database) or non-searchable (all the others). It was observed in several works (e.g., in [6]) that there are structural differences between searchable and non-searchable forms. For example, the average number of text fields in non-searchable forms is higher than those in searchable forms. Thus, we can build a binary (domain-independent) classifier and use the differences for the classifier training.

However, forms with one or two visible fields might be problematic since such forms give us very little information about their structure. For instance, forms for site search[3] that typically have only one visible text field are non-searchable while the form with two (select and text) visible fields shown in Figure 2 is searchable. To overcome this issue, we divide all forms into two groups: those with one or two visible fields of select or text types (we call them *u-forms* for short as searchable u-forms are often interfaces to unstructured web databases), and those with more than two visible fields (called *s-forms* as searchable s-forms often lead to structured databases). Apparently, two binary classifiers for u- and s-forms should exist and be trained on slightly different sets of form features.

The next task is to find which subject categories cover a web database content (that accessible via an identified search interface) in the best way. Currently, we classify web databases into ten domains: airfare, auto, book, travel, job, movie, music, real estate, rental, science. The classification of u- and s-forms into subject categories is done separately. In both cases, the result of classification of a page

---

[2] Software that takes a web content, parses it and displays on the screen. A layout engine (e.g., Gecko [18]) is typically used by web browsers or other applications that require displaying of web contents.

[3] Site search forms allowing to search through indexable site's web pages are not considered to be interfaces to online databases.

Fig. 2. PubMed's search interface

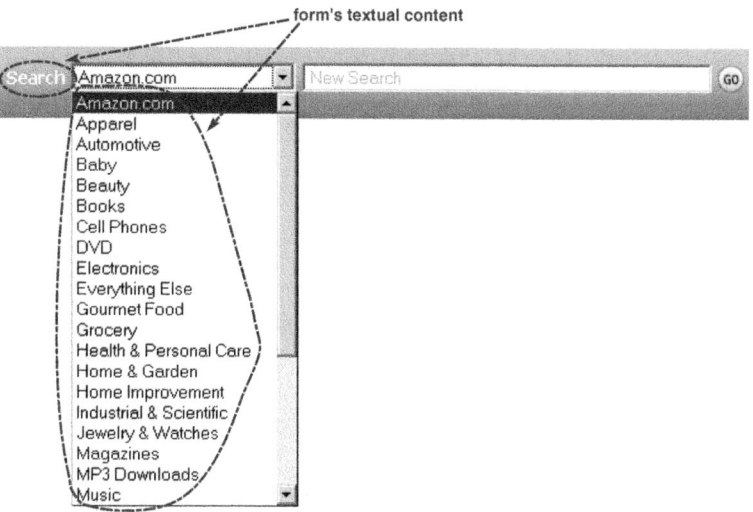

Fig. 3. Textual content of the form on the front page of `Amazon.com`

with a search interface is only supplemental because a page in the travel category can often contain an airfare search form. U-forms are somewhat problematic as they typically have little or no meaningful textual content[4] and, moreover, often have to be classified into several domains. For example, consider search form on the front page of `Amazon.com` shown in Figure 3. Ideally, this form with one text and one select fields has to be classified into three categories: book, movie, and music. However,the textual content of the form is domain-independent: the text string "Search" and the option values of select field such as "Books", "Apparel", "Automotive", etc. (see Figure 3).

   Our solution to this problem is to classify u-forms using the post-query approach initially proposed by Gravano et al. [10]. The idea of the post-query classification is issuing probing queries via a searchable form and retrieving counts of matches which are returned for each probing query. If each probing query corresponds to some category than the number of returned matches points out the coverage of the database for this category (for example, if no matches are

---

[4] In case of HTML forms, the textual content of a form is the text enclosed by the start and end FORM tags after the HTML markup is removed.

returned for a car-related query then database is not in the 'auto' domain). Unlike u-forms, s-forms are easier to classify since, evidently, much more information about underlying database can be extracted from a searchable s-form. In this way, we extract meaningful textual content of s-forms and pass it to the text classifier. Additionally, we can extract the form field labels and use them in the classification process as well. Particularly, He et al. [11] used the field labels to cluster searchable forms. Though we do not use the clustering approach in the current implementation of our system, one can expect that the clustering based on the field labels might be a good supplement to the text classifier based on the form's textual content.

Next section describes the architecture of the system called I-Crawler (Interface Crawler) for automatic finding and classifying search interfaces.

5   Architecture of I-Crawler

Based on our approach described in the previous section we designed the I-Crawler system, which architecture is shown in Figure 4. The I-Crawler consists of four main components: *Site/Page Analyzer*, *Interface Identification*, *Interface Classification*, and *Form Database*. The goal of the I-Crawler is to crawl suggested pages or web sites (as a typical crawler does), extract all web forms from the visited pages, mark the extracted forms as searchable or non-searchable, and store them in the Form Database. Additionally, searchable forms are classified into subject hierarchies.

The Site/Page Analyzer component is responsible for the form crawling efficiency. For a particular page it analyzes a page's site, links located on a page, etc. and suggests which to be processed first (for instance, those that are most likely to lead to search interfaces) and which to be ignored. Currently we do not pay much attention to the Site/Page Analyzer since we concentrate on finding as many search interfaces as possible and, thus, prefer to perform mostly unrestricted crawling. However, if the task is to find search interfaces to web databases in one particular domain then the role of the Site/Page Analyzer is highly important.

The second component, Interface Identification, is the most important in the current implementation. It includes three parts: *Interface Detector*, *Structure Extractor*, and *Binary Classifier*. The Interface Detector is responsible for detecting a form within a web page. Since both HTML and non-HTML forms[5] have to be further extracted from a page, the Interface Detector processes a page like a web browser does. If no form is detected then nothing is passed to the underlying modules; otherwise the code describing a detected form on a web page is passed to the Structure Extractor and the code of a web page with the form's code removed is passed to the Interface Classification component (namely, to the *Page Classifier*). The Structure Extractor extracts the structural features

---

[5] Such as forms implemented as Java applets or in Flash. In the current implementation, only non-HTML forms in Flash are handled. Technically, SWF-files are parsed using the Perl library *Perl::Flash* [24].

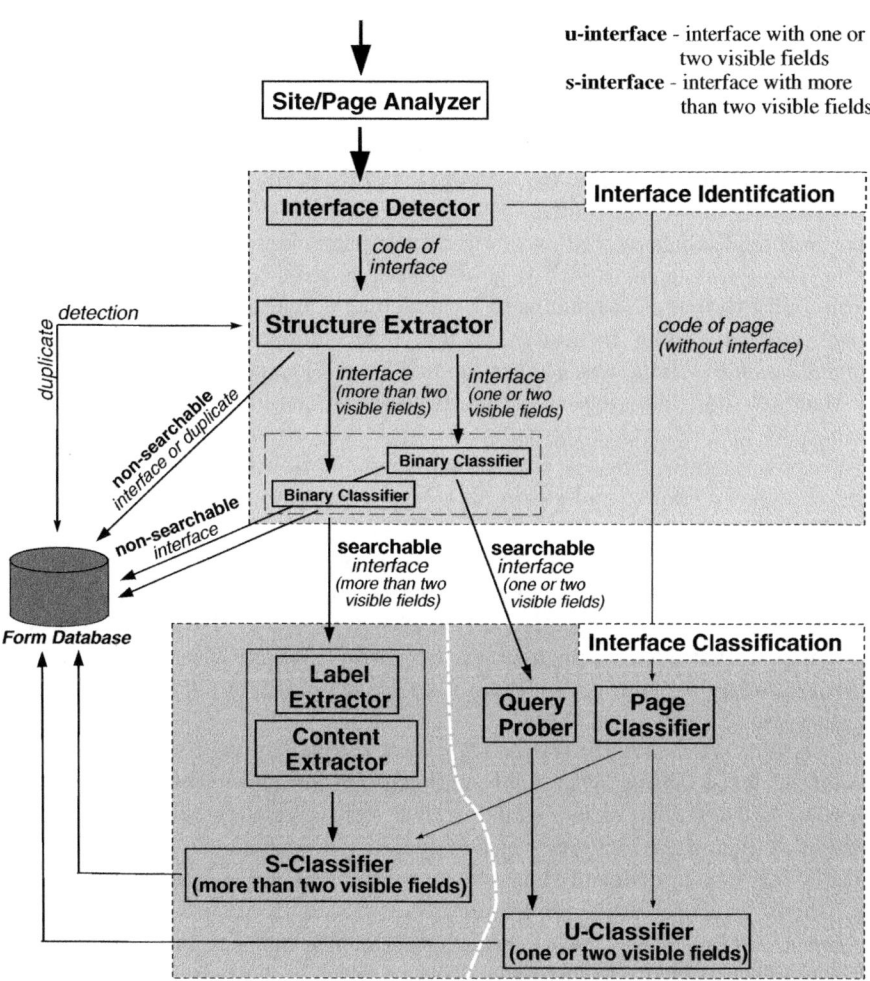

Fig. 4. Architecture of I-Crawler

of a form such as the form's URL, the total number of fields, the number of text fields, etc. Information about the form structure is explicitly defined in the form code and, hence, the form features' extraction requires no specific techniques. The Structure Extractor communicates with the Form Database to detect any duplicates that are already stored in the Form Database. It also has simple rules (e.g., a form with a password field is non-searchable) and stores non-searchable forms in the Form Database. If a non-searchable or duplicate form is identified then the I-Crawler stops processing at this stage; otherwise, structural features of a form are passed to the Binary Classifier. We implemented two binary classifiers – the first is for forms with one or two visible fields of select or text types (u-forms) and the second is for the forms with more than two visible fields (s-forms). Both classifiers determine if a form is searchable or non-searchable. The

I-Crawler stops processing if a non-searchable form is identified; otherwise, a searchable form is passed to the Interface Classification component. Note that searchable forms of each type (u-forms and s-forms) are processed differently (see Figure 4).

The Interface Classification component is responsible for classification of searchable forms. U-forms are classified based on the results of form probing and page classification. S-forms are classified based on the extracted form content and field labels as well as the results of page classification. The Page Classifier module analyzes a web page and assigns to it a score which defines the probability that a page belongs to a particular domain. In our experiments, we used the Bow toolkit for statistical language modeling [16] to implement the Page Classifier. The *Query Prober* module is an adopted version of the QProber system [10] that makes classification decisions by sending query probes through an u-form and analyzing the number of matches reported for each query. The *U-Classifier* aggregates the classification information from the Page Classifier and the Query Prober and stores an u-form and its topic (or a set of topics) in the Form Database.

Unlike u-forms s-forms are processed by the module which recognizes the field labels of a s-form and extract the textual content of a form (e.g., predefined values of select fields). This information is then passed to the *S-Classifier*, which used it (together with supplementary data from the Page Classifier) to classify a s-form into subject hierarchies. Finally, a s-form and its classification information is stored in the Form Database.

Last but not least, the Form Database component stores full information about all forms (either searchable and non-searchable) encountered by the I-Crawler system. This means that for each form all its features recognized and extracted during the form identification and classification can easily be accessed by any other component of the I-Crawler. Non-searchable forms are also stored as it helps to detect duplicate forms.

In the next section we describe our experiments with the Interface Identification component of the I-Crawler and report some preliminary results obtained.

6   Experimental Results

The Interface Identification component of the I-Crawler was implemented in Java (except the Interface Detector module written in Perl) and was running on Pentium IV 1.7GHz and 512MB of RAM under Ubuntu 7.10. For the Binary Classifier we considered the following machine learning techniques: support vector machine, decision tree, and multilayer perceptron. All classifiers have been constructed with help of the WEKA package [25]. We used the following four datasets:

Dataset 1: 216 searchable web forms from the UIUC repository (http://meta querier.cs.uiuc.edu/repository) plus 90 searchable web forms (30 of which are JavaScript-rich and non-HTML forms) collected by us and 300 non-searchable forms also collected by us.

Dataset 2: Dataset 1 with all u-forms excluded.

Dataset 3: 264 searchable forms from the collection of Russian search interfaces collected in [19] and 264 non-searchable forms in Russian collected by us.

Dataset 4: 90 searchable and 120 non-searchable u-forms collected by us.

For each form in the datasets we retrieved the following 20 structural features: whether a form is HTML or non-HTML; presence of the string *"search"*, *"find"* or similar one within the FORM tags for HTML forms; the submission method; the number of fields of each type (there are twelve types: text, select, etc.); the number of items in selects; the length of action attribute; the sum of text sizes; the presence of Javascript-related attributes; and the number of tags within the FORM tags. The learning was performed using randomly selected two thirds of each dataset and the testing using the remaining third. The error rates on test sets for each learning algorithm are shown in Table 1. Note that the error rate for the decision tree classifier (the second row of Table 1) on the dataset 1 was estimated using the n-fold cross-validation technique [13]. We also notice that the accuracy of our classifier increases if the dataset contains only s-forms and, thus, the separation of forms into u- and s-forms is worthwhile.

For comparison we considered the classifier described in [1] (last row of Table 1). It used 14 form features (that are mostly overlapping with the ones used by our learning algorithms) and its learning was performed using two thirds of dataset 1 (except they did not have additional 90 searchable forms, not deal with JavaScript-rich and non-HTML forms, and used the distinct set of non-searchable forms) and the testing using the remaining third of dataset 1. Our classifier outperformed the one in [1] since its error rate is slightly lower and, more importantly, obtained using the n-fold cross-validation. Besides, our classifier successfully processed thirty JavaScript-rich and non-HTML interfaces which were completely ignored by the approach in [1].

We selected the decision tree algorithm (built on dataset 1) and applied it to finding search interfaces on real web sites. Three groups of web sites were studied: 1) 150 deep web sites randomly selected from the collection in [19]; 2) 150 sites randomly selected from the *"Recreation"* category of http://www.dmoz.org; and 3) 150 sites randomly selected based on IP addresses. All sites in each group were crawled by the I-Crawler to depth five (note that we ignored already known search interfaces on pages from the sites of group 1). We then identified search interfaces and counted the numbers of found web databases. Also, to count the

Table 1. Error rates for learning algorithms

Learning algorithm	Dataset			
	1	2	3	4
SVM	14.8%	12.9%	15.3%	18.6%
Decision tree	**7.8%** *(n-fold cross-validation)*	**6.2%**	**9.1%**	15.7%
MultiLayer Perceptron	10.9%	10.7%	11.9%	**14.3%**
Decision tree in [1]	8.0% *(no cross-validation)*	-	-	-

Table 2. Number of web databases found and missed within each site group

Site group	Num of correctly found databases	Num of missed databases	Error rate
(1)	39	5	10.1%
(2)	31	2	8.8%
(3)	3	0	10.7%

number of false negatives (i.e., how many databases were not found by the algorithm) and false positives (i.e., how many databases are wrongly predicted), we manually inspected all forms analyzed by the classifier. The results, the numbers of found and missed databases and error rates for each group of sites, are presented in Table 2.

The results clearly demonstrate that finding search interfaces (and eventually web databases) is more efficient if a crawler uses a certain strategy for visiting pages. Particularly, root pages of "already discovered" deep web sites are good start points for discovering new web databases. Additionally, it is worth to investigate if the classifier itself could be improved by providing it with some characteristics of previously crawled pages (e.g., if they themselves have forms).

7   Conclusion and Future Work

Due to the large scale of the Web the ability to automatically locate search interfaces to web databases becomes a key requirement for any application accessing the deep Web. In this paper, we described the architecture of the I-Crawler, a system for finding and classifying search interfaces. Specifically, the I-Crawler is intentionally designed to be used in the deep web characterization studies and for constructing directories of deep web resources. Unlike almost all other approaches known to us, we recognized and analyzed JavaScript-rich and non-HTML searchable forms. Though dealing with JavaScript-rich and non-HTML interfaces is technically challenging it is an urgent issue as such interfaces are going to reach a sizable proportion of searchable forms on the Web. Our preliminary experiments showed that on similar datasets we were able to discover search interfaces more accurately than classifiers described in earlier works. Reliable classification of web databases into subject hierarchies will be the focus of our future work.

References

1. Barbosa, L., Freire, J.: Searching for Hidden-Web Databases. In: Proc. of WebDB 2005, pp. 1–6 (2005)
2. Barbosa, L., Freire, J.: Combining Classifiers to Identify Online Databases. In: Proc. of WWW 2007, pp. 431–440 (2007)
3. Bergholz, A., Childlovskii, B.: Crawling for Domain-Specific Hidden Web Resources. In: Proc. of WISE 2003, pp. 125–133 (2003)

4. Broder, A.: A Taxonomy of Web Search. SIGIR Forum 36(2), 3–10 (2002)
5. Chakrabarti, S., van den Berg, M., Dom, B.: Focused Crawling: a New Approach to Topic-Specific Web Resource Discovery. Computer Networks 31(11-16), 1623–1640 (1999)
6. Chang, K., He, B., Li, C., Patel, M., Zhang, Z.: Structured Databases on the web: Observations and Implications. SIGMOD Rec. 33(3), 61–70 (2004)
7. Cope, J., Craswell, N., Hawking, D.: Automated Discovery of Search Interfaces on the Web. In: Proc. of ADC 2003, pp. 181–189 (2003)
8. Flanagan, D.: JavaScript: The Definitive Guide, 4th edn. O'Reilly Media, Sebastopol (2001)
9. Galperin, M., Cochrane, G.: Nucleic Acids Research Annual Database Issue and the NAR online Molecular Biology Database Collection in 2009. Nucl. Acids Res. 37(Suppl. 1), 1–4 (2009)
10. Gravano, L., Ipeirotis, P., Sahami, M.: QProber: A System for Automatic Classification of Hidden-Web Databases. ACM Trans. Inf. Syst. 21(1), 1–41 (2003)
11. He, B., Tao, T., Chang, K.: Organizing Structured Web Sources by Query Schemas: a Clustering Approach. In: Proc. of CIKM 2004, pp. 22–31 (2004)
12. Jayapandian, M., Jagadish, H.V.: Automating the Design and Construction of Query Forms. Trans. Knowl. Data Eng. 21(10), 1389–1402 (2009)
13. Kohavi, R.: A Study of Cross-validation and Bootstrap for Accuracy Estimation and Model Selection. In: Proc. of IJCAI 1995, pp. 1137–1143 (1995)
14. Lage, J., da Silva, A., Golgher, P., Laender, A.: Automatic Generation of Agents for Collecting Hidden Web Pages for Data Extraction. Data Knowl. Eng. 49(2), 177–196 (2004)
15. Madhavan, J., Ko, D., Kot, L., Ganapathy, V., Rasmussen, A., Halevy, A.: Google's Deep Web crawl. In: Proc. of VLDB 2008 (2008)
16. McCallum, A.: Bow: A toolkit for statistical language modeling, text retrieval, classification and clustering, http://www.cs.cmu.edu/~mccallum/bow
17. Raghavan, S., Garcia-Molina, H.: Crawling the Hidden Web. In: Proc. of VLDB 2001 (2001)
18. Reis, C., de Mattos Forte, R.: An Overview of the Software Engineering Process and Tools in the Mozilla Project. In: Proc. of Open Source Software Development Workshop, pp. 155–175 (2002)
19. Shestakov, D.: Characterization of National Deep Web. TUCS Technical Report 892 (2008)
20. Shestakov, D.: Deep Web: Databases on the Web. In: Entry in Handbook of Research on Innovations in Database Technologies and Applications. IGI Global (2009)
21. Shestakov, D., Bhowmick, S., Lim, E.-P.: DEQUE: Querying the Deep Web. Data Knowl. Eng. 52(3), 273–311 (2005)
22. Shestakov, D., Salakoski, T.: Host-IP Clustering Technique for Deep Web Characterization. In: Proc. of APWeb 2010 (2010)
23. Shestakov, D., Salakoski, T.: On Estimating the Scale of National Deep Web. In: Wagner, R., Revell, N., Pernul, G. (eds.) DEXA 2007. LNCS, vol. 4653, pp. 780–789. Springer, Heidelberg (2007)
24. Wistow, S.: Deconstructing Flash: Investigations into the SWF File Format. Technical Report (2000)
25. Witten, I., Frank, E.: Data Mining: Practical Machine Learning Tools and Techniques, 2nd edn. Morgan Kaufmann, San Francisco (2005)
26. Wu, P., Wen, J.-R., Liu, H., Ma, W.-Y.: Query Selection Techniques for Efficient Crawling of Structured Web Sources. In: Proc. of ICDE 2006 (2006)

Building Specialized Multilingual Lexical Graphs Using Community Resources

Mohammad Daoud[1], Christian Boitet[1], Kyo Kageura[2], Asanobu Kitamoto[3],
Mathieu Mangeot[1], and Daoud Daoud[4]

[1] Grenoble Informatics Laboratory, GETALP, Université Joseph Fourier, 385,
rue de la Bibliothèque, 38041 Grenoble, France
{Mohammad.Daoud,Christian.Boitet,Mathieu.Mangeot}@imag.fr
[2] Library and Information Science Laboratory, Graduate School of Education,
The University of Tokyo, 7-3-1 Hongo, Bunkyo-ku, Tokyo, 113-0033, Japan
kyo@p.u-tokyo.ac.jp
[3] The National Institute of Informatics, 2-1-2 Hitotsubashi, Chiyoda-ku, Tokyo 101-8430
Kitamoto@nii.ac.jp
[4] Princess Sumaya University, P.O. Box 1438 Al-Jubaiha 11941 Jordan
Daoud@batelco.jo

Abstract. We are describing methods for compiling domain-dedicated multilingual terminological data from various resources. We focus on collecting data from online community users as a main source, therefore, our approach depends on acquiring contributions from volunteers (explicit approach), and it depends on analyzing users' behaviors to extract interesting patterns and facts (implicit approach). As a generic repository that can handle the collected multilingual terminological data, we are describing the concept of dedicated Multilingual Preterminological Graphs MPGs, and some automatic approaches for constructing them by analyzing the behavior of online community users. A Multilingual Preterminological Graph is a special lexical resource that contains massive amount of terms related to a special domain. We call it preterminological, because it is a raw material that can be used to build a standardized terminological repository. Building such a graph is difficult using traditional approaches, as it needs huge efforts by domain specialists and terminologists. In our approach, we build such a graph by analyzing the access log files of the website of the community, and by finding the important terms that have been used to search in that website, and their association with each other. We aim at making this graph as a seed repository so multilingual volunteers can contribute. We are experimenting this approach with the Digital Silk Road Project. We have used its access log files since its beginning in 2003, and obtained an initial graph of around 116000 terms. As an application, we used this graph to obtain a preterminological multilingual database that is serving a CLIR system for the DSR project.

1 Introduction

Discovering and translating domain specific terminology is a very complicated and expensive task, because (1) it depends on human terminologists [1], which increases

Z. Lacroix (Ed.): RED 2009, LNCS 6162, pp. 94–109, 2010.

the cost, (2) terminology is dynamic [2], thousands of terms are coined each year, and (3) it is difficult to involve subject matter experts in the construction process. That will not only increase the cost, but it will reduce the quality, and the coverage (linguistic and informational) of the produced term base. Databases like [3-5] are built by huge organizations, and it is difficult for a new domain with a smaller community to produce its own multilingual terminological database.

There is some work on constructing lexical resources by using Machine-readable dictionaries "MDRs" [6] [7], however for a domain-specific terminology, the involvement of the community and domain experts is essential, and associating several multilingual repositories into a specialized database may affect the integrity of the data and the domain relevance. TransGraph [8] is another attempt to associate various MDRs into a graph of words and its translations, effective for finding translation equivalences for general purpose lexical units. However, such a graph cannot handle relations between terms for a specific domain. Besides, MDRs do not suffice to determine such relations between lexical units available in the terminological sphere of a domain.

We are trying to analyze various resources in order to replace the traditional way of extracting related terminology. We introduce the concept of multilingual preterminological graphs, which are constructed by analyzing the interaction between domain-related resources on one side, and domain experts on the other side. Basically, we analyze the access log files to find important terms used to access the website, and relations between them. This approach falls under the category of implicit user contribution. reCAPTCHA [9] is an example of using this kind of contribution. After constructing the initial graph, we try to multilingualize it by using online multilingual resources at the beginning, and then by accepting progressive enhancements from community users in an explicit contribution approach.

Multilingual knowledge in a specific domain may not be available in any format (MDRs, printed dictionaries…). But such knowledge might be known and used by specialized multilingual people. We claim that discovering them, and encouraging them to contribute (explicitly and implicitly) is as important as discovering digital resources, or web services…

The remainder of this paper is organized as follows. The second section introduces the MPGs and the implicit and explicit approaches to construct them. The third section describes the extraction and contribution platform and its applications. Then section four reports the experimental results. And finally, section five draws some conclusions.

2 Multilingual Preterminological Graphs: Construction and Evolution

2.1 Definitions

We begin by describing multilingual preterminological graphs in detail, and present the approaches to initialize and multilingualize them.

A multilingual preterminological graph $MPG(N,E)$ is a finite nonempty set $N=\{n1,n2, …\}$ of objects called Nodes together with a set $E=\{e1,e2, …\}$ of unordered pairs of distinct nodes of MPG called edges. MPG of domain X, contains possible

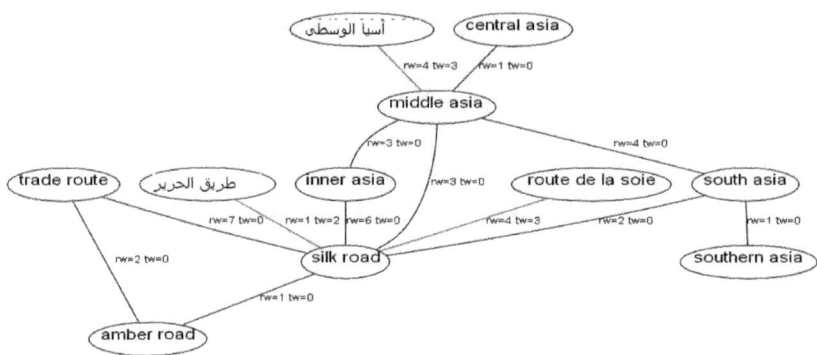

Fig. 1. A small MPG

multilingual terms related to that domain connected to each other with relations. A multilingual lexical unit and its translations in different languages are represented as connected nodes with labels.

In an *MPG* the set of nodes **N** consists of *p,l, s, occ,* where *p* is the string of the term, *l* is the language, *s* is the code of the first source of the term, and *occ* is the number of occurrences. Note that *l* could be undefined. For example: *N={[silk road, en, log],[Great Wall of China, en, ,wikipedia, 5], [الصين, ar, contributorx,6]},* here we have three nodes, 2 of them are English and one in Arabic, each term came from a different source. Note that English and Arabic terms belong to the same *N* thus, the same MPG.

An *Edge e={n, v}* is a pair of nodes adjacent in an *MPG*. An edge represents a relation between two terms represented by their nodes. The nature of the relation varies. However, edges are weighted with several weights (described below) to indicate the possible nature of this relation.

The following are the weights that label the edges on an MPG: *Relation Weights rw*: For an edge *e={[p1,l1,s1], [p2,l2,s2]}, rw* indicates that there is a relation between the preterm *p1* and *p2*. The nature of the relation could not be assumed by *rw*. *Translation Weights tw*: For an edge *e={[p1,l1,s1], [p2,l2,s2]}, tw* suggests that *p1* in language *l1* is a translation of *p2* in language *l2*. *Synonym Weights sw*: For an edge *e={[p1,l1,s1], [p2,l1,s2]}, sw* suggests that *p1* and *p2* are synonyms. Weights are measures calculated based on (1) analyzing log files, (2) terminology extraction, (3) automatic lexical translation, and (4) volunteer contribution, as we will describe in the following subsections. A *tedge* is an edge where *tw* is more than zero, *tdegree(n)* is the number of *tedges* that connect to n. A *redge* is an edge where *rw* is more than zero, *rdegree(n)* is the number of *regdes* that connect to n.

Figure 1 shows a simple MPG. The shown nodes represents terms related to the historical Silk Road [10]. For example, "inner Asia" and "middle Asia" are synonyms, so *rw* between them is 3 while *tw* equals zero. "Route de la soie" is the French equivalent of "Silk Road"; hence *tw* is more than 1.

2.2 Implicit Approach

Access log files constitute a very useful resource that is related to a specific domain, as they register the interactions between a domain-related online community on one side and users (who might include domain experts) on the other side. A server access log file keeps track of the requests that have been made to the server, along with other information like request time, IP address, referred page.

We analyze two kinds of requests that can provide us with information to enrich the MPG: (1) requests made to a local search engine devoted to a website and its documents, and (2) requests with reference from a web-based search engine (like Google, Yahoo!...).

From these requests we can obtain the search terms that visitors have used to access the website. Moreover, we can understand the way users interpret a concept into lexical units. Finding a pattern in their requests may lead to find a relation between the terms used in requests. For example, if we find that five different users send two consecutive search requests t1 and t2, then there is a possibility that t1 and t2 have a lexical relation.

As the pseudo code of "*analysing_searchlogfiles()*" illustrates we construct the initial MPG from access log files after filtering their records to find the search requests. The graph constructor analyzes the requests to make the initial graph by creating edges between terms available within the same session. The relation weight between x and y, $rw(x,y)$, is set to the number of sessions containing x and y within the log file. For example, $rw(x,y) = 10$ means that 10 people thought about x and y within the same search session.

```
analysing_searchlogfiles()
    for each search session of the log file Session_n
        for each term_n in Session_i
            if there is an edge between term_i and term_j then
                rw(term_i, and term_j)++;
            elseif there is no edge
                construct edge(term_i, term_j);
                rw(term_i, term_j)=1;
```

Figure 2 shows an example of a log file and the produced graph. The proposed method did not discover the kind of relation between the terms. However it discovered that there is a relation, for example, three users requested results for "yang" followed by "yin" within the same session. Hence, edge with weight of 2 was constructed based on this fact.

2.3 Explicit Approach

Explicit user interaction is the intentional contribution from the community user. The motive to contribute is initiated by associating the contribution process to an interesting and attractive activity.

User contribution $C(x,y,s,t)$ will increase the confidence that x is a translation of y s is the source language and t is the target language. Hence, $tw(x,y)$ (initialized at the multililingualization process) will be increased, accordingly. Accumulating the contributions will result in enlarging the graph and enhancing the confidence in its translation equivalences.

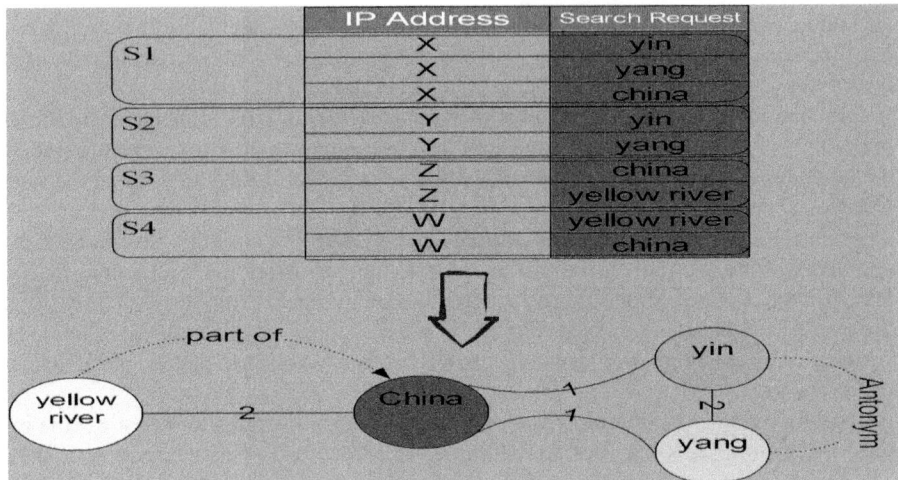

Fig. 2. Example of constructing an MPG from an access log file

3 Graph Multilingualization

After constructing the initial MPG, we expand it by translating the terms using multilingual online resources. In the case of terminology, we are using Wikipedia [11], IATE, and Google Translate [12]. The choice of Wikipedia comes from the fact that it could be helpful for cultural terminology [13], as it is rich with proper names.

Each translation into each language is represented as a new node in the graph, an edge between the term and its translation is established, and *tw (initially equals 0)* is modified accordingly.

The translation weight between x and y equals the number of resources indicating that x is a translation of y.

Therefore, if $tw(x,y) > k$, where k is a confidence threshold, then x is a *direct translation* equivalence of y.

More generally, if there is a path p between x and y, where all edges on p have $tw > k$, then x is an *indirect translation* (see next subsections) of y.

Based on figure 1, if k=1, then "آسيا الوسطى" is an Arabic equivalent of "middle Asia" because *tw* is larger than 1.

3.1 Finding Synonyms

There are two kinds of information to indicate that two terms may be synonym in a graph. The first one is the *rw* between both of them, and the second is the number of translations overlapping the two terms. The second information was used by Trans-Graph to resolve word sense inflation. However, in a domain-dedicated terminology, the first information is very important to find that some terms represent the same concept.

Figure 3 shows that X1 and X2 have a relation *rw* and they have three shared translations. The probability that X1 and X2 are synonym increases if the number of translation overlaps is high, based on [8], and if the *rw(X1,X2)* is high, therefore we need to find a modified weight for synonyms.

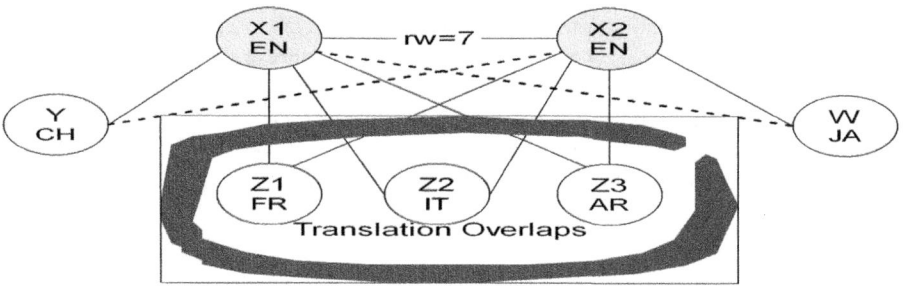

Fig. 3. An MPG where there is a possibility that X1 and X2 are synonyms

The following formula computes the new weights:

$$synonym\,weight\,(X1,X2)=\frac{(rw(X1,X2))}{(min(rdegree(X1),rdegree(X2)))}+$$
$$\frac{(\#\,translation\,overlaps)}{(min(tdegree(X1),tdegree(X2)))} \qquad (1)$$

Where *rdegree(x)* is the number of edges that connect to x with *rw* > 0, and *tdegree(x)* is the number of edges that connect to x with *tw* > 0. For example, in figure 3, *sw(X1, X2)=(1/1+3/4)=7/4*.

3.2 Indirect Translations

If the graph has a term *t1* and its synonym *t2*, then edges with high *tw* can connect *t1* to *t2* and vice versa. In other words, *t1* and *t2* correspond to the same concept and it is possible that they have the same translations. We call this *indirect translation* because there is no direct edge between the term and translationally equivalent terms.

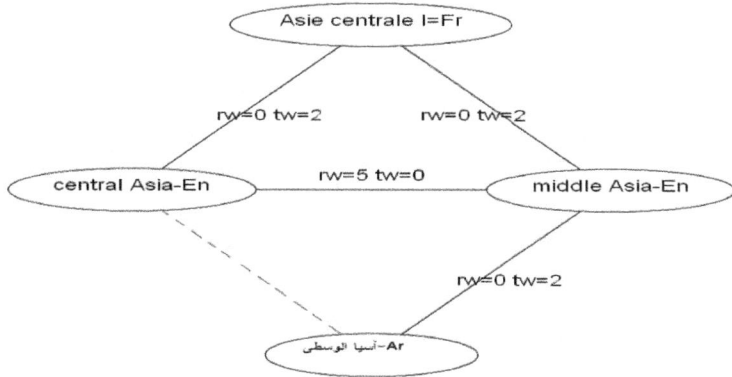

Fig. 4. An MPG with indirect translation

Therefore, x is an indirect translation of y, if *x* connects to *x1*, and there is a path *p* from *x1* to *y*, where *tw(x1,x)* > *k*, *k* being a confidence threshold, and where all edges of *p* have *sw* > *k1*, *k1* being a synonymy confidence threshold.

For example, in figure 4, "آسيا الوسطى" is considered as an Arabic translation of "central Asia" if *k=1*, and *k1=1*. This is because *tw("آسيا الوسطى"*, *middle Asia)=2*, *and sw(central Asia, middle Asia)=5/1+1=6*, based on formula 1.

4   Platform

As figure 5 shows, the terminological lexical sphere for a domain, is constructed from different resources. And it is represented as an MPG, the MPG is used as it is for several applications that will serve the online community and the same applications are capable of attracting contribution.

The produced graph is represented as a GraphML file (graphml.graphdrawing.org). GraphML offers a structure that is compatible with MPG, and it can be easily produced by the system, adopting this format is important to make the graph more scalable and useful for other applications, beside many systems and tools have been developed to manipulate and visualize graphs in GraphML format.

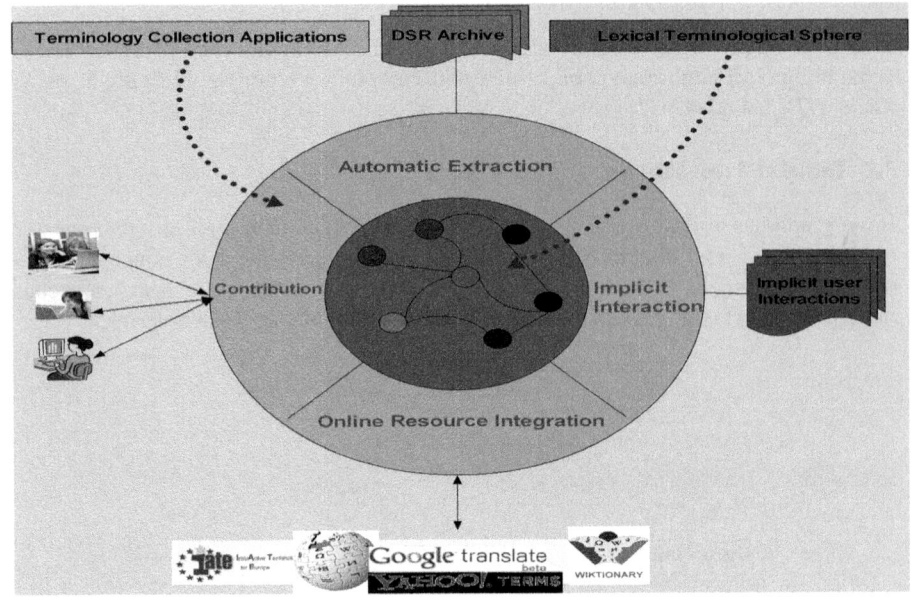

Fig. 5. Platform for constructing MPG

4.1   The Case of the Digital Silk Road

The Digital Silk Road project [14] is an initiative started by the National Institute of Informatics (Tokyo) in 2002, to archive cultural historical resources along the Silk Road, by digitizing them and making them available and accessible online.

One of the most important sub-projects is the Digital Archive of Toyo Bunko Rare Books [15] where tens of old rare books available at Toyo Bunko library have been digitized using OCR (Optical Character Recognition) technology. The digitized collection contains books from different languages (English, French, Russian…), all of them related to the historical Silk Road, like the 2 volumes of the Ancient Khotan by Marc Aurel Stein.

We are trying to build a collaborative multilingual terminological database dedicated to the DSR project and its resources [16]. To conduct such a study, there are two approaches, implicit and explicit, as described in [17]. We used the implicit approach as we have the access log files of the website since 2003, which contain many interesting facts.

DSR-MPG is synchronized with a multilingual pre- terminological database pTMDB that interacts with users who search the data base and contribute.

Each term represented as a node in the graph corresponds to a record in the Solr-based index along with some useful term related and concept related information.

For a historical archive like the DSR, we find that reading and searching were the most important for users. Log files since 2003 show that 80% of the project visitors were interested in reading the historical records. Moreover, around 140000 search requests have been sent to the internal search engine. We are trying to derive indirect motivation to the pTMDB through the interesting resources of the DSR itself. So we implemented two applications (1) "contribute-while-reading" and (2) "contribute-while-searching", explained in the next subsection. They are available at http://dsr.nii.ac.jp/pTMDB/

4.2 Applications

4.2.1 Contribute While Searching
As shown in figure 6, historical physical books have been digitized and indexed into a SOLR-based search engine.

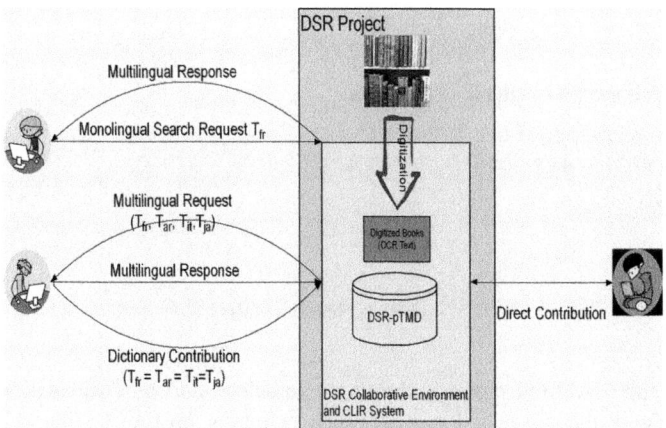

Fig. 6. General architecture of the environment [16]

We expect users to send monolingual search requests in any language supported by our system to get multilingual answers. Having a term base of multilingual equivalences could achieve this [18] [19]. A bilingual user who could send a bilingual search request could be a valid candidate to contribute. In fact, the same bilingual request could be a valid MPG contribution, and also multilingual requests. We plan that users who use our search engine will use the DSR-pTMDB to translate their requests and will contribute to the graph spontaneously.

Digital Silk Road Archive search

○ English		Search
○ French		
◉ Japanese	十二宮	

Fig. 7. A Japanese user translating his request

As figure 7 shows, a Japanese user would translate the search request, to receive the results, as shown in figure 8.

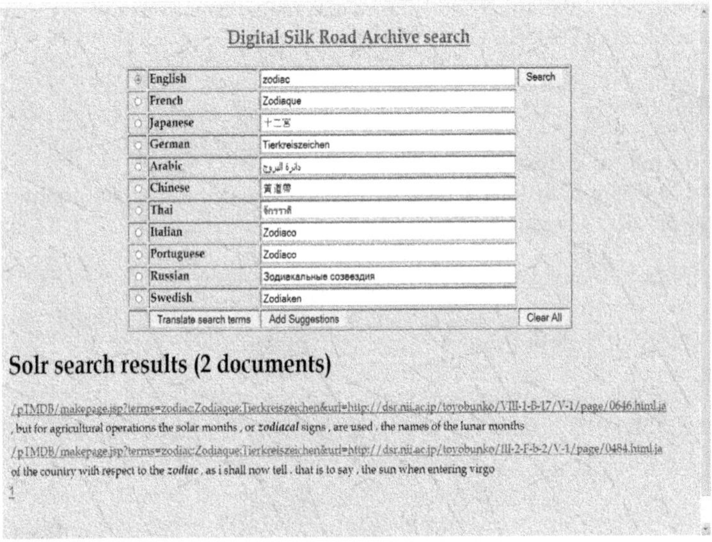

Digital Silk Road Archive search

English	zodiac	Search
French	Zodiaque	
Japanese	十二宮	
German	Tierkreiszeichen	
Arabic	دائرة البروج	
Chinese	黄道带	
Thai	ราศี	
Italian	Zodiaco	
Portuguese	Zodiaco	
Russian	Зодиакальные созвездия	
Swedish	Zodiaken	
Translate search terms	Add Suggestions	Clear All

Solr search results (2 documents)

/pTMDB/makepage.jsp?terms=zodiac;Zodiaque;Tierkreiszeichen&url=http://dsr.nii.ac.jp/toyobunko/VIII-1-B-17/V-1/page/0646.html.ja , but for agricultural operations the solar months , or *zodiacal* signs , are used . the names of the lunar months

/pTMDB/makepage.jsp?terms=zodiac;Zodiaque;Tierkreiszeichen&url=http://dsr.nii.ac.jp/toyobunko/III-2-F-b-2/V-1/page/0484.html.ja of the country with respect to the *zodiac* , as i shall now tell . that is to say , the sun when entering virgo
1

Fig. 8. Search results

During the searching process, the user can ask to add new translation if s/he was not happy with the suggested translation, by clicking on "Add Suggestions" to view the page showed at figure 9.

Digital Silk Road preTerminological Multilingual Database

	Language	pTMDB	Google	Suggestion
⊙	English	caliphate	caliphate	caliphate
○	French	Califat	califat	
○	Japanese		カリフ	
○	German	Kalifat	Kalifat	
○	Arabic		الخلافة	الخلافة الإسلامية
○	Chinese		哈里发	
○	Thai			
○	Italian		califfato	
○	Portuguese		califado	
○	Russian	Халифат	халифат	
○	Swedish	Kalifat	kalifat	
	Add Suggestions	Clear All		

Solr search results (1 documents)

score	3.7358246	
ar	*****	
ao	*****	
de	Kalifat	
en	caliphate	

Fig. 9. Contribution page

4.2.2   Contribute While Reading

The other interesting application is trying to help users from different linguistic backgrounds to translate some of the difficult terms into their languages while they are reading, simply by selecting a term from the screen.

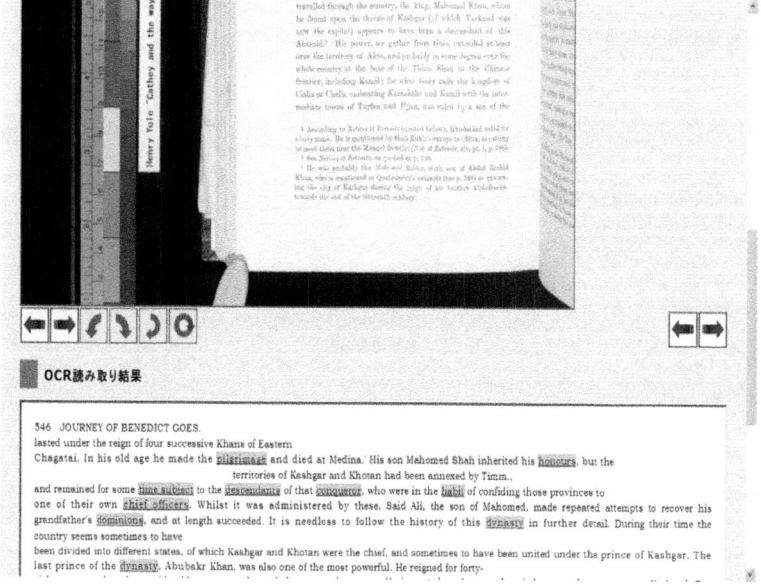

Fig. 10. Translate while reading

As shown in figure 10, readers will see a page from a book as an image, with its OCR text. Important terms will be presented with yellow background. Once a term is clicked, a small child contribution/lookup window will be open, similar to the one in figure 9. Also user can lookup/translate any term from the screen by selecting it.

This application helps covering all the important terms of each book.

5 Experiment

To build the initial DSR-MPG, we used the access log files of the DSR website (dsr.nii.ac.jp) from December 2003 to January 2009. The initial graph after normalization contained 89,076 nodes; most of them being for English terms, we filtered the logs (semi automatically) to analyze only access requests with search queries, the initial graph was produced in less than 5 hours, using a PC with Intel Pentium 4 processor. We also sent the OCR text of the archived books of Toyo Bunko library to a term extraction engine, in this experiment Yahoo! Terms. We extracted 81,204 terms. 27,500 of them were new terms that were not discovered from the access log files. So, the total number of nodes in the initial graph was 116,576 nodes, see figure 11 for sample nodes.

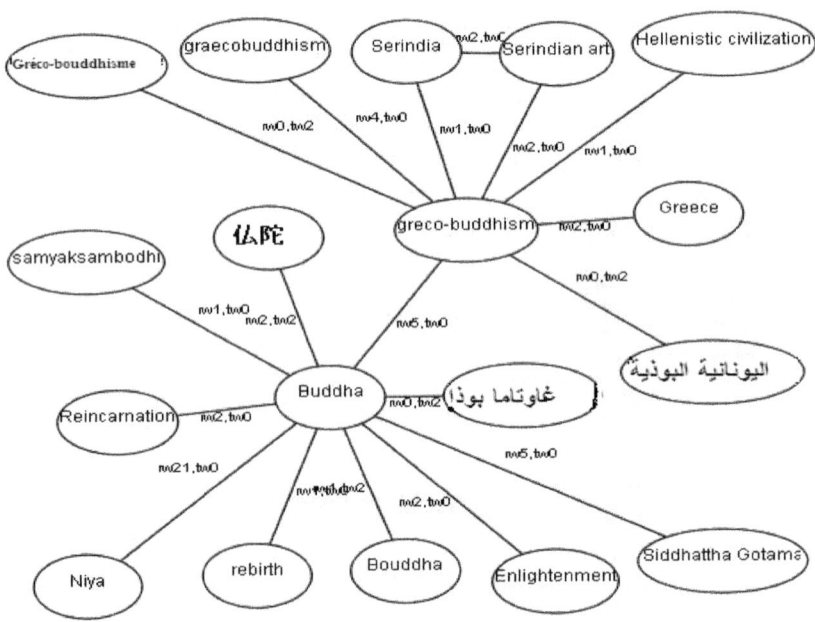

Fig. 11. Sample nodes from DSR-MPG

After the multilingualization process described in section 3, the graph has 210,781 nodes containing terms from the most important languages. The graph has now 779,765 edges with $tw > 0$.

The important languages are the languages of the majority of the visitors, the languages of the archived books, and representative languages a long the Silk Road. DSR-MPG achieved high linguistic coverage as 20 languages have more than 1000 nodes on the graph.

To evaluate the produced graph, we extracted 350 English terms manually from the index pages of the following books:

- Ancient Khotan, vol.1:
- http://dsr.nii.ac.jp/toyobunko/VIII-5-B2-7/V-1/
- On Ancient Central-Asian Tracks, vol.1:
- http://dsr.nii.ac.jp/toyobunko/VIII-5-B2-19/V-1
- Memoir on Maps of Chinese Turkistan and Kansu, vol.1: http://dsr.nii.ac.jp/toyobunko/VIII-5-B2-11/V-1

We assume that the terms available in these books are strongly related to the DSR. Hence, we tried to translate them into Arabic and French.

Figure 12 compares between DSR-MPG, and various general purpose dictionaries. Out of the 350 terms, we found 189 correct direct translations into Arabic. However, the number reached 214 using indirect translations.

On the other hand, the closest to our result was PanImages, which uses Wikitionaries [20] and various dictionaries, with only 83 correct translations.

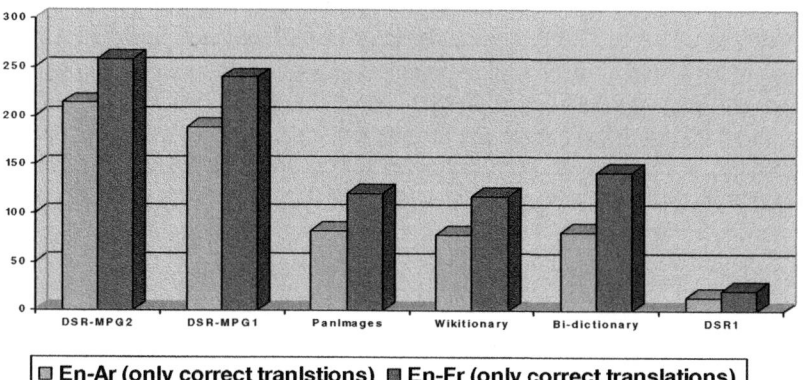

Fig. 12. A comparison between DSR-MPG, and other dictionaries. The En-Ar bi-dictionary is Babylon [21], and the En-Fr bi-dictionary was IATE.

DSR-MPG1 is the translations obtained from formula 1, DSR-MPG2 represents the translations obtained from indirect translations, which increased the amount of correct translation by 25 terms in the case of En-Ar.

The result can be progressively enhanced by accepting contributions from volunteers through the applications we described in the section three and the generic nature of MPG makes it easy to accept contributions from any dictionary or terminological database.

6 Conclusions and Perspectives

We described the explicit and implicit approaches that we are using to extract and discover domain dedicated terminology from human interaction with a related web-community. We presented a new lexical resource that can handle multilingual terms for a specialized domain. Multilingual Preterminological Graphs are constructed based on domain dedicated resources, and based on volunteer contributions. We described the approach for using access log files to initialize such graphs by finding the trends in the search requests used to access the resources of an online community.

Aiming at a standardized multilingual repository is very expensive and difficult. Instead of that, MPGs tries to use all available contributions. This way will enhance the linguistic and informational coverage, and tuning the weights (*tw*, *rw*, and *sw*) will give indications for the confidence of the translation equivalences, as the *tedges* accumulate the agreements of the contributors and MDRs (online resources).

We experimented the concept of MPGs on the domain of the historical Silk Road. We used the resources of the Digital Silk Road Project to construct a DSR-MPG and some applications that attract further contribution to the MPG. DSR-MPG achieved high linguistic and informational coverage compared to other general purpose dictionaries. Furthermore, the generic structure of the MPG makes it possible to accept volunteer contributions, and it facilitates further study of computing more lexical functions and ontological relations between the terms.

We are packaging the platform for constructing the DSR-MPG to be used in other domains as a tool for "Multilingual Terminology Elicitation" this platform will construct an MPG for a set of textual resources to collect its preterminology. Currently we are working on constructing an MPG for the domain of Arabic dreams interpretation, this MPG will serve a service for interpreting dreams (in Arabic), a beta version is available at this website [22]. Furthermore, we are investigating more scenarios of contribution to enrich the graph; one of them is based on playful methods using a *game with a purpose (GWAP)* [23] where users contribute to a knowledge repository while playing an online game, the knowledge repository in our case is a lexical graph.

References

1. Cabré, M.T., Sager, J.C.: Terminology: Theory, methods and applications. J. Benjamins Pub. Co. xii, 247 (1999)
2. Kageura, K.: The Dynamics of Terminology: A descriptive theory of term formation and terminological growth. Terminology and Lexicography Research and Practice 5, 322 (2002)
3. IATE. Inter-Active Terminology for Europe (2008), http://iate.europa.eu (cited 2008 10/10/2008)
4. UN. United Nations Multilingual Terminology Database (2008), http://unterm.un.org/ (cited 2008 10/10/2008)
5. IEC. Electropedia (2008), http://dom2.iec.ch/iev/iev.nsf/welcome?openform (cited 2008 10/10/2008)
6. Gopestake, A., et al.: Acquisition of lexical translation relations from MRDS. Machine Translation 9(3-4), 183–219 (1994)

7. Helmreich, S., Guthrie, L., Wilks, Y.A.: The use of machine readable dictionaries in the PANGLOSS project. In: Proceedings of the AAAI Spring Symposium on Building Lexicons for Machine Translation, Stanford Univ., Stanford (1993)
8. Etzioni, O., et al.: Lexical translation with application to image searching on the web. In: MT Summit XI, Copenhagen, Denmark (2007)
9. Anh, L.V.: Human Computation. In: Computer Science, p. 87. Carnegie Mellon University, Pittsburgh (2005)
10. Ono, K., et al.: Memory of the Silk Road -The Digital Silk Road Project. In: Proceedings of (VSMM 2008), Project Papers, Limassol, Cyprus (2008)
11. Wikipedia. Wikipedia (2008), http://www.wikipedia.org/ (cited 2008 June 1, 2008)
12. Google. Google Translate (2008), http://translate.google.com (cited 2008 June 1, 2008)
13. Jones, G.J.F., et al.: Domain-Specific Query Translation for Multilingual Information Access Using Machine Translation Augmented With Dictionaries Mined From Wikipedia. In: Proceedings (CLIA 2008), Hydrabad, India (2008)
14. NII. Digital Silk Road (2003), http://dsr.nii.ac.jp/index.html.en (cited 2008 1/9/2008)
15. NII. Digital Archive of Toyo Bunko Rare Books (2008), http://dsr.nii.ac.jp/toyobunko/ (cited 2008 June 1, 2008)
16. Daoud, M., et al.: A CLIR-Based Collaborative Construction of Multilingual Terminological Dictionary for Cultural Resources. In: Translating and the Computer, London-UK, vol. 30 (2008)
17. Stermsek, G., Strembeck, M., Neumann, G.: A User Profile Derivation Approach based on Log-File Analysis. In: Arabnia, H.R., Hashemi, R.R. (eds.) IKE. CSREA Press (2007)
18. Chen, A.: Cross-Language Retrieval Experiments at CLEF 2002. In: CLEF 2002 working notes (2002)
19. Oard, D.: Global Access to Multilingual Information. In: Fourth International Workshop on Information Retrieval with Asian Languages, Taipei-Taiwan (1999)
20. Wikitionary. Wikitionary (2008), http://en.wikipedia.org/wiki/Wiktionary (cited 2008 1/9/2008)
21. Babylon. Babylon Dictionary (2009), http://www.babylon.com/define/98/English-Arabic-Dictionary.html (cited 2009 5/5/2009)
22. Daoud, D., Al Ahlam, T.: (2010), http://www.maherinfo.com/ (cited 2010)
23. Ahn, L.v.: Games With A Purpose. IEEE Computer Magazine, 96–98 (2006)

Appendix: MPG as a GraphML

The following is a sample MPG in GraphML format:
————XML STARTS————————————

```
<?xml version="1.0" encoding="UTF-8"?>
<GraphML>
<key id="d0" for="node" attr.name="preterm" attr.type="string"></key>
<key id="d1" for="node" attr.name="language_code" attr.type="string">
<default>eng</default></key>
<key id="d2" for="node" attr.name="source" attr.type="string">
<default>unknown</default></key>
<key id="d3" for="node" attr.name="occ" attr.type="string">
<default>1</default></key>
<key id="d4" for="edge" attr.name="rw" attr.type="double">
<default>0</default></key>
```

```xml
<key id="d5" for="edge" attr.name="sw" attr.type="double">
<default>0</default></key>
<key id="d6" for="edge" attr.name="tw" attr.type="double">
<default>0</default></key>

<graph isAcyclic="true" id="dsr" >
<node id="2353" >
<data key="d0">great wall of China</data>
<data key="d1">eng</data>
<data key="d2">dsr_log</data>
<data key="d3">11</data>
</node>
<node id="2354" >
<data key="d0">سور الصين العظيم</data>
<data key="d1">ara</data>
<data key="d2">wikipedia</data>
<data key="d3">3</data>
</node>
<node id="2355" >
<data key="d0">万里の長城</data>
<data key="d1">jpn</data>
<data key="d2">dsr_log</data>
<data key="d3">4</data>
</node>
<node id="2356" >
<data key="d0">Grande Muraille de Chine</data>
<data key="d1">fra</data>
<data key="d2">wikipedia</data>
<data key="d3">3</data>
</node>

<edge source="2353" target="2354">
<data key="d4">0</data>
<data key="d5">0</data>
<data key="d6">3</data>
</edge>
<edge source="2353" target="2355">
<data key="d4">1</data>
<data key="d5">0</data>
<data key="d6">2</data>
</edge>
<edge source="2353" target="2356">
<data key="d4">0</data>
<data key="d5">0</data>
<data key="d6">2</data>
</edge>
</graph>
</GraphML>
```
————————XML ENDS————————

The above XML graph corresponds to the graph in Figure 13.

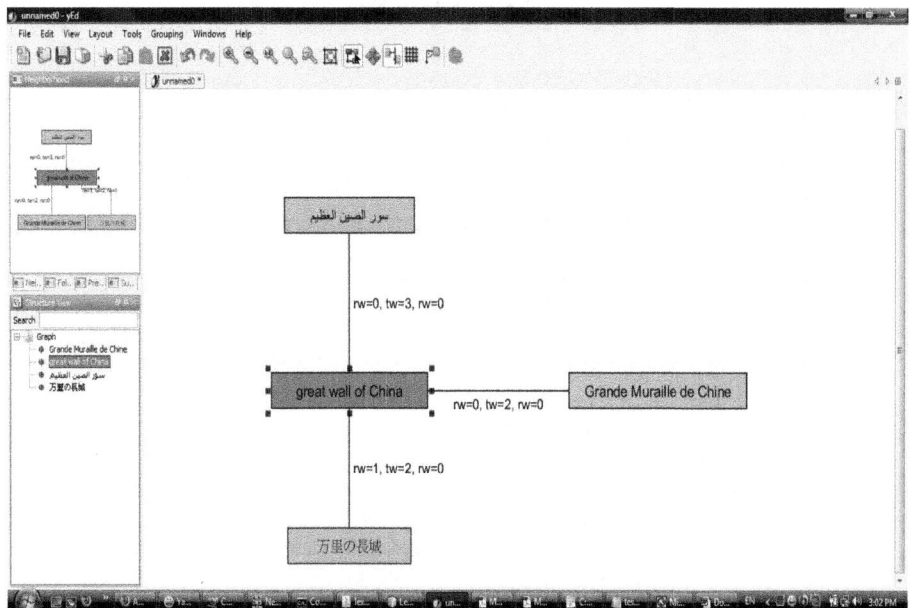

Fig. 13. Sample graph

An Efficient Semantic Web Services Matching Mechanism

Jing Li[1,2], Dianfu Ma[1,2], Zhuo Zhao[1,2], Hong Zhu[1,2], and Lusong Li[2]

[1] Institute of Advanced Computing Technology, Beihang University, Beijing, China
{lijing,dfma}@nlsde.buaa.edu.cn,
{zhaozhuo,zhuhong}@act.buaa.edu.cn
[2] State Key Lab. of Software Development Environment, Beihang University, Beijing, China
lilvsong@nlsde.buaa.edu.cn

Abstract. Bringing semantics to Web Services description and matching re-markably improves the precision and recall performance of service discovery. However, it greatly increases the service matching time by executing semantic reasoning, and makes the real-time service selection and composition harder than before. To shorten service matching time, this paper presents an efficient Semantic Web Services matching mechanism with semantic information pre-treatment. It shifts part of the reasoning process from service matching phase to service publishing phase. A prototype of Semantic Web Services matchmaker has been implemented based on this mechanism. The experiments on two service datasets show that our mechanism outperforms existing methods.

Keywords: Semantic Web Services, Service Matching, Pretreatment.

1 Introduction

Web Services are autonomous and modular applications deployed, interoperated and invoked over Internet. A rapid increase of Web Services [1] makes services discovery become harder. To retrieve services in an accurate and automatic way among a large numbers of candidates, researchers have presented some efforts [2-4]. Among these contributions, Semantic Web Services have received a lot of attention in recent years. Bringing semantics to Web Service has greatly improved the recall and precision performance of service discovery.

Nowadays, Semantic Web Services discovery approaches can be classified into three main types, which are logic-based approaches, non-logic based approaches and hybrid approaches [5]. Logic-based approaches describe services with semantic service description languages such as OWL-S and do service matching based on se-mantic reasoning. Non-logic based approaches use methods such as latent semantic analysis to exploit semantic information from service description. In contrast, hybrid approaches employ combinations of both. However, these intricate service matching methods increase the query response time of service retrieval and hardly support dy-namic real-time service selection. Experiments show that semantic service match-maker search consumes about 5 seconds more time than a typical keyword-based search [6]. For example, in the S3 contest 2008 [7], the best service discovery

Z. Lacroix (Ed.): RED 2009, LNCS 6162, pp. 110–119, 2010.

system's average query response time was 5.26 seconds with only 1000 services in the service registry.

To shorten service matching time, this paper proposes an efficient Semantic Web Services matching mechanism that shifts part of process from service matching phase to service publish phase. Given an ontology based service advertisement, it extracts the semantic information from the advertisement and creates matrixes named service semantic feature matrixes (SSFM) to express the semantic information of the service. When a service request arrives, it extracts the semantic information in the request and generates request semantic feature matrixes. It filters out service ads according to the ontology which the request uses and the structure of request. Then it calculates the similarity between the left ads' and request's semantic feature matrixes. The final output is a list of services which are ranked by this similarity value. A serial of evaluations on two Semantic Web Services data corpuses suggest that this matching mechanism offers better performance.

The remainder of this paper is structured as follows. Section 2 presents the semantic information pretreatment process. In Section 3, the matrix based Semantic Web Services matching algorithm is introduced in detail. Section 4 describes a prototype and a series of experiments. Section 5 is the conclusion.

2 Semantic Information Pretreatment

To an online Web Services discovery system, the most important evaluation criterions are high precision-recall performance and short query response time. In the meanwhile, service publish time is important too. Based on the fact that the frequency of service requesting is much higher than the frequency of service publishing, in this paper, our motivation is for getting shorter query response time, we can appropriately increase the service publishing time. So we adopt the semantic pretreatment strategy which does part of the semantic reasoning in the service publishing step and store this semantic information in a special data structure.

When the service provider submits a service ad file (OWL-S), it firstly publishes the ontologies which are imported by this service into the semantic registry, and then checks the semantic consistency between the ontologies and service description to make sure the concepts which service refers exist. This step guarantees that services which refer the ontologies or concepts that do not exist will not be accepted. After the semantic consistency check, it publishes the service semantic information and creates the semantic feature matrixes for this service. When the requester submits a query, it first checks its semantic consistency and then creates the semantic feature matrixes for this query. At last, it does the matrix operations to calculate the similarity between services and query.

This section presents the ontology and service/request semantic information pretreatment and section 3 describes how to calculate the similarity between services and query.

2.1 Semantic Information Pretreatment for Ontology

In Semantic Web Services discovery, the most important semantic information is the ontology concepts which are referred by services and the relationship between these concepts. Normally, given an ontology description file, such as an OWL file, the full relationship between all concepts has not presented directly. For example, when a OWL file defines concept A is a subclass of concept B and concept A is an equivalence class of concept C, it probably will not directly define that C is a subclass of B. This is one of the reasons for why it needs time to do the reasoning. To shorten the reasoning time in service matching, we deal with the ontologies and supplement the full relationships between concepts, then store these relationships before the service publishing. The relationships which we consider include subclass relationship, super class relationship and equivalence class relationship. Because comparing to other relationships, these three are more important and can turn the scales. At the same time, we extract all the concepts and individuals from the ontology description, and store them in the semantic registry.

2.2 Semantic Information Pretreatment for Service and Query

In order to achieve fast service matching, this mechanism pre-reasons on the semantic information during service publishing and keeps the reasoning results in matrix forms. To record the functional parameter information, we separate the inputs and outputs of a service into two individual matrixes, which are input functional matrix *ISFM (S)* and output functional matrix *OSFM (S)*. Both of *ISFM (S)* and *OSFM (S)* are called *SSFM*.

We represent the service as a triad $SEV = <IN,ON,ONT>$, the input set $IN = \{in_1, in_2...in_m\}$ $(m{\geq}0)$, m is the input number of the service. The output set $ON = \{on_1, on_2, ...on_n\}$ $(n{\geq}0)$, n is the output number of the service. And the ontology set referred by inputs $IONT=\{iont_1, iont_2...iont_k\}$ $(k{\geq}0)$, here k is the number of ontologies referred by the service inputs. the ontology set referred by outputs $OONT=\{oont_1, oont_2...oont_t\}$ $(t{\geq}0)$, here t is the number of ontologies referred by the service outputs. We define the concept number set $CN=\{cn_1, cn_2...cn_x\}$ $(x{\geq}0)$, cn_i is the concept number of ontology $iont_i$ or $oont_i$. So the concepts in $iont_i/oont_i$ can be identified as concept sets $iont_{i\_}cont = \{iont_i.concept_1, iont_i.concept_2...iont_i.concept_{cn_i}\}$ and $oont_{i\_}cont = \{oont_i.concept_1, oont_i.concept_2...oont_i.concept_{cn_i}\}$.

When a new service S is submitted, its functional matrixes $ISFM(S)$ and $OSFM(S)$ are generated according to formula (1) and formula (2). $ISFM(S).v_{pq}$ is the element in the pth row and the qth column of matrix $ISFM(S)$. $OSFM(S).v_{pq}$ is the element of the pth row and the qth column of matrix $OSFM(S)$.

$$ISFM(S).v_{pq} = \begin{cases} 1. & \text{if and only if } in_q = iont_q.concept_p (0 \leq q \leq m, 0 \leq p \leq cn_q) \\ 0. & \text{else} \end{cases} \quad (1)$$

$$OSFM(S).v_{pq} = \begin{cases} 1. & \text{if and only if } on_q = oont_q.concept_p (1 \leq q \leq n, 1 \leq p \leq cn_q) \\ 0. & \text{else} \end{cases} \quad (2)$$

We give an example to explain how to generate the matrixes for a service. *Service A* is a novel price searching service. It has 2 inputs and 1 output. The inputs are annotated by the concept *novel* and the concept *press*. The output is annotated by the concept *recommendprice*. These 3 concepts are from 3 ontologies: *reading* (includes *novel*), *company* (includes *press*) and *price* (includes *recommendprice*). Ontology is regarded as a vector. The vector's length is the concepts number in the ontology. We generate one input semantic feature matrix (ISFM) and one output semantic feature matrix (OSFM). The ISFM has two columns which instead of *reading* ontology (vector 1) and *company* ontology (vector 2). In the beginning, all the elements in the vectors are "0". We set "1" at the concept *novel*'s position in the vector 1, and set "1" at the concept *press*'s position in the vector 2. The number of rows in the ISFM or OSFM is the sum of the number of elements in each ontology that is used. Then we generate the OSFM in the same way.

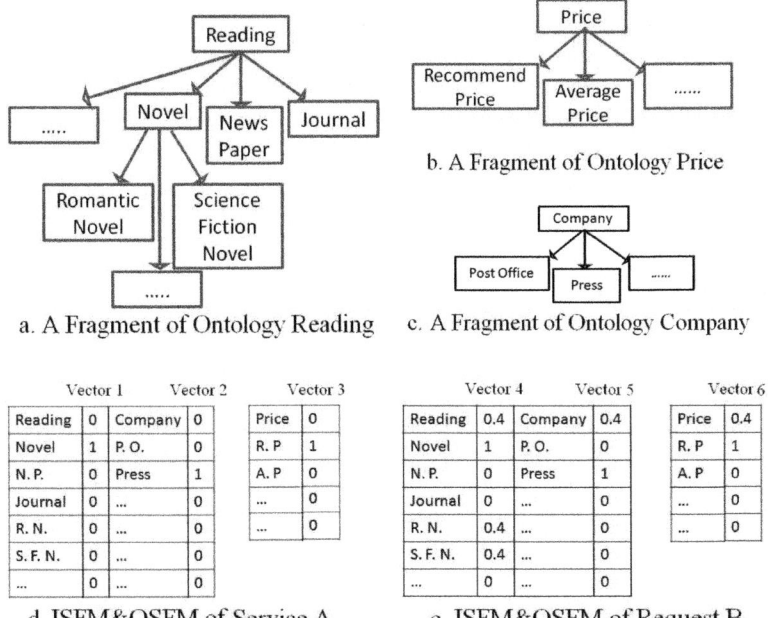

a. A Fragment of Ontology Reading   c. A Fragment of Ontology Company

b. A Fragment of Ontology Price

	Vector 1		Vector 2		Vector 3
Reading	0	Company	0	Price	0
Novel	1	P. O.	0	R. P	1
N. P.	0	Press	1	A. P	0
Journal	0	...	0	...	0
R. N.	0	...	0	...	0
S. F. N.	0	...	0		
...	0	...	0		

d. ISFM&OSFM of Service A

	Vector 4		Vector 5		Vector 6
Reading	0.4	Company	0.4	Price	0.4
Novel	1	P. O.	0	R. P	1
N. P.	0	Press	1	A. P	0
Journal	0	...	0	...	0
R. N.	0.4	...	0	...	0
S. F. N.	0.4	...	0		
...	0	...	0		

e. ISFM&OSFM of Request B

Fig. 1. Fragments of ontologies and ISFM&OSFM

When the service ad is published, its ISFM and OSFM are generated and stored in the semantic registry. In the request's ISFM and OSFM, we consider the similarity between concepts. For example, now we take this *Service A* as the *Request B*, in *ISFM(R)*, when we set "1" at the concept *novel*'s position in vector 4, we also set a pure decimal $k \in (0,1)$ at *novel*'s super class/subclass position. In the OSFM, we set "1" at the concept *recommendprice*'s position; we also set k at *recommendprice*'s super class position. We can apply some existing concept similarity algorithm to calculate the pure decimal k. In our work, we use Generalized Cosine-Similarity Measure [8] to calculate the semantic distance d and $k = 1/(d+1)$. The formula (3) and formula (4) show how to calculate the element value in *ISFM(R)* and *OSFM(R)*. In figure 1, we present the fragments of the two ontologies, the *ISFM* and *OSFM* of *Service A* and *Request B*.

$$ISFM(R).v_{pq} = \begin{cases} 1. & \text{if and only if } in_q = iont_q.concept_p\,(0 \le q \le \text{m}, 0 \le p \le cn_q) \\ k. & \text{if } in_q \supset iont_q.concept_p \text{ or } in_q \subset iont_q.concept_p \\ 0. & \text{else} \end{cases} \quad (3)$$

$$OSFM(R).v_{pq} = \begin{cases} 1. & \text{if and only if } on_q = oont_q.concept_p\,(0 \le q \le n, 0 \le p \le cn_q) \\ k. & \text{if } on_q \supset oont_q.concept_p \text{ or } in_q \subset oont_q.concept_p \\ 0. & \text{else} \end{cases} \quad (4)$$

The set of ontology that annotated request outputs is $O_R = \{or_n|\ n{\ge}0\}$, and the set of ontology that annotated request inputs is $I_R = \{ir_m|\ m{\ge}0\}$. The set of ontology that annotated a service outputs is $O_S = \{os_i|\ i{\ge}0\}$, and the set of ontology that annotated service inputs is $I_s = \{is_j|\ j{\ge}0\}$. When a request arrives, we first generate its *ISFM* and *OSFM*, according to requester's requirement and then filter out part of the services which do not satisfy the conditions (5).

$$O_s \bigcap (\bigcup_{k=1}^{n} or_k) \neq \Phi, \ I_s \bigcap (\bigcup_{k=1}^{m} ir_k) \neq \Phi \quad (5)$$

3 Semantic Web Services Matching Algorithm

A Matrix based Semantic Web Services matching algorithm is presented in figure 2, in which *r* is the request's *SSFM*, ad is the service's *SSFM*, *OResult* is the matching relationship matrix between *r.OSFM* and *ad.OSFM*, *IResult* is the matching relationship matrix between *r.ISFM* and *ad.ISFM*, *OVector* is the similarity vector of outputs and *IVector* is the similarity vector of inputs. $t(x,y)$ and $h(x,y)$ are the element of xth row and y^{th} column of *OResult* and *IResult*. $t(,y)$ is the yth column of *OResult* , $t(x,)$ is the xth row of *OResult*. $h(,y)$ is the yth column of *IResult* and $h(x,)$ is the xth row of *IResult*. *n* and *m* are the output and input numbers of request. $\sum ovector_k$ and $\sum ivector_j$ are the elements' value sum of *OVector* and *IVector*.

$$Similarity = a \times (\frac{\sum ovector_k}{m}) + b \times (\frac{\sum ivector_j}{n}) \quad (6)$$

$$a + b = 1,\ a{>}0,\ b{>}0 \quad (7)$$

$$a + b = -1,\ a{<}0,\ b{<}0 \quad (8)$$

There are two main steps in this algorithm:

(i)   Calculate the matching relationship matrixes between service and request;
(ii) Get the similarity value from the matching relationship matrixes.

It first matches the service and the request by calculating matrix product and the two result matrixes are the matching relationship matrixes. Then, it picks up the biggest *k* and *j* (*k* and *j* are the matched output and input numbers) non-zero elements from *OResult* and *IResult*, saves them into *OVector* and *IVector*. At last, it returns the similarity of the service and request. The similarity is calculated by the formula (6). Here, *a* and *b* are the weight values of output and input, and satisfy either the formula (7) (when the matching type is completely matched or similar matched) or formula (8) (when the matching type is reverse completely matched or reverse similar matched). We adjust a and b to get the best ranking list. The similarity between the request and each service can be in the interval [-1, 1].

SWS Matching Algorithm
---
function SWSMatching(*SSFM r, SSFM ad*)
    OResult = r.OSFM⁻¹×ad.OSFM
    while(*t(x,y)* is maximum element in *OResult*){
        OVector.add(*t(x,y).value*)
        delete *t(x,)* and *t(,y)* of *OResult*
    }until (*t(x,y)* = 0)
    IResult = r.ISFM⁻¹×ad.ISFM
    while(*h(x,y)* is maximum element in *IResult*){
        IVector.add(*h(x,y).value*)
        delete *h(x,)* and *h(,y)* of *IResul*
    }until (*h(x,y)* = 0)
    return a * ($\sum ovector_k$/m) + b*($\sum ivector_j$/n)

Fig. 2. Matrix based Semantic Web Services matching algorithm

Table 1. Similarity analysis

No.	Range of similarity	Description	Conditions
1	Similarity = 1	Complete matched	$|S._{ON}|>=|R._{ON}|$, $|S._{IN}|<=|R._{IN}|$; all the matched parameters are completely matched
2	Similarity$\in$ (0,1)	Similar matched	$|S._{ON}|>=|R._{ON}|$, $|S._{IN}|<=|R._{IN}|$; part/all of the matched parameters are similar matched, the else are completely matched
3	Similarity = -1	Reverse complete matched	$|S._{ON}|<|R._{ON}|$, $|S._{IN}|<=|R._{IN}|$; or $|S._{ON}|>=|R._{ON}|$, $|S._{IN}|>|R._{IN}|$; all the matched parameters are completely matched
4	Similarity$\in$ (-1,0)	Reverse similar matched	$|S._{ON}|<|R._{ON}|$, $|S._{IN}|<=|R._{IN}|$; or $|S._{ON}|>=|R._{ON}|$, $|S._{IN}|>|R._{IN}|$, part/all of the matched parameters are similar matched, the else are completely matched
5	Similarity = 0	Not matched	If it doesn't satisfy the above conditions

Table 1 gives the analysis for all the matching types. $|S._{ON}|$ is service output number, $|R._{ON}|$, $|S._{IN}|$ and $|R._{IN}|$ are the request output number, service input number and the request input number. If two parameters (input or output) refer the same concept or the equivalent concept, the two parameters are completely matched; if two parameters refer different concepts, and the two concepts have the subclass relationship, the two parameters are similar matched. When the request and the service have the same outputs but the service's input's number are more than the request's input's number, we call it "Reverse matched". The ranking method is as follows, the order is from (1) to (5). (1) The complete matched services; (2) Similar matched services that sorted by the similarity; (3) Reverse complete matched services; (4) Reverse similar matched services sorted by the absolute value of similarity; (5) Not matched services.

In this work, we also consider about service precondition and effect matching. If both of precondition and effect are described by ontologies, we can describe and match them in the same way as the way we describe and match input and output. So we have two more SSFM matrixes which are precondition functional matrix (PSFM) and effect functional matrix (ESFM). And this step should be done before we match input and output. If the matching result of precondition or effect is not 1, we should stop matching input and output. The matching result of this service and request is 0 (not matched). If the precondition and effect are described by other rule languages, we do not support the PE matching.

4   Prototype Implementation and Experiments

We implemented a prototype, which we called MEMORY, based on our matching mechanism. The structure of MEMORY is shown in figure 3. The front-end contains two major parts. One is the service publishing interface for service provider, namely Publish Interface, and the other is the service requests interface for service consumer, called Request Interface. Publish Interface extracts the semantic information from service description document and starts the process of service publishing. MEMORY supports OWL-S based service description. Request Interface gets the semantic service request which is written by the service consumer and triggers the service matching process. The request of MEMORY is also an OWL-S file.

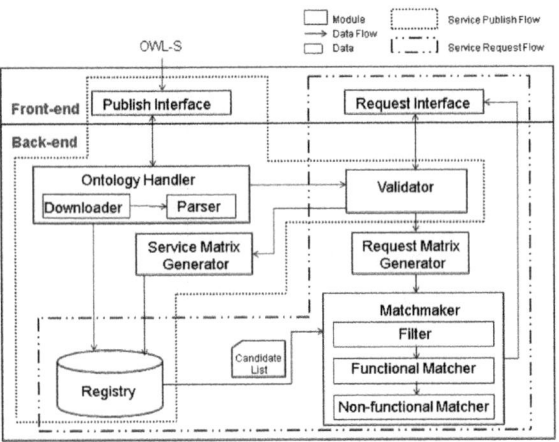

Fig. 3. The structure of MEMORY

Experiments are conducted on Pentium IV 3.0GHz machines with 1 Gigabyte of memory. The system is implemented with Java (JDK1.6.0). The MySQL 5.0 Community Server database is used as a registry. Our experiments are based on two corpuses. One is from DFKI, which has been used in the International Semantic Service Selection (S3) contest in 2008(owls-tc2) [7]. Because the scale of owls-tc2 is too small to show the performance of our system, we also do the experiments on the other bigger corpus which is created by us.

4.1 Experiments on OWLS-TC2

To compare the precision-recall ratios and performance of MEMORY, we do our experiments on owls-tc2, which contain 1007 services that are well-annotated by 32 ontologies manually. Besides, this corpus also contains 29 queries and their relevance services sets. OWLS-iMatcher2, OWLS-MX 2.0 and JIAC-OWLSM are the top three systems in S3 contest 2008. These three systems adopted hybrid approaches, while MEMORY adopts logical approach. Figure 4 presents the precision-recall curves of these three systems and MEMORY.

Table 2. Compare of total publish-matching time and average query response time

System	Total runtime	Average query response time
OWLS-iMatcher2	11.2 min	22.94 secs
OWLS-MX 2.0	14.4 min	5.26 secs
JIAC-OWLSM	3.9 min	7.54 secs
MEMORY	9.6 min	0.496 secs

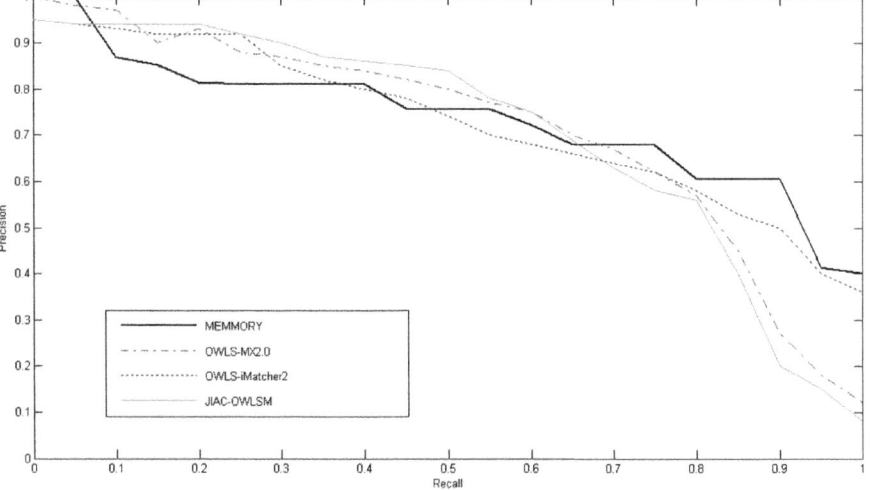

Fig. 4. Comparison of R/P performances

Table 2 gives the total runtime and average query response time of these three systems and MEMORY. The total runtime includes service registrations and service matching & ranking time for 1007 services and 29 queries. Average query response time includes service matching & ranking time for one query. The precision-recall curves in figure 4 illustrates that MEMORY has a bit better PR performance than the other three systems. To Web Services discovery, the short query response time is more important than the short service publishing time. The results in Table 2 show that MEMORY doesn't have the shortest total runtime, but has the shortest average query response time, which is less than 10% of the time of OWLS-MX 2.0.

4.2 Experiments on Our Corpus

We have collected 5,023 different WSDL files from Google and some Web Services portals. There are 2,788 active services which contain 25,752 operations. We automatically transform the WSDL files into OWL-S files with our WSDL2OWLS tool, and take each operation as one single OWL-S file. After annotating these operations automatically with 70 ontologies from some famous research institutes, we get 25,752 annotated OWL-S files. Our experiments are based on five service sets with different sizes: 4000, 80000, 12000, 16000 and 20000. We pick up 90 OWL-S files as the queries to test the average query response time. In these 90 queries, 30 queries have one input and one output, 30 queries have two inputs and one output, and the last 30 queries have three inputs and one output.

Figure 5 shows the increasing trend of the average query response time with the increasing OWL-S files number and queries with different numbers of inputs. The result shows that the average response time slowly increases along with the service set scale. The relationship between the query response time and service number is nearly linear. And with bigger numbers of input, the response time is increasing. But the increasing region in reduced. These results prove that our mechanism has good scalability.

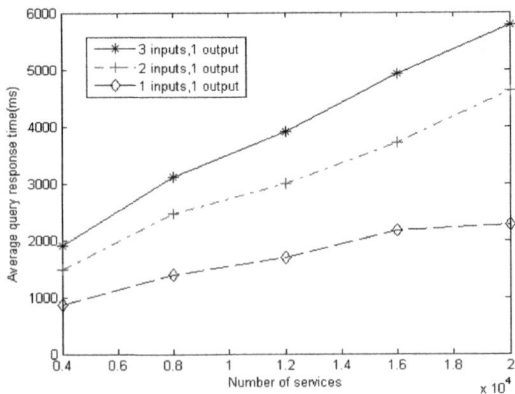

Fig. 5. Average query response time

5 Conclusion

This paper proposed an efficient Semantic Web Services matching mechanism which can retrieve services in an accurate and rapid way. Based on this mechanism, we developed a prototype named MEMORY. Experiments on MEMORY proved that our mechanism is scalable and outperforms existing methods.

Acknowledgments. Acknowledge the support of the un-structure data management system program of China and the BaiMai Project between Thales (France) and China.

References

1. Al-Masri, E., Mahmoud, Q.H.: Investigating Web Service on WWW. In: WWW 2008, pp. 795–804 (2008)
2. Paolucci, M., Kawamura, T., Payne, T.R., Sycara, K.: Semantic Matching of Web Services Capabilities. In: Horrocks, I., Hendler, J. (eds.) ISWC 2002. LNCS, vol. 2342, pp. 36–47. Springer, Heidelberg (2002)
3. Jaeger, M., Rojec-Goldmann, G., Liebetruth, C., Mühl, G., Geihs, K.: Ranked matching for service descriptions using owl-s. In: The 14. GI/VDE Fachtagung KiVS (2005)
4. Klusch, M., Fries, B., Sycarac, K.: OWLS-MX: A hybrid Semantic Web service matchmaker for OWL-S services. JWoS 7(2), 121–133 (2009)
5. Klusch, M.: Semantic Service Coordination. In: Schumacher, M., Helin, H., Schuldt, H. (eds.) CASCOM - Intelligent Service Coordination in the Semantic Web, ch. 4. Birkhaeuser Verlag, Springer (2008)
6. Kawamura, T., Hasegawa, T., Ohsuga, A., Paolucci, M., Sycara, K.: Web services lookup: a matchmaker experiment. IT Professional 7(2), 36–41 (2005)
7. International Contest S3 on Semantic Service Selection (2008), http://www-ags.dfki.uni-sb.de/~klusch/s3/html/2008.html
8. Ganesan, P. (eds.): Exploiting hierarchical domain structure to compute similarity. ACM Transactions on Information Systems 21(1), 64–93 (2003)

Efficiently Selecting the Best Web Services

Marlene Goncalves[1], Maria-Esther Vidal[1], and Alfredo Regalado[1],
and Nadia Yacoubi Ayadi[2]

[1] Computer Science Department, Universidad Simón Bolívar, Caracas, Venezuela
{mgoncalves,mvidal,aregalado}@ldc.usb.ve
[2] RIADI Laboratory, National School of Computer Science, 2010 La Manouba
nadia.yacoubi@asu.edu

Abstract. Emerging technologies and linking data initiatives have motivated the publication of a large number of datasets, and provide the basis for publishing Web services and tools to manage the available data. This wealth of resources opens a world of possibilities to satisfy user requests. However, Web services may have similar functionality and assess different performance; therefore, it is required to identify among the Web services that satisfy a user request, the ones with the best quality. In this paper we propose a hybrid approach that combines reasoning tasks with ranking techniques to aim at the selection of the Web services that best implement a user request. Web service functionalities are described in terms of input and output attributes annotated with existing ontologies, non-functionality is represented as Quality of Services (QoS) parameters, and user requests correspond to conjunctive queries whose sub-goals impose restrictions on the functionality and quality of the services to be selected. The ontology annotations are used in different reasoning tasks to infer service implicit properties and to augment the size of the service search space. Furthermore, QoS parameters are considered by a ranking metric to classify the services according to how well they meet a user non-functional condition. We assume that all the QoS parameters of the non-functional condition are equally important, and apply the Top-k Skyline approach to select the k services that best meet this condition. Our proposal relies on a two-fold solution which fires a deductive-based engine that performs different reasoning tasks to discover the services that satisfy the requested functionality, and an efficient implementation of the Top-k Skyline approach to compute the top-k services that meet the majority of the QoS constraints. Our Top-k Skyline solution exploits the properties of the Skyline Frequency metric and identifies the top-k services by just analyzing a subset of the services that meet the non-functional condition. We report on the effects of the proposed reasoning tasks, the quality of the top-k services selected by the ranking metric, and the performance of the proposed ranking techniques. Our results suggest that the number of services can be augmented by up two orders of magnitude. In addition, our ranking techniques are able to identify services that have the best values in at least half of the QoS parameters, while the performance is improved.

Keywords: Service Discovery, Ranking, Top-k Skyline, Deductive Reasoning.

Z. Lacroix (Ed.): RED 2009, LNCS 6162, pp. 120–139, 2010.

1   Introduction

During the last decade, emerging technologies such as the Semantic Web, Linked Data initiatives, affordable computation and network access, have made available a great number of public resources. Health and Life sciences are good examples of this phenomenon. These domains constantly evolve, and have generated publicly available information resources and services whose number and size have dramatically increased during the last years. A good survey of existing bioinformatics catalog of resources can be found in [26].

Web services are usually defined in terms of functional parameters (input and output attributes) that express what the service is able to do, and non-functional or Quality of Service parameters (QoS) that describe the service behavior. Additionally, Web services are enriched with annotations of domain ontology concepts, that describe the semantics of their attributes [19,30]. Web service annotations are used during discovery tasks to infer implicit properties and identify services that meet a user functional request. A Web service discovery task receives as input a query as well as a service registry consisting of service descriptions, and returns as output a list of matched services. A user request or discovery query specifies the functional and non-functional requirements of the requested services. Functional requirements express the functionality of the desired services in terms of its inputs and outputs declared as semantic concepts; also preconditions and effects of executing the services can be specified. QoS parameters can be used to rank services according to non-functional criteria or to restrict the quality of the requested services.

In existing approaches for Web service discovery, logical inference tasks are performed to deduce matches between parameters of the query and the service descriptions; new Web service properties are deduced by exploiting semantic service descriptions as well as domain knowledge [5,29]. However, reasoning-based approaches for service discovery are not tailored to select the top-k skyline services that best meet the non-functional parameters in a request; this feature is particularly important when a large number of incomparable services satisfy the non-functional criteria of the user request, and only a small subset maybe useful to the user. We have aimed at this problem, and we have proposed a hybrid approach that combines reasoning tasks with Top-k Skyline-based ranking techniques.

Web service functionalities are described in terms of ontology annotated input and output attributes, non-functionality is represented as Quality of Services (QoS) parameters, and user requests correspond to conjunctive queries whose sub-goals impose restrictions on the functionality and quality of the services to be selected. Services and ontologies are implemented as a deductive database. Predicates in the deductive database represent knowledge explicitly expressed in the ontology, and the semantics of the language used to describe the ontologies and to annotate the services. Ontology annotations are used in different reasoning tasks to infer service implicit properties and to augment the size of the search space of the available services; QoS parameters are considered by a ranking metric to classify the services according to how well they meet the query QoS constraints.

Our approach relies on a two-fold technique to select the top-k skyline services that satisfy a set of functional and non-functional requirements, i.e., the services that meet the non-functional requirements and have the best values in the majority of the QoS parameters used in the non-functional condition. Our approach differs from existing solutions [5,17,19,36]: first for being able to identify the top-k skyline services, and second, for applying reasoning and ranking techniques to efficiently identify them. In the first phase, an ontology-driven approach is used to select the services that satisfy the functional conditions; reasoning tasks are implemented on top of a deductive database and they provide the basis to infer implicit properties of the available services and to augment the size of the search space. This approach extends the deductive solution presented in [5] with six new reasoning tasks to derive new service descriptions based on the ontology annotations. Three of the six reasoning tasks infer new types of the service input attributes, while the other three derive new types of the output attributes. In the second phase, the top-k services that best satisfy the non-functional request are identified from the set of incomparable services or skyline. The Skyline Frequency metric (SFM) [16] distinguishes the best services by measuring the number of times a service is part of the skyline induced by the subsets of the QoS parameters in the non-functional condition. The algorithm Web Top-k Skyline Frequency (WTKSF) is performed to identify the top-k services in terms of this metric. The WTKSF algorithm is an extension of the index-based algorithm TKSI proposed in [18]. TKSI computes the top-k services in a set of skyline points, where top-k services are identified in terms of a user score function whose properties are unknown. Thus, the WTKSF algorithm exploits the properties of SFM to speed up the process of computing the top-k services by just computing the SFM for a small subset of the incomparable services. We have conducted an experimental study to compare the performance of the WTKSF algorithm with respect to a state-of-the-art algorithm named BUS that computes the SFM, and we have observed that WTKSF outperforms this approach. Additionally, we have studied the quality of the services identified by our two-fold approach. In our experiments, the top-k services distinguished by SFM have the highest values in at least half of the non-functional parameters, while the number of operations required to compute the top-k skyline services is reduced.

The rest of the paper is organized as follows. Section 2 reviews related work in the fields of Service Discovery, Skyline and Top-k ranking techniques. In Section 3, we motivate the importance of using the Top-k Skyline approach to discover the top-k services that best meet user request functional and non-functional conditions. Section 4 defines our approach. Section 5 reports our experimental results. Finally, section 6 concludes and outlines our future work.

2   Related Work

2.1   Semantic Web Service (SWS)

In order to describe the semantic of a set of available services, different frameworks have been defined [3,4,5,22,33]. These approaches aim at providing richer semantic specifications of Web services and reasoning tasks, in order to enable the flexible automation of service processes. However, because of a lack of generality, some important service selection specific reasoning tasks cannot be supported. First, OWL-S is an OWL ontology to describe Web services in terms of their properties and capabilities. The OWL-S ontology is comprised of three main components: the service profile that describes the service functionality; the service model that establishes how the service works; and the service grounding that specifies how the service has to be accessed. The Web Service Modeling Ontology (WSMO) [33] defines services that can be requested or provided, and the agreements between the providers and requesters. A WSMO instance describes a service in terms of non-functional properties; the ontologies used to describe the service; mediators that can deal with protocol and process related mismatches between Web services; and the functional description of the service. In addition, the model supports the definition of the objectives or goals that a client needs to satisfy when consulting a Web service, and the specification of the mediators that can be used to handle heterogeneity between goals specifications and service descriptions. On the other hand, SAWSDL defines mechanisms to annotate elements with a model reference that establishes the meaning of each element. These semantics can help to disambiguate the description of Web services during automatic discovery and composition of the Web services. Although OWL-S, WSMO and SAWSDL are able to express the semantic of the services, they do not support service specific reasoning tasks.

Lacroix and Aziz [26] analyze BioMoby, a service repository that supports syntactic resource description and discovery in the bioinformatics domain. To enhance the service description task with semantics, they also propose a semiautomatic solution to express the functionality of the services in terms of existing datatypes [26]. Although the proposed techniques successfully achieve the goal of semantically annotating services in terms of a give set of datatypes, knowledge implicitly encoded in ontologies is not exploited. Thus, solutions provided by these techniques may be incomplete. In addition, no information about the quality of the discovered services is considered during the description or discovered process.

In [3,4], the logic-based deductive framework Deductive Web Service (DWS) is proposed and the approach BiOnMap illustrates the usage of this framework. DWS offers a canonical representation of service descriptions that is modeled as a Datalog deductive database. Each DWS database is comprised of generic meta-level predicates that express the information encoded in the language used to define the service properties; thus, DWS does not require the usage of any particular formalism to describe the services. Semantic descriptions of Web services are represented as Datalog extensional predicates and are able to model all the information specified by SAWSDL standards. Datalog intensional predicates are used to express the properties of framework operators. In [5], the DWS generic framework is extended with intensional predicates to support the task of resource discovery and to represent domain constraints. Also, a discovery-specific reasoning engine has been implemented on top of DWS, and reasoning tasks that combine properties of the services with domain constraints, has been developed. In this paper, we extend the BiOnMap approach with six new reasoning tasks and empirically study their effects on the size of the search space. In addition, we propose a ranking technique able to distinguish the services that best meet a user request on a set non-functional conditions.

2.2   Service Matching and Discovery

Algorithms to matching and discovery resources can be classified according to their search and reasoning capabilities. On one hand, some approaches rely on keyword-based search languages as well as category browsing, and Google is one of the Web search engines that provides a significantly higher number of files for a given keyword-based user request [6]. These approaches are based on information registered in the Universal Description, Discovery and Integration (UDDI) registry, an important catalyst in the evolution of Web services. However, such syntactic approaches based on UDDI or Google are not well suitable for Web service discovery because, services are selected in terms of keyword-based searches, which are ranked by using link-based metrics that do not necessarily reflect the goodness of the solutions with respect to the user requirements.

On the other hand, the majority of resource discovery approaches use Request Functional Profiles that represent user requirements, and rely their computations on reasoning engines that depending on the service semantic descriptions, offer a semantic-based solution. Paolucci et al. [29] propose a solution that relies on the information published in the OWL-S Service Profile to identify matches between services. Although semantic descriptions can be used to discover the resources that meet a user request, the main disadvantage of this approach arises from the limited capability of the Service Profiles to describe the properties of a service. For instance, information of the control structures used in a service is not available; thus, incorrect matches could be identified [7]. To overcome some of these limitations, Sycara et al. [35] have developed a matchmaker that uses freely available UDDI servers to store DAML-S advertisements, and enhances the matching task in UDDI with information about service capabilities; however, reasoning capabilities are limited to the reasoning tasks implemented at DAML-S. Pathak et al. [30] describe an ontology-based framework for discovery semantically heterogeneous Web services. The approach relies on user-supplied and context-specific mappings to specify Web services. User-specified functional requirements are considered during the discovery process, and user-specified criteria are used to rank the discovered services. The reasoning engine just computes the set of triples implied by the ontologies, and mappings between user and integrated ontologies are used to interoperate among different service descriptions.

The FUSION [23] semantic registry is based on a combination of three standards: UDDI, for storing and retrieving syntactic and semantic information about services and service providers, SAWSDL for creating semantically annotated descriptions of service interfaces, and OWL, for modelling service characteristics and performing fine-grained service matchmaking via DL reasoning. In contrast with prominent approaches, FUSION relies on service functional and non-functional properties for service matchmaking. However, FUSION only considers service input and output attributes, and the categorization of the service with respect to some semantically represented classification scheme. OWLS-MX [19] is a hybrid approach that complements logic based reasoning with approximate matching based on syntactic IR based similarity computations. OWLS-MX uses the OWL-DL description logic reasoner Pellet for logic based filtering, and a great variety of similarity metrics for complementary approximate matching. Kuster et al. [24] propose an approach that integrate service composition into service discovery and matchmaking to match service requests that ask for multiple connected effects. Services are described in DSD (DIANE Service Description language) in terms of operational, aggregating, selecting and rating elements. The reasoning tasks are implemented as active compositions and are able to consider semantic information represented in the DSD descriptions. Similarly, the approach described in [11] implements the reasoning tasks as a problem of constraint composition, where only OWL-S information is represented as constraints. Also, the solution proposed by Kona et al. [21] uses Constraint-based Logic Programming to efficiently represent how an atomic service affects the external world; service descriptions are modeled as Prolog facts and the discovery engine problem is to discovery the list of services that satisfy the restrictions expressed in the user request. Although these approaches may be efficient and semantically described the services and user requests, they do not provide a complete solution to the discovery problem because in case of existing a large number of choices for a given user request, they are not able to identify the most suitable ones.

2.3   Service Selection

The problem of selecting the services that implement an abstract workflow and best fit the QoS-based criteria is known as the QoS-aware service selection or composition problem, which has been shown to be NP-hard [38]. Several heuristics have been proposed to find a relatively good solution. Rahmani et al. [32] present a distance metric-based heuristic that guides a backward search algorithm; this metric induces an order of the services in a way that sink nodes are unlikely to be visited. In a series of papers, Berardi and others [8,9,10] describe services and workflows in terms of deterministic finite-state machines that are encoded using Description Logic theories whose models correspond to solutions of the problem; scalability or performance of the proposed solution has not been reported. Ko et al. [20] propose a constraint-based approach that encodes the non-functional permissible values as a set of constraints whose violation needs to be minimized; to traverse the space of possibly optimal solutions, a hybrid algorithm that combines tabu search and simulated annealing meta-heuristics is implemented. Experimental results show that the proposed solution is able to scale up to a large number of services and abstract processes. Cardellini et al. [13] encode one part of the QoS-aware service composition problem as a Linear Programming problem [13]. Wada el at. [38] treat the problem as a multi-objective optimization problem where the different QoS parameters are considered equally important instead of aggregating them into a single function; then, a genetic-based algorithm is proposed to identify a set of non-dominated service compositions that best fit all the QoS requirements. Alrifai and Risse [2] propose a two-fold solution that uses a hybrid integer programming algorithm to find the decomposition of global QoS into local constraints, and then, selects the services that best meet the local constraints. Finally, Kuter and Golbeck [25] extend the SHOP2 planning algorithm to select the trustworthy composition of services that implement a given OWL-S process model, while Sohrabi and McIlraith [34] propose a HTN planning-based solution where user preference metrics and domain regulations are used to guide the planner into the space of relevant compositions. Although these solutions are able to solve the optimization problem and scale up to a number of abstract processes, none of them are tailored to perform reasoning tasks that exploit the knowledge encoded in the ontology annotations of the services or apply ranking techniques able to distinguish the top-k services that best meet the non-functional requirements of a user request.

WSMX 1.0 [17] is a middleware framework for covering all the Semantic Web Services life cycle: monitoring for Semantic Web Services for fault handling and estimation of quality of service; ranking engine to identify the services according to user preferences; service grounding engine based on W3C SAWSDL recommendations. WSMX 1.0 makes uses of a ranking approach that uses semantic descriptions of non-functional properties to select the most suitable service for a given service request, where services are semantically described using WSMO and WSML. The core of the non-functional property (NFP) specification is a set of ontologies that provide the terminology used to specify NFPs aspects of services. NFP's are modeled as logical expressions in WSML similar to pre-post conditions, and assumptions and effects. Services are ranked in terms of a semantic ranking and multi-criteria ranking, where the ranking engine determines the importance of the particular NFP for the requester, and the logical definition of the NFP is used to compute the value of the parameter each service as well as its importance. An aggregated score is computed for each service by summing the normalized values of non-functional weighted by importance values; scores are sorted according to the ordering sense extracted from the goal and the final list of services is returned. Similar to WSMX 1.0, we assume that the NFP values are computed or estimated by using a monitoring or sampling technique. However, our approach differs from WSMX 1.0 for considering all the NFP's equally important, and finding the services that meet the majority of the NFP's.

2.4   Ranking Approaches

Skyline [12] and Top-k [14] approaches have been defined in the context of databases to distinguish the best points that satisfy a given ranking condition. A Skyline-based technique identifies a partially ordered set of services whose order is induced by criteria comprised of conditions on equally important parameters. Top-k approaches select the top-k elements based on a score function or discriminatory criteria that induces a totally ordered of the input set. A new hybrid approach that combines the benefits of Skyline and Top-k has been proposed in [18] and it is known as Top-k Skyline. Top-k Skyline identifies the top-k services using a discriminatory criteria that induces a total order of the services that compose the skyline of points that satisfy a given multi-dimensional criterium. Top-k Skyline has became necessary in many real-world situations [37], and a variety of ranking metrics have been proposed to discriminate among the points in the skyline, e.g., Skyline Frequency [16], k-dominant skyline [15], and k representative skyline [28]. Skyline Frequency is one of the most significant metrics that ranks skyline points in terms of how many times a skyline point belongs to the skyline induced by the subsets of the multi-dimensional criteria; it measures how much a skyline point satisfies the different parameters in the multi-dimensional criteria. Intuitively, a high Skyline Frequency value indicates that a point may be dominated on smaller subsets of the multi-dimensional criteria, and it can be considered a very good point because it may dominate in many of the other subsets; in contrast, a skyline point with a low Skyline Frequency value shows that other skyline points dominate it in subsets of the multi-dimensional criteria. Approaches in [31,39] propose two algorithms to compute Skyline Frequency values by building the Skycube or the union of the skylines of the non-empty subsets of the multidimensional criteria. The Bottom-Up Skycube algorithm (BUS) [39] identifies the Skycube of d dimensions in a bottom-up fashion. BUS sorts dataset on each dimension of the multi-dimensional criteria in a list and it calculates the skyline points from one to d dimensions. BUS makes use of the skyline point properties to speed the Skycube computation. On the other hand, the Top-Down Skycube algorithm (TDS) [31] computes the Skycube in a top-down manner based on a Divide and Conquer (DC) Skyline algorithm [12]. TDS computes a minimal set of paths in the lattice structure of the Skycube and then, it identifies skylines in these paths. Thus, multiple related skylines are built simultaneously. BUS and TDS can be used to compute the Top-k Skyline. However, some overhead may have to be paid, because both algorithms compute the Skycube completely. Goncalves et al. [18] propose an index-based technique called TKSI, to compute the Top-k Skyline points by just probing the minimal subset of incomparable points and using a given score function to distinguish the best points. Since the properties of the function used to identify the Top-k Skyline are unknown, the algorithm requires to compute the values of all the points. In contrast, the WTKSF algorithm selects the Top-k Skyline services in terms of the Skyline Frequency metric; thus, by exploiting the properties of this metric, WTKSF just requires the computation of the metric for a small subset of points, thus, its performance is improved.

3   Motivating Example

In order to study the homology between a human gene and genes from other species, a scientist has to compare the DNA sequence of the gene against genomic sequences from multiple species. In the first step, she uses a Web service that retrieves a DNA sequence given a human gene name. Then, she uses an alignment Web service to perform sequence alignments and extract from the alignment report the most similar sequences to the input DNA sequence.

Suppose, we assume that the domain knowledge is represented through a domain ontology which captures the semantics and properties of bioinformatics concepts. Domain ontology depicted in Figure 1 is used to annotate input and output parameters of a set of services. Service annotations correspond to semantic functional descriptions of the services as it has been proposed in the semantic model presented in [27]. Such annotations will be used to describe the services registered in existing sites and portals such as the BioCatalogue.[1] Services annotations are manually generated based on their textual descriptions, and the service behavior is described in terms of Quality of Service (QoS) parameters such as response time, cost, reliability, throughput, or trust. Sampling techniques may be used to accurately estimate the QoS values of the available services.

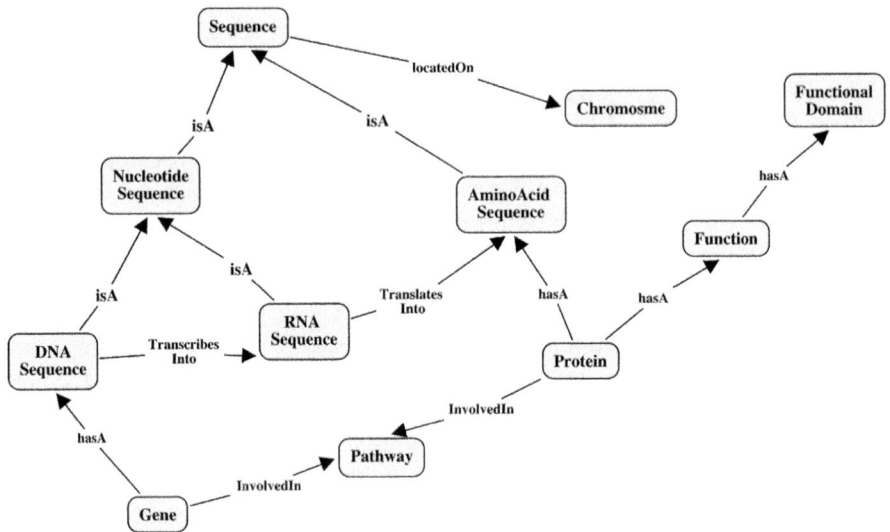

Fig. 1. Fragment of a Domain Ontology

A discovery query specifies a set of functional and non-functional constraints that need to be satisfied. Functional constraints express the semantic types accepted and returned by a Web service. For example, in the first step of the homology study, the scientist needs a service that receives as input a *gene name* and returns as output a *DNA Sequence*. An exact matching between a user query and Web services descriptions is not a very common case. In this paper, we propose a technique that relies on reasoning tasks in order to relax the properties of semantically described services and allow flexible matchmaking between user's queries and Web service descriptions. For example, if a service s receives as input a Biological Sequence, then one can relax this property to all the subclasses of the concept *Sequence*, i.e., *Nucleotide Sequence, Aminoacid Sequence, DNA Sequence* and *RNA Sequence*. Moreover, if s is a service that returns as output

---

[1] http://www.biocatalogue.org/

a *DNA Sequence*, then it is possible to infer that all the super-classes of the concept *DNA Sequence* are also output types of the service *s*.

A large number of Web services can be selected to implement each step of the homology study. Then, it is important to select among the services that functionally satisfy the user request the *"best"* services in terms of non-functional properties. Non-functional properties are represented in our approach by a set of QoS parameters. Suppose our scientist is only interested in the top-2 services that perform sequence alignment and meet the following non-functional criteria: *(Availability)* must be greater or equal than *90*; *(Response Time)* should be less or equal than *3* seconds; and *(Throughput)* should be greater or equal than *10*. Our scientist considers all the non-functional parameters in the query criteria are equally important. In consequence, it may exist a set of incomparable services, i.e., none of them is better than the rest in terms of the values of the parameters *Response Time*, *Availability*, and *Throughput*. This set is known as skyline [12], and it has been shown that for criteria on a large number of dimensions, this set can be very large [16]. Thus, it may be necessary to discriminate the top-k services among the ones in this set. In the next section, we propose a new solution to the problem of selecting the top-k services among a skyline or top-k skyline services.

4   Our Approach

In this section we describe the problem of selecting the top-k skyline services that best satisfy a user request. Finally, we describe the Web Top-k Skyline Frequency (WTKSF) algorithm.

We implement the set of the available service descriptions as a deductive database *DWS=(ESB,ISB)* where, *ESB* is comprised of extensional predicates that describe the properties of the services explicitly declared, and *ISB* corresponds to the set of rules that implicitly define the properties of the services in terms of the reasoning service tasks and the axioms that describe the properties of the operators used to describe the services. Rules in *ISB* are safe Horn clauses free of negations, and the meaning of a *DWS* program corresponds to the minimal model of *DWS* [1].

Definition 1. Service Description. *A service s is a 3-tuple (i, o, nf), where:*

- *i corresponds to a set of pairs (a,t) where, a is an input attribute and t is a datatype, i.e., i is the set of the datatypes of the input attributes of s;*
- *o refers to a set of pairs (b,d) where, b is an output attribute and d is a datatype, i.e., o is the set of the datatypes of the output attributes of s;*
- *nf is a set of triples (p,v,u), where p is a QoS parameter, v is a value associated with the parameter p, and u is the unit in which the value v is expressed, i.e., nf is the set of the QoS parameters that describe s.*

Table 1 is comprised of a set of built-in predicates to describe the available services. The "inputType" and "outputType" built-in predicates declare the

Table 1. A Sample of Built-in Predicates

Built-in Predicate	Description
inputType(s,a,t)	Service s with an input attribute a of type t
outputType(s,b,d)	Service s with an output attribute b of type d
qos(s,p,v)	Service s has a value v for the QoS parameter p
Op($v1,v2$)	Op is an arithmetic connector, e.g., $>$, $<$, and so on

semantic types of the input and output attributes of a service, respectively. The "qos" built-in predicate declares that a service has a QoS parameter and indicates its value.

Example 1. The *Emboss Transeq*[2] Web service performs the translation of nucleotique sequences into their corresponding protein sequences in all six frames. Based on the domain ontology depicted in Figure 1, the functionality of this service is described as follows: (a) it has an input attribute $i1$ of type *Nucleotide Sequence* and an output attribute $o1$ of type *Protein Sequence*. Additionally, suppose that a sampling process is performed to estimate the QoS parameter values of the service, and the following values were collected: *Response Time* is 4 seconds, *Availability* is 98 % and *Throughput* is 10 invocations/second. Additionally, the service *backTranseq*[3] translates a protein sequence into a nucleotide sequence, and suppose it has the same QoS parameter values than *Emboss Transeq*, i.e., *Response Time* is 4 seconds, *Availability* is 98 % and *Throughput* is 10 invocations/second. Thus, both services will be described in terms of these functional and non-functional properties, and at the implementation level, we will use built-in predicates in Table 1 to explicitly describe these functional and non-functional properties of these services as follows:

```
inputType('Emboss Transeq',i1,'Nucleotide Sequence').
outputType('Emboss Transeq',o1,'Protein Sequence').
qos('Emboss Transeq','Availability',98).
qos('Emboss Transeq','ResponseTime',4).
qos('Emboss Transeq','Throughput',10).
inputType('backTranseq',i2,'Protein Sequence').
outputType('backTranseq',o2,'Nucleotide Sequence').
qos('backTranseq','Availability',98).
qos('backTranseq','ResponseTime',4).
qos('backTranseq','Throughput',10).
```

Definition 2. A Discovery Query. *A discovery query is expressed as a conjunctive query $Q(X)$:-$\exists Y G(X,Y)$ where X and Y are sequences of variables, and $G(X,Y)$ represents a conjunction of built-in predicates in Table 1.*

Example 2. Suppose a user is interested in services that perform the reverse translation of a protein sequence to its corresponding nucleotide sequence; also he is interested in services that satisfy the following non-functional requirements:

---

[2] http://www.ebi.ac.uk/soaplab/typed/services/nucleic_translation.transeq?wsdl
[3] http://www.ebi.ac.uk/soaplab/typed/services/nucleic_translation.backtranseq?wsdl

Response Time is at most 6 seconds and *Availability* is at least 96. Thus, the discovery query is expressed as follows, where upper case letters denote variables:

q(S):-inputType(S,I,'Protein Sequence'), outputType(S,O,'Nucleotide Sequence'),
    qos(S,'ResponseTime',V1), <(V1,6), qos(S,'Availability',V2),>(V2,96).

Intuitively, a service *s* belongs to the answer of a discovery query *q*, if the predicates that describe *s* satisfy the conditions expressed in *q*. Thus, in our running example, service *Emboss Transeq* does not satisfy the query in Example 2, while *backTranseq* does meet the query conditions, and it will be the only service in the answer.

Definition 3. The Top-k Skyline Service Discovery Problem. *Let* q : $Q(X)$:-$\exists Y G(X,Y)$ *be a discovery query. Let* k *be an integer number. Let SW be a set of services. The Top-k Skyline Service Discovery problem corresponds to the problem of identifying a set of services* $SW' = \{S_1, S_2, ..., S_k\}$ *such that,* $SW' \subseteq SW$ *and:*

- *For each service* s *in* SW', *s satisfies the functional and non-functional requirements expressed in* q,
- *The* k *services in* SW' *have the best values in the Skyline Frequency metric, and these services belong to the skyline set induced by the satisfaction of the non-functional requirements in* q. *A service* s *belongs to the skyline if and only if, there is no a different service* s' *with better values than* s *in the QoS parameters of the non-functional condition in* q.

Example 3. Suppose that our scientist is also searching for services able to perform sequence alignment and that meet the following non-functional criteria: *Availabitity* must be greater or equal than 96 and *Response Time* should be less or equal to 5 seconds. Consider the services *NCBIBlastService*,[4] *runBlat*[5] and *WSFASTA*,[6] which meet the functional scientist's requirement. Now suppose these services are described in terms of the QoS properties shown in Table 2. Then, these three services also satisfy the non-functional criteria.

Table 2. QoS Properties of Web Services

Services	Availability	Response Time
NCBIBlastService	98 %	4 seconds
RunBLAT	97 %	2 seconds
WSFASTA	96 %	1 seconds

Additionally, suppose the scientist is only interested in the best (top-1) service. First, considering *Availability*, *RunBLAT* is better than *WSFASTA*, and *NCBIBlastService* is better than *RunBLAT*. However, if *Response Time* is

---

[4] http://www.ebi.ac.uk/Tools/webservices/wsdl/WSNCBIBlast.wsdl?kjkj
[5] http://biomoby.org/services/wsdl/inb.bsc.es/runBlat
[6] http://www.ebi.ac.uk/Tools/webservices/wsdl/WSFasta.wsdl

considered, *WSFASTA* is better than *RunBLAT*, and *RunBLAT* is better than *NCBIBlastService*. Since none of these services is better than the rest in all the QoS parameters, they are incomparable, i.e., they are part of the skyline induced by the non-functional condition of the query. Thus, to select the best service, a discriminative criterium is required. In this paper, we propose a ranking technique that effectively and efficiently provides a solution to this problem.

4.1 Selecting Services That Meet Functional Requirements

In this section we describe a set of reasoning tasks that allow to derive new properties of the available services. These reasoning tasks are represented as Horn clauses in the deductive database *DWS* that models the services.

Hierarchy Input relaxation: if a is an input attribute of service s, and a is annotated with class C, then a is also annotated with all the sub-classes of C.

Hierarchy Output relaxation: if b is an output attribute of service s, and b is annotated with class C, then b is also annotated with all the super-classes of C.

Functional Input relaxation: if a is an input attribute of service s, and a is annotated with class C and there is a functional property from D to C, then a is also annotated with D.

Inverse Functional Input relaxation: if a is an input attribute of service s, and a is annotated with class C and there is a functional property from C to D and this property has inverse, then a is also annotated with D.

Functional Output relaxation: if b is an output attribute of service s, and b is annotated with class D and there is a functional property from D to C, then b is also annotated with C.

Inverse Functional Output relaxation: if b is an output attribute of service s, and b is annotated with class C and there is a functional property from D to C and this property has inverse, then b is also annotated with D.

To illustrate how the number of annotations is augmented by firing these reasoning tasks, consider the Web services *DDBJGetEntry*[7] and *NCBIBlastService* in Figure 2. *DDBJGetEntry* retrieves DNA sequences given a gene name, while *NCBIBlastService* is an alignment Web service that detects similarity between sequences. Both services are linked to their input and output attributes by thick arrows labelled *hasInput* and *hasOutput*, respectively. Thick arrows labelled *rdf:type*, represent the explicitly expressed ontology annotations of the input and output attributes of these two services. Dotted arrows denote annotations that are inferred by applying the reasoning tasks of Hierarchy Input and Output relaxation. In this simple example, these two reasoning tasks increased the number of annotations by up to three times. In section 5 we report the results of an experimental study where we observe that the size of the number of annotations can be increased by almost two orders of magnitude.

---

[7] http://xml.nig.ac.jp/wsdl/GetEntry.wsdl

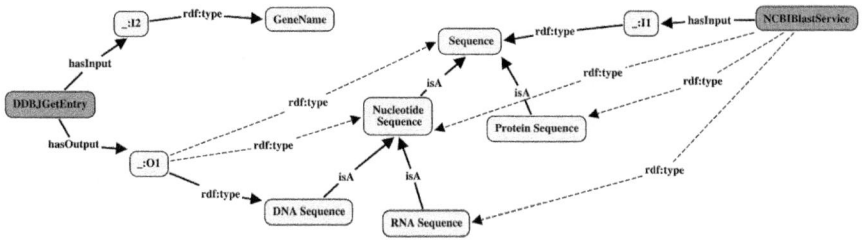

Fig. 2. Derived Properties Applying Hierarchy Input and Hierarchy Output relaxation

4.2   Selecting Services That Meet Non Functional Requirements

The *Top-k Skyline* approach is used to identify the services that best meet the non-functional criteria. We propose the usage of the Web Top-k Skyline Frequency (WTKSF) algorithm to identify a set of services that satisfy an instance of the Top-k Skyline Service Discovery Problem. The WTKSF algorithm exploits the properties of the Skyline Frequency metric (SFM) to identify among the set of skyline of services, the ones with the highest values of this metric. Intuitively, the result of executing the WTKSF is the top-k services that satisfy the functional requirements in a discovery query, and that have the best values in the majority of the non-functional requirements of the query. The WTKSF resembles the Top-k SkyIndex (TKSI) algorithm introduced in [18], because in both algorithms the number of skyline points that are computed to produce the top-k skyline is minimized. However, WTKSF differs from TKSI for using properties of the SFM to guide the search into the space of the skyline services that maximize the values of this metric. Thus, in addition to limit the number of computed skyline services, the computation of the SFM is also reduced. WTKSF assumes that the available services are in d ordered lists according to their values of the QoS parameters, where d is the number of QoS parameters used in the query non-functional criteria. Then, WTKSF considers the following rules to decide if a service s_i is better than a service s_j:

- s_i is an extreme point in more than $\frac{d}{2}$ QoS parameters, i.e., s_i has the best values in half or more of the QoS parameters of the query. A service is an extreme point in a dimension m, if it has the best value of the QoS parameter associated with the dimension m.
- There is no service s_k better than s_i in $(d - l)$ dimensions, where l is the number of dimensions in which s_j is an extreme point.
- There exists service s_k better than s_j in $(d - l)$ dimensions, where l is the number of dimensions in which s_i is an extreme point.

In case none of these rules holds, WTKSF computes the values of the Skyline Frequency metric for s_i and s_j, to decide which of these two services is the best. WTKSF stops when k services are produced. Thus, the skyline of services is partially built, and the Skyline Frequency metric is computed only for some of the skyline services.

5   Experimental Study

Dataset and Query Benchmark: the study was conducted on datasets of randomly generated services where input and output parameters were annotated with the MeSH controlled vocabulary[8] and the Protein Ontology (PRO). [9] Services were associated with ten QoS parameters; values ranged from 0.0 to 1.0. Also, 30 queries were randomly generated by defining the conditions on the functional and non-functional parameters that describe the service datasets. In all cases, a uniform distribution was followed.

Evaluation Metrics: we report on the number of discovered services, Number of Probes (NP) and the Normalized Skyline Frequency value (NSF). NP is the number of the probes of the non-functional criteria and Skyline Frequency metric evaluations performed by the algorithm. NSF is a quality metric that represents a percent of non-empty subspaces of the non-functional criteria; it indicates how good is a Skyline service. NSF is computed as follows: $\frac{SFM}{2^d-1}$. The experiments were evaluated on a SunFire V440 machine equipped with 2 processors Sparcv9 of 1.281 MHZ, 16 GB of memory and 4 disks Ultra320 SCSI of 73 GB running on SunOS 5.10 (Solaris 10).

Implementations: to study the quality of the reasoning tasks, the reasoning engine was developed as a Prolog bottom-up meta-interpreter that implements a semi-naive evaluation engine, and computes the minimal model of the rules that implement the reasoning tasks presented in Section 4.1. Queries were expressed as conjunctive queries and evaluated by a top-down meta-interpreter implemented by extending the sideways-passing of information inherent to Prolog rules; once a service that satisfied the functional request expressed in the query was produced, the computation was forced to fail, and backtracking took place to discover a new service. Finally, WTKSF and BUS were implemented in Java (64-bit JDK version 1.5.0 12). Services were stored in relational tables on Oracle 9i, and sorted based on each QoS parameter.

5.1   Effectiveness of the Reasoning Task

We studied the effectiveness of the reasoning tasks by executing the number of selected services when the reasoning tasks are performed. In Figure 3(a) we compare the average number of discovered services (logarithmic scale), when the discovered process is evaluated using the reasoning tasks (RT) and without reasoning tasks (WRT). We ran 30 queries and we considered datasets of 1,000; 2,000; 4,000; 6,000 and 16,000 services. We can observe that number of discovered services is up to two orders of magnitude higher when the reasoning tasks described in Section 4.1 are executed.

---

[8] http://www.nlm.nih.gov/mesh/meshhome.html
[9] http://proteinontology.org.au/hierarchy.htm

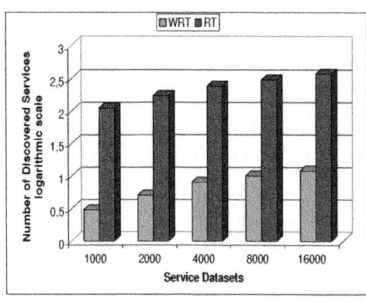

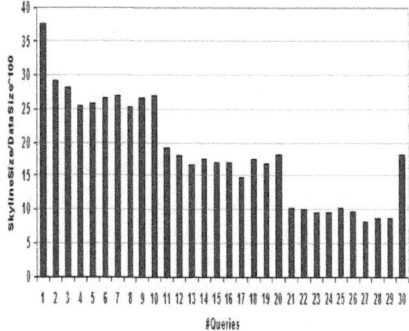

(a) Average Number of Discovered Ser- (b) Skyline Size versus Available Services
vices (logarithmic scale)

Fig. 3. Quality of the Proposed Approach

5.2 Quality and Performance of the Top-Skyline Technique

We studied the quality of the WTKSF, and we compare its performance with
respect to the BUS algorithm. We ran 30 queries on a dataset of 10,000 services;
each query has ten equally important QoS parameters.

In Figure 3(b), we report the ratio of the skyline size to the total number of
services that satisfy the functional conditions of the query. In general, we observe
that the skyline size is larger for high dimensional queries. In the studied queries,
the skyline size ranges from 9% to 37% of the total number of services that satisfy
the functional conditions.

Figure 4(a) reports on the number of probes performed by WTSKF and BUS
(logarithmic scale). We can observe that WTKSF reduces the number of probes
by at least three orders of magnitude with respect to the bottom-up solution
implemented by the BUS algorithm. This is because, WTKSF does not build

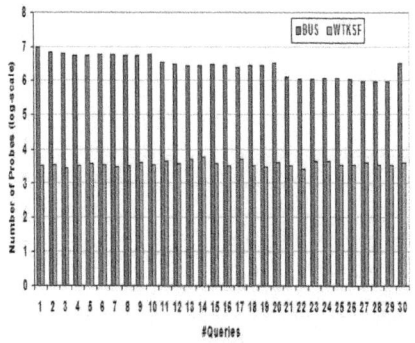

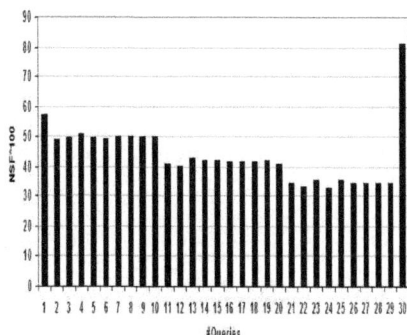

(a) Number of Probes (logarithmic scale) (b) Quality of the Top-k Skyline Services

Fig. 4. Performance of the Proposed Ranking Approach

the skyline completely or computes the Skyline Frequency metric for all the services that meet the functional requirements.

Additionally, the quality of the top-k skyline services identified by the ranking engine is shown in Figure 4(b). NSF values are between 0.3 and 0.8, i.e., the discovered services dominate in at most 80% of the sub-spaces of the non-functional criteria and they may be of good quality. For Top-k Skyline queries for ten and nine dimensions, NSF is near to 0.5; this indicates that selected services dominate in almost 50% of the sub-spaces of the non-functional criteria. For Top-k Skyline queries with eight dimensions, NSF is around to 0.4; thus, selected services are less dominators. Finally, Top-k Skyline queries with seven dimensions, have a NSF about 0.3. NSF of the last query is 0.8, and this is because the skyline size is larger than the size of the other Top-k Skyline queries with seven dimensions.

6   Conclusions and Future Work

In this paper we proposed a ranking-based framework to efficiently discover the services that best meet the functional and non-functional requirements of a user request. The proposed framework is based on an ontology-driven approach that is able to infer the properties of the available services and deduce which of them satisfy the user functional requirement. Furthermore, the Top-k Skyline approach is used to identify the top-k services among the services that best meet a set of equally important QoS parameters. We reported initial experimental results, and showed that our approach is able to identify good quality services and outperform state-of-the-art solutions. In the future, we plan to implement the proposed reasoning tasks on a cluster of machines, and exploit the benefits of existing Cloud-based paradigms as Map/Reduce.

References

1. Abiteboul, S., Hull, R., Vianu, V.: Foundations of Databases. Addison-Wesley, Reading (1995)
2. Alrifai, M., Risse, T.: Combining global optimization with local selection for efficient QoS-aware service composition. In: WWW, pp. 881–890 (2009)
3. Ayadi, N., Lacroix, Z., Vidal, M.: A Deductive Approach for Resource Interoperability and Well-Defined Workflows. In: Meersman, R., Tari, Z., Herrero, P. (eds.) OTM-WS 2008. LNCS, vol. 5333, pp. 998–1009. Springer, Heidelberg (2008)
4. Ayadi, N., Lacroix, Z., Vidal, M., Ruckhaus, E.: Deductive Web Services: An Ontology-Driven Approach for Service Interoperability in Life Science. In: Meersman, R., Tari, Z., Herrero, P. (eds.) OTM-WS 2007, Part II. LNCS, vol. 4806, pp. 1338–1347. Springer, Heidelberg (2007)
5. Ayadi, N.Y., Lacroix, Z., Vidal, M.-E.: BiOnMap: A Deductive Approach for Resource Discovery. In: iiWAS, pp. 477–482 (2008)
6. Bachelechner, D., Siorpaes, K., Fensel, D., Toma, I.: Web Service Discovery- A Reality Check. In: Demos and Posters of the 3rd European Semantic Web Conference, ESWC (2006)

7. Bansal, S., Vidal, J.M.: Matchmaking of web services based on the DAML-S service model. In: AAMAS 2003: Proceedings of the Second International Joint Conference on Autonomous Agents and Multiagent Systems, pp. 926–927. ACM, New York (2003)

8. Berardi, D., Calvanese, D., De Giacomo, G., Hull, R., Mecella, M.: Automatic composition of transition-based semantic web services with messaging. In: VLDB 2005: Proceedings of the 31st international conference on Very large data bases, VLDB Endowment, pp. 613–624 (2005)

9. Berardi, D., Cheikh, F., Giacomo, G.D., Patrizi, F.: Automatic Service Composition via Simulation. Int. J. Found. Comput. Sci. 19(2), 429–451 (2008)

10. Berardi, D., Giacomo, G.D., Mecella, M., Calvanese, D.: Composing Web Services with Non deterministic Behavior. In: IEEE International Conference on Web Services, pp. 909–912 (2006)

11. Biswas, D.: Web Services Discovery and Constraints Composition. In: Marchiori, M., Pan, J.Z., Marie, C.d.S. (eds.) RR 2007. LNCS, vol. 4524, pp. 73–87. Springer, Heidelberg (2007)

12. Börzsönyi, S., Kossmann, D., Stocker, K.: The skyline operator. In: Proceedings of the 17th International Conference on Data Engineering, Washington, DC, USA, pp. 421–430. IEEE Computer Society, Los Alamitos (2001)

13. Cardellini, V., Casalicchio, E., Grassi, V., Presti, F.L.: Flow-Based Service Selection for Web Service Composition Supporting Multiple QoS Classes. In: ICWS, pp. 743–750 (2007)

14. Carey, M.J., Kossmann, D.: On saying "Enough already!" in SQL. SIGMOD Rec. 26(2), 219–230 (1997)

15. Chan, C.-Y., Jagadish, H.V., Tan, K.-L., Tung, A.K.H., Zhang, Z.: Finding k-dominant skylines in high dimensional space. In: SIGMOD 2006: Proceedings of the 2006 ACM SIGMOD International Conference on Management of Data, pp. 503–514. ACM, New York (2006)

16. Chan, C.Y., Jagadish, H.V., Tan, K.-L., Tung, A.K.H., Zhang, Z.: On High Dimensional Skylines. In: Ioannidis, Y., Scholl, M.H., Schmidt, J.W., Matthes, F., Hatzopoulos, M., Böhm, K., Kemper, A., Grust, T., Böhm, C. (eds.) EDBT 2006. LNCS, vol. 3896, pp. 478–495. Springer, Heidelberg (2006)

17. Facca, F.M., Komazec, S., Toma, I.: WSMX 1.0: A Further Step toward a Complete Semantic Execution Environment. In: Aroyo, L., et al. (eds.) ESWC 2009. LNCS, vol. 5554, pp. 826–830. Springer, Heidelberg (2009)

18. Goncalves, M., Vidal, M.-E.: Reaching the Top of the Skyline: An Efficient Indexed Algorithm for Top-k Skyline Queries. In: Bhowmick, S.S., Küng, J., Wagner, R. (eds.) Database and Expert Systems Applications. LNCS, vol. 5690, pp. 471–485. Springer, Heidelberg (2009)

19. Klusch, M., Fries, B., Sycara, K.: Automated semantic web service discovery with OWLS-MX. In: AAMAS 2006: Proceedings of the Fifth International Joint Conference on Autonomous Agents and Multiagent Systems, pp. 915–922. ACM, New York (2006)

20. Ko, J.M., Kim, C.O., Kwon, I.-H.: Quality-of-Service Oriented Web Service Composition Algorithm and Planning Architecture. Journal of Systems and Software 81(11), 2079–2090 (2008)

21. Kona, S., Bansal, A., Gupta, G., Hite, T.: Efficient Web Service Discovery and Composition using Constraint Logic Programming. In: Proc. ALPSWS (2006)

22. Kopecký, J., Vitvar, T., Bournez, C., Farrell, J.: SAWSDL: Semantic Annotations for WSDL and XML Schema. IEEE Internet Computing 11(6), 60–67 (2007)
23. Kourtesis, D., Paraskakis, I.: Combining SAWSDL, OWL-DL and UDDI for Semantically Enhanced Web Service Discovery. In: Bechhofer, S., Hauswirth, M., Hoffmann, J., Koubarakis, M. (eds.) ESWC 2008. LNCS, vol. 5021, pp. 614–628. Springer, Heidelberg (2008)
24. Küster, U., König-Ries, B., Stern, M., Klein, M.: DIANE: an integrated approach to automated service discovery, matchmaking and composition. In: WWW 2007: Proceedings of the 16th International Conference on World Wide Web, pp. 1033–1042. ACM, New York (2007)
25. Kuter, U., Golbeck, J.: Semantic Web Service Composition in Social Environments. In: Bernstein, A., Karger, D.R., Heath, T., Feigenbaum, L., Maynard, D., Motta, E., Thirunarayan, K. (eds.) ISWC 2009. LNCS, vol. 5823, pp. 344–358. Springer, Heidelberg (2009)
26. Lacroix, Z., Aziz, M.: Resource Descriptions, Ontology and Resource Discovery. International Journal of Metadata, Semantics and Ontologies (IJMSO) Special Issue on Resource Discovery (to appear 2010)
27. Lacroix, Z., Raschid, L., Vidal, M.-E.: Semantic Model to Integrate Biological Resources. In: ICDE Workshops, pp. 63–67 (2006)
28. Lin, X., Yuan, Y., Zhang, Q., Zhang, Y.: Selecting Stars: The k Most Representative Skyline Operator. In: ICDE, pp. 86–95 (2007)
29. Paolucci, M., Kawamura, T., Payne, T.R., Sycara, K.: Semantic Matching of Web Services Capabilities. In: Horrocks, I., Hendler, J. (eds.) ISWC 2002. LNCS, vol. 2342, pp. 333–347. Springer, Heidelberg (2002)
30. Pathak, J., Koul, N., Caragea, D., Honavar, V.G.: A framework for semantic web services discovery. In: WIDM 2005: Proceedings of the 7th Annual ACM International Workshop on Web Information and Data Management, pp. 45–50. ACM Press, New York (2005)
31. Pei, J., Yuan, Y., Lin, X., Jin, W., Ester, M., Wang, Q.L.W., Tao, Y., Yu, X., Zhang, Q.: Towards multidimensional subspace skyline analysis. ACM Trans. Database Syst. 31(4), 1335–1381 (2006)
32. Rahmani, H., GhasemSani, G., Abolhassani, H.: Automatic Web Service Composition Considering User Non-functional Preferences. Next Generation Web Services Practices, 33–38 (2008)
33. Roman, D., Keller, U., Lausen, H., de Bruijn, J., Lara, R., Stollberg, M., Polleres, A., Feier, C., Bussler, C., Fensel, D.: Web Service Modeling Ontology. Appl. Ontol. 1(1), 77–106 (2005)
34. Sohrabi, S., McIlraith, S.A.: Optimizing Web Service Composition While Enforcing Regulations. In: Bernstein, A., Karger, D.R., Heath, T., Feigenbaum, L., Maynard, D., Motta, E., Thirunarayan, K. (eds.) ISWC 2009. LNCS, vol. 5823, pp. 601–617. Springer, Heidelberg (2009)
35. Sycara, K., Paolucci, M., Ankolekar, A., Srinivasan, N.: Automated discovery, interaction and composition of semantic web services. Journal of Web Semantics 1, 27–46 (2003)
36. Toma, I., Roman, D., Fensel, D., Sapkota, B., Gomez, J.M.: A Multi-criteria Service Ranking Approach Based on Non-Functional Properties Rules Evaluation. In: Krämer, B.J., Lin, K.-J., Narasimhan, P. (eds.) ICSOC 2007. LNCS, vol. 4749, pp. 435–441. Springer, Heidelberg (2007)

37. Vlachou, A., Vazirgiannis, M.: Link-based Ranking of Skyline Result Sets. In: Proceedings of the 3rd Multidisciplinary Workshop on Advances in Preference Handling, M-Pref (2007)
38. Wada, H., Champrasert, P., Suzuki, J., Oba, K.: Multiobjective Optimization of SLA-Aware Service Composition. In: SERVICES 2008: Proceedings of the 2008 IEEE Congress on Services - Part I, Washington, DC, USA, pp. 368–375. IEEE Computer Society, Los Alamitos (2008)
39. Yuan, Y., Lin, X., Liu, Q., Wang, W., Yu, J.X., Zhang, Q.: Efficient computation of the skyline cube. In: VLDB 2005: Proceedings of the 31st International Conference on Very Large Data Bases, VLDB Endowment, pp. 241–252 (2005)

Author Index

GPSR Compliance

The European Union's (EU) General Product Safety Regulation (GPSR) is a set of rules that requires consumer products to be safe and our obligations to ensure this.

If you have any concerns about our products, you can contact us on ProductSafety@springernature.com

In case Publisher is established outside the EU, the EU authorized representative is:

Springer Nature Customer Service Center GmbH
Europaplatz 3
69115 Heidelberg, Germany

Batch number: 09490872

Printed by Printforce, the Netherlands